What People Are Saying About
The Highly Sensitive Person's Workbook

"A very useful tool for exploring many facets of your HSP personality . . . in a focused, organized, private manner." —E. G.

"Elaine Aron's workbook enabled me to privately examine unexplored areas in my life. A few hours once a week helped me understand and deal with issues I had ignored for years. Dr. Aron's concern and personality came alive in her writing style. Her workbook became my friend and counselor." —C. J.

"Do you feel your antennae are out for every nuance? That subtlety and detail are magnified for you and lost to others? Do you think you are the only one like this? In her workbook, Elaine Aron has articulated what we have wanted to hear—there are others like us! And that our trait has benefits and gifts." —E. R.

"This workbook will help you recognize your sensitivity for the gift it is, heal the wounds which are holding you back, and assist you in finding the place of empowerment from which your gifts may be freely given." —J. V.

"When I took the test at the beginning and found that all but one of the statements applied to me, it was like coming home to family I'd never known. Dr. Aron's new workbook is tough going, in a way, because so many negative stereotypes about sensitivity, absorbed in childhood, have to surface and be reframed. But the ability to see oneself in a new, clearer light makes it well worth the effort." —J. G.

"I don't usually do the exercises in self-help books, but I did do most of these. They helped me better understand myself, and those in the chapter on close relationships I credit with improving my relationship with my partner—certainly cheaper than going to a marriage counselor." —F. W.

"A valuable companion to Dr. Aron's groundbreaking *The Highly Sensitive Person,* her workbook contains clear step-by-step instructions designed to help you explore and appreciate your unique characteristic. It is a pleasure to recommend it to other HSPs." —E. E.

"Elaine Aron's effectiveness is two-pronged. She diffuses our defensiveness about being 'sensitive,' while providing tangible tools." —N. G.

"My father called me *Pikon,* 'super sensitive' in Filipino, and implied I was abnormal. My sisters took the cue and teased me endlessly. As a result, I felt flawed and looked for solutions in books and tapes that urged me to think positively. But I still felt a piece was missing—one Dr. Aron provided with this workbook." —J. S.

"*The Highly Sensitive Person Workbook* has been a self-paced and private way to heal from prior misconceptions about myself. In this workbook, Elaine Aron demystifies psychotherapy and shows what you can do to understand and accept yourself. Now I can also add the workbook to the books I recommend and give as gifts. It is the perfect companion to *The Highly Sensitive Person.*" —E. M.

"After feeling like a square peg in a round hole for most of my life, working through Dr. Aron's workbook made me feel like I am valued and can add value to others. The exercises provide a safe, fun, well-guided pathway to our inner selves." —P. P.

The Highly Sensitive Person's Workbook

The Practical Guide for Highly
Sensitive People and HSP Support
Groups by the Bestselling Author
of *The Highly Sensitive Person*

The Highly Sensitive Person's Workbook

Elaine N. Aron, Ph.D.

Broadway Books New York

BROADWAY

THE HIGHLY SENSITIVE PERSON'S WORKBOOK. Copyright © 1999 by Elaine N. Aron, Ph.D. All rights reserved. Printed in the United States of America. No part of this book may be reproduced or transmitted in any form or by any means, electronic or mechanical, including photocopying, recording, or by any information storage and retrieval system, without written permission from the publisher. For information, address Broadway Books, a division of Random House, Inc., 1540 Broadway, New York, NY 10036.

Broadway Books titles may be purchased for business or promotional use or for special sales. For information, please write to: Special Markets Department, Random House, Inc., 1540 Broadway, New York, NY 10036.

BROADWAY BOOKS and its logo, a letter B bisected on the diagonal, are trademarks of Broadway Books, a division of Random House, Inc.

Visit our website at www.broadwaybooks.com

FIRST EDITION

ISBN 0-7679-0337-4

99 00 01 02 03 10 9 8 7 6 5 4 3 2 1

Contents

Contents

ix

Acknowledgments

I am deeply grateful to the San Francisco Bay Area *Comfort Zone* subscribers who volunteered to go through this workbook to test it out, either on their own or in a group. They were thorough, even when I needed their response quickly, and their feedback improved this workbook a great deal.

Betsy Amster, my agent, and Tracy Behar, my editor, have been extraordinarily wise, sensitive, and friendly with their HSP author. It is such a pleasure to work with them.

I want to explicitly acknowledge here that Dr. Irene Pettit was the first person to utter the words "highly sensitive" in my presence. Without her, well, things would not be as good for many of us.

Finally, I hope I never cease to be astounded by the support of my husband, Art Aron. His energy, cheerfulness, and calm are the essential complement to myself! His brains have greatly refined the evidence for this trait. He's a good man.

The Highly Sensitive Person's Workbook

Introduction

"You're overly sensitive." "You're just too sensitive." "You are so hyper- sensitive."

Other variations on the same theme:

"Tired *already?*"

"You aren't *scared,* are you?"

"What's the matter with you? Shy?" "No sense of fun?" "No self-confidence?"

And the theme behind it all: *"What's wrong with you?"*

Sound familiar? If you were like me, you heard these so often from well-meaning parents, teachers, and friends that you began to accept them as true—"Something's the matter with me." And since you knew you couldn't change, you developed a sense of possessing some hidden fatal flaw. You began to see your life as a constant compromise with that flaw, a struggle against failure.

This workbook has one essential message: *There's nothing wrong with high sensitivity.* There's nothing wrong with you for being sensitive. If you answer true to twelve or more of the items in the self-test on page 10, you have a highly sensitive nervous system—a nervous system designed to notice subtleties in the environment, a great asset in many situations.

Yes, a sensitive nervous system also means that inevitably you are more easily overwhelmed by intense levels of stimulation. That's part of the package. But being highly sensitive is no "syndrome" or basic personality flaw.

A highly receptive, highly sensitive nervous system is inherited by about 15 to 20 percent of humans, and that proportion is the same in other animal species as well. Males and females inherit this trait equally (although sensitive men certainly have an especially difficult time in our culture). And there's no evidence of any difference in its presence among the races.

So many sensitive nervous systems can't be wrong, flawed, or genetic mistakes. There must be a purpose to this trait—for example, in any group, how good it is to have some who notice things others don't. To fulfill that purpose, however, you have some important and uplifting work ahead of you. You have to undo, bit by bit, the subtle and not-so-subtle harm to your self-concept inflicted by all those well-meant but erroneous criticisms of what is really just your natural, innate, useful style. This workbook—created from my years of experience with hundreds of highly sensitive people or "HSPs," and personally tested by fifty more— is dedicated to helping you free yourself of that harm and develop your sensitive potential.

Of course, maybe you are highly sensitive but think you never heard any criticism of yourself for being sensitive. Or you think you've got my general point—it's a positive trait, and you'll remember that. Or you certainly aren't shy or lacking in confidence, so this has nothing to do with you. But stay with me for a moment more. High sensitivity is not the same as shyness or even introversion—30 percent of HSPs are, in fact, extroverted. And you may not consciously feel flawed, but it is unlikely, given our culture, that you escaped internalizing an unconscious assumption that you had to hide your real personality, that you were at least odd, if not abnormal. Most HSPs report that it has required months or years of inner work to recognize the many negative, wrong ideas they held about themselves and then slowly eliminate those from their unconscious emotional reactions as well as their conscious intellects. The purpose of this workbook is to help you through this process.

WHAT EXACTLY DO I MEAN BY SENSITIVITY?

HSPs are born with a trait that makes them aware of all kinds of subtle messages from outside and inside. It's not that our eyes or ears are sharper. It's that we process more deeply the information we receive. We *like* to reflect. This sensitivity bestows advantages in many situations. According to research, HSPs are more intuitive, aware, and conscientious (always considering consequences, like "what if I don't get this done?" or "what if everybody broke this rule?"). We are good with infants, animals, and plants—and in any situation in which it helps to notice subtle signs. We are great at detail work and spotting errors, yet we are also "big picture" visionaries, unusually aware of the workings of the past and of likely future outcomes. We report rich, complex inner lives, unusual dreams, a concern for social justice, and a spiritual or philosophical talent.

If we are going to pick up on more subtleties, however, it follows that we also would have to be more easily overwhelmed by non-subtle or strong stimulation: Noise. Visual clutter. Scratchy fabrics. "Funny" odors and food that's slightly "off" or tainted. Temperature extremes and all sorts of sudden changes. Emotionally evocative situations. Crowds. Strangers. And if we process information more deeply, we are going to dwell longer on the meaning of criticisms, rejections, betrayals, losses, and deaths. Some other plain facts about us: We tend to have more allergies and more sensitivity to pain, medications, caffeine, and alcohol. We are usually more affected by hunger and need to eat regularly. None of this makes us weak—just different.

In short, sensitivity is an advantage in many situations and for many purposes, but not in other cases. Like having a certain eye color, it is a neutral, normal trait inherited by a large portion of the population, although not the majority.

WHAT YOU NEED TO KNOW ABOUT YOUR TRAIT—OR, WHY THIS BOOK

When I began my research on high sensitivity, I never planned to write books about it. I was a research psychologist suddenly working on something very personally relevant—my own reasons for feeling so different from others. But other HSPs soon convinced me that they too needed some basic knowledge about themselves. Their campaign to get me to publish something on HSPs began when a local newspaper described my findings, and several hundred HSPs tracked me down and insisted that I give a public lecture, then teach a course, then write a book, which I did—*The Highly Sensitive Person*. It was difficult to find a publisher, but now that book has sold over 100,000 copies and has seen thirteen printings to date, with almost no national media coverage, selling just by word of mouth among HSPs. Over and over HSPs told me, and still tell me, that this information has changed their lives. This is the kind of ethical call to action no scientist can refuse.

Still, I thought the first book would be the end of it. But it wasn't. People read it and wanted even more—courses, consultations, support groups, and any other tools for assimilating these ideas which, as one HSP put it, "completely rearrange the inner furniture."

This need for even more information makes sense to me now. You don't change your entire view of yourself after reading one book. But since I'm only one person, and an HSP, I can't be out teaching and speaking all the time. So I am trying to clone myself through this workbook, providing any HSP, anywhere, with whatever I would have provided in a course, personal consultation, or support group.

From my experience with so many HSPs, here's what you need:

- *Basic knowledge about your trait. The Highly Sensitive Person* provides that in depth, and this workbook does too, in an equally useful but different format, with even greater emphasis on self-exploration of the meaning of the trait for you, especially in chapters 1 and 2.
- *Help with self-care.* HSPs have different nervous systems than others. If we try to live by the same operating instructions that others use, we develop all kinds of chronic illnesses, as so many of you have learned the hard way. Yet if we overprotect ourselves, our assets go unexpressed, and that can also lead to stress and illness. Chapter 3 in particular focuses on HSP self-care.
- *Help reframing your life.* A rethinking of your life, especially the "failures," in light of your sensitivity will happen spontaneously to some degree, but because it is so important, HSPs find it is worth doing systematically and consciously. Obviously the purpose of this entire workbook is to reframe your life in terms of your trait. But this is done step-by-step for each area of your life in chapters 1, 2, 4, 5, 6, 7, and 9.
- *Help healing past traumas.* Research suggests that HSPs living in normal, not-too-stressful environments can actually be healthier

than others. But if our childhoods were troubled or there were special traumas any time in our lives, we are prone to more anxiety and depression than others. Much of this can be healed, and needs to be for the sake of our bodies and happiness, but it requires conscious effort. Chapter 8 helps with that process and encourages the continuation of it elsewhere.

- *Help integrating the trait with specific aspects of life.* Having a nervous system that is different affects everything you do. Therefore, this workbook helps you work with your trait in each area of life—your social life in general (Chapter 5), your close relationships (Chapter 7), vocation and workplace issues (Chapter 6), your relations with health-care professionals (Chapter 9), and of course your inner or spiritual life (Chapter 10).

THIS IS A DEPTH WORKBOOK—HOW TO USE IT

You should use this workbook in any way you darn well please. You can use it without ever reading *The Highly Sensitive Person,* or you can go through this book as you read that one (the chapter topics match), or you can go through this book any time after reading the other.

You can just read this workbook, without doing any of the tasks. Yes, you have my full permission. Or you can do all of them, in order. Or out of order. Or do the ones that appeal to you, in any order.

I suggest, however, that whatever you do, you try to do it consciously. Try to be aware of the inner voice that perhaps says, "you need this book," and also be aware of the one that may later say, "I do *not* want to do that." Find out *why,* especially when you feel inclined to skip something. So the issue is not whether you do it, but how conscious you can be about why.

This is a *depth* workbook. It is written by a depth psychologist. To me, depth psychology means that my goal is to help you honor the ignored, neglected, and even despised parts of yourself. Your personal history and your culture have taught you that certain aspects of yourself are best ignored, forgotten. The depth approach attempts to reclaim some of that (all of it would be impossible). We try to invite it back, host it, listen to it. This frees the energy used to repress it, and more important, frees whatever was of value in what has been lost. Often the very thing a person most needs in life is to be found among the qualities rejected in child-hood—perhaps a woman's "too masculine" assertiveness or a man's "too feminine" sense of subtle feeling, to use two overworked examples.

For many of us, until very recently, a very ignored and repressed part of ourselves was our sensitivity. For some of us, this sensitivity remains partly or wholly shameful or distasteful. (I still receive requests to have the HSP newsletter *Comfort Zone* sent in a brown paper cover.) Thus, to me, restoring this trait to an honored place in your life requires depth work.

Depth work is rewarding, but not always easy. This is why this work-book contains a series of what I call "tasks," not "activities" or even "ex-ercises." There may even be some private heroism required. One of the HSP volunteers who pretested the workbook wrote in her evaluation that "I read your book [*The Highly Sensitive Person*] a year and a half ago and while it did affect me tremendously, I was still somehow very emotionally disconnected from it." After six months of therapy, exploring her child-hood more deeply, she said she thought when she "volunteered for this it would be a breeze—even fun!—but I am really surprised by the effect it has had." She found some tasks required considerable willpower to return to and finish. "I wouldn't have thought this possible a year or so ago."

Not every tester reported such intense experiences, but even when this workbook is playful, it is playing with your core self. You are al-lowed and encouraged to skip those places that seem heavy going. Just be aware of why you are doing it. "This hurts." "This scares me." Or whatever you are feeling.

Much of this workbook involves writing. In fact, one HSP volunteer who tested the workbook thought everyone should keep a separate jour-nal of reactions to the tasks. You might want to do that. But if you are not used to journaling or stream-of-consciousness writing, you need to know that the writing you do here or along with this workbook should go un-judged and unedited. Just let it come out. No one is going to see or grade it. If your own inner critic won't allow that, we will soon be dealing with that troublemaker, starting on page 18.

The secret to journaling is to take your time to feel before you write. Here's the experience of one of the volunteer workbook testers:

*I've noticed that I have a persistent habit of wanting to have
a "correct," "interesting," or "right" response to the exercises. I*

> *have to get past this tendency in order to feel okay about what I'm really feeling. Often, these are unpleasant feelings: defensiveness, shame, anger, rage. It takes me a long time to calm down and regain my bearings in order to think of responses useful to me.*

This volunteer also suggested a "nonlinear" and even preverbal approach may be needed at times:

> *With some exercises, I found it best to read the entire description once or twice, letting things "simmer" and then "bubble up," and returning to the exercises as things occurred to me. I find it hard, if not impossible, to approach these exercises in a linear way. Also, sometimes only intense feelings come up, with no words, not even images that I could describe.*

Opening up to preverbal or nonverbal thought is exactly what depth work is about. So consider her suggestion to take your time and give yourself permission to just observe whatever happens.

At the end of each task you will find an "In Conclusion" section, which provides an opportunity for you to reflect upon and sum up the effect that the task had or how you wish to apply it. This may seem like extra effort, but these sections will serve as wonderful summaries of your work when looking through the book months or years later. So take this chance to reflect, an act that is something of a rarity in today's fast-paced world, but one of your HSP specialties.

By the way, if you are like me and find handwriting laborious, don't feel obliged to write in this book. Use a word processor.

Finally, *it is extremely important* that if you become seriously distressed while doing these activities, you stop and get good professional help. Chapter 8 discusses how to do that.

A SPECIAL FEATURE—WORKING WITH OTHER HSPs

HSPs need to get to know each other. Many of you have sensed this and asked for support groups, courses, or just a chance to meet other HSPs. I make a particular effort to meet this need with Chapter 11 in this workbook. It leads you through the steps of organizing and conducting a six-week leaderless discussion group for HSPs. Once begun, the group can continue indefinitely if it so chooses, discussing on its own or working through the tasks in this workbook as a group. Chapter 11 provides a careful, detailed, tested structure for those crucial first six weeks.

Of course you can organize a group, go through the workbook, and not follow the six-week structured plan, but I personally suggest you do that only if you hire a professional group facilitator, at least to get you started.

I also encourage you to find another HSP and go through this workbook with that person—perhaps your best friend or spouse, if he or she is another HSP. Or you might find such a person by organizing a group for HSPs, or through a note in the "Contact Center" of the HSP newsletter *Comfort Zone* referenced in the back of this book, or on your own among your friends.

The only problem with working through this book with others is that some tasks may be too personal to discuss with people you do not know well. Therefore, for each task I indicate if it is appropriate for a pair or group not well acquainted, called As; just getting acquainted, Bs; or well acquainted, Cs. Some tasks are only for Cs, some fine for Bs and Cs but not As. Some are fine for all three. So:

- Tasks for As are those ideal for the early stage of a pair or group, soon after meeting.
- Tasks for Bs are ideal for well-established relationships, but ones in which you personally do not feel completely safe and ready to open up completely about everything. There are plenty of tasks that can be done in such an environment.
- Tasks for Cs are ideal for the advanced stage of a relationship, where the pair or group has worked through its issues to the point that it can really "work"—that is, listen and help each other—without too much interference from mistrust, misunderstandings about assumptions, competitiveness, envy, and the like.

TO THE NOT-SO-SENSITIVE

To those who have picked up this book because you have a partner, friend, or family member who seems highly sensitive, you are welcome here too, to read or to give the workbook as a gift. According to the letters I receive from HSPs, it will be just that—a gift to the other of confidence and pride about what once may have been a cause for self-doubt. In giving it, or reading it yourself, you and this person who is more sensitive than you—*not* in the sense of empathy or kindness, but in a very physical way—will also gain a far better understanding of your relationship. That should be a gift to you as well.

DEDICATING THIS BOOK

Authors always get to dedicate their books. Since you will write most of this one, you should dedicate it—maybe to an HSP you especially admire. Like yourself.

I Dedicate This Book To:

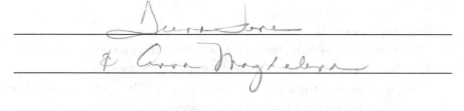

Are You Highly Sensitive?

A SELF-TEST*

Answer each question according to the way you feel. Answer true if it is at least somewhat true for you. Answer false if it is not very true or not at all true for you.

T F   I seem to be aware of subtleties in my environment.

T F   Other people's moods affect me.

T F   I tend to be very sensitive to pain.

T F   I find myself needing to withdraw during busy days, into bed or into a darkened room or any place where I can have some privacy and relief from stimulation.

T F   I am particularly sensitive to the effects of caffeine.

T F   I am easily overwhelmed by things like bright lights, strong smells, coarse fabrics, or sirens close by.

T F   I have a rich, complex inner life.

T F   I am made uncomfortable by loud noises.

T F   I am deeply moved by the arts or music.

T F   I am conscientious.

T F   I startle easily.

T F   I get rattled when I have a lot to do in a short amount of time.

T F   When people are uncomfortable in a physical environment I tend to know what needs to be done to make it more comfortable (like changing the lighting or the seating).

T F   I am annoyed when people try to get me to do too many things at once.

T F   I try hard to avoid making mistakes or forgetting things.

T F   I make it a point to avoid violent movies and TV shows.

T F   I become unpleasantly aroused when a lot is going on around me.

T F   Changes in my life shake me up.

T F   I notice and enjoy delicate or fine scents, tastes, sounds, and works of art.

T F   I make it a high priority to arrange my life to avoid upsetting or overwhelming situations.

*From *The Highly Sensitive Person: How to Thrive When the World Overwhelms You* by Elaine N. Aron. Copyright © 1996 by Elaine N. Aron. Published by arrangement with Carol Publishing Group. A Birch Lane Press Book.

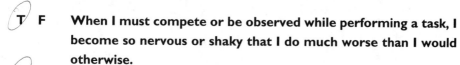

T F When I must compete or be observed while performing a task, I become so nervous or shaky that I do much worse than I would otherwise.

T F When I was a child, my parents or teachers seemed to see me as sensitive or shy.

SCORING YOURSELF

If you answered true to twelve or more of the questions, you're probably highly sensitive.

But frankly, no psychological test is so accurate that you should base your life on it. If only one or two questions are true of you, but they are *extremely* true, you might also be justified in calling yourself highly sensitive.

1

Getting to Know
Your Sensitivity

With the tasks in this chapter, you will become better acquainted with your sensitive self and some of the basic skills HSPs need, like how to speak up in defense of your sensitivity and how to understand your role in your world. But to do that, you need a little more information about your trait. So your very first task is simply to read and absorb.

IF IT'S SO NORMAL, WHY DO I
SOMETIMES FEEL SO DIFFERENT?

The following five points are very important for all HSPs to grasp and remember:

1. *Overstimulation means overarousal.* In everyone, sensitive or not, overstimulation always leads to physiological overarousal. You know you are overaroused when you feel overwhelmed or exhausted in a total-body, can't-work, can't-coordinate, can't-relax, brain-frazzled way. You may have a pounding heart; churning stomach; trembling hands; shallow breath; or hot, flushed, damp, or cold skin.

2. *It's important to maintain an optimal level of arousal.* Absolutely everyone, sensitive or not, always performs worse and feels bad when overaroused. They can't hit a ball, think of witty things to say, or enjoy what's going on around them. Everyone dislikes being underaroused too. That's boredom. Again, you'll be too dull to hit the ball, make the remark, or enjoy the show. Starting at birth, organisms seek an *optimal level of arousal*, not too much or too little, and they seek it as incessantly

and eagerly, and usually unconsciously, as they seek air, food, and water. They do that by regulating how much stimulation or input they receive.

3. *HSPs are more easily overaroused.* In the Introduction I defined this trait as being aware of subtleties by more deeply processing stimulation. If we HSPs are going to be aware of stimulation others would not even notice, in a highly stimulating situation we will necessarily receive more input and become overaroused more quickly. Once we are overaroused, we are like anyone else overaroused—we perform and feel worse. We almost *have* to blow it when the supervisor is watching, or say something inane during the opening moments of a first date. These settings may push some blasé non-HSPs out of lethargy into their optimal level of arousal and performance. But we HSPs are more likely to be pushed beyond our optimal level, into overarousal.

Since we are more easily overaroused, we have more experiences of "failing" under pressure and not enjoying what we are "supposed to" enjoy. No wonder we begin to seem lacking in confidence, not much "fun," sensitive to criticism, or shy (in particular, see Chapter 5 for a discussion of the origins of shyness in HSPs).

The bottom line here is that although we and those around us do enjoy the assets that come with our sensitivity—our extra awareness, empathy, creativity, spirituality, and so forth—we and others must also accept the inevitable downside, the tendency to be more easily overwhelmed. *It's a package deal.*

4. *Sensitivity is not our culture's ideal.* Most of you reading this happen to live in a highly competitive, technological, media- and consumer-driven culture that is now influencing values throughout the globe. And right now it values the ability to handle high levels of stimulation over the ability to detect subtleties.

In some cultures sensitivity is highly admired. For example, a study found that Chinese elementary children who are "sensitive and quiet" are among the most respected and liked by their peers, but in Canada they are among the least respected and liked. Sensitivity is valued in *traditional* China, Japan, and Europe, and also in most cultures living close to the earth, which need their trackers, herbalists, and shamans. But cultures that are very aggressive, expansive, or stressed, or have many immigrants value insensitive, tough, risk-taking personalities to work long hours, go to war, and so forth.

5. *HSPs are more affected than others by being raised in bad home environments.* My research has shown that HSPs who have experienced traumas or troubled home environments in childhood are more depressed, anxious, and tense than HSPs with easier personal histories, and also more distressed than non-HSPs with similar histories. This is often another reason why HSPs feel different—they are still troubled by events or circumstances that others would be over by now. And because HSPs who have had troubled childhoods are especially distressed as adults, the trait becomes associated for everyone with anxiety and depression. But HSPs without a troubled past are no more psychologically distressed than anyone else—sometimes *less* so. That's important to remember. Depression or anxiety is *not* the basic trait of an HSP and they *can* be healed. Although that type of healing work is not the main focus of this workbook, Chapter 8 will provide a few nudges along the path.

SENSITIVITY IN A CULTURAL CONTEXT

Our culture needs us more than it knows, so there's an important social as well as personal reason for you to feel more empowered. A little history shows why this is. Aggressive, expansive cultures—the kind that do not value sensitivity—appeared about five thousand years ago in Europe and Asia, when nomadic herding tribes emerged from the steppes of Eurasia and took over the more peaceful peoples then living in Europe, the Middle East, and India. The usurpers spoke a language, Indo-European, which was the precursor of Greek, Latin, English, German, French, Spanish, Hindi, and many other languages as well. They brought a culture that, like the language, would spread into North and South America and eventually dominate most of the globe. There were similar incursions of nomads moving eastward, into China (hence the protective Great Wall was built) and Japan. The ancestors of the Greeks and Romans were the same sort of nomadic upstarts. Still later waves of nomadic "barbarians" such as the Huns and Mongols destroyed the empires of those who had gone before.

The nomads' philosophy was more herds, requiring more land, requiring attacks on other tribes, resulting in more captured women (they killed captured men and children) to have more sons to capture more herds, more land, more women to have more sons, more herds, and so forth. When the nomads took over the prosperous but unfortified cities of the agrarian and trading people that had attracted them out of their arid plains, they transformed the people into slaves and soldiers, the towns into fortresses, and the societies into empires. The order of the day: The best defense is a good offense, and survival requires an expanding economy. Sound familiar?

The Indo-European language and culture has taken over most of the globe. The more peaceful cultures such as the Native Americans and Australian aborigines have kind of been eaten for breakfast. Not all of these "prehistoric" cultures were primitive either. In Europe, the Middle East, India, and parts of North and South America, these earlier societies had developed large cities, sometimes with running water, metallurgy, and the beginnings of written language. But at least in Europe, the Middle East, and India, most of these cities were without kings, slaves, castles, or fortifications. There were no wars and very few signs of class distinctions among the people. Government was simple: In good times, food was brought into a temple complex and in hard times it was distributed. Except for overseeing trading activities, that seems to have been the extent of the central authorities.

In contrast, consider Indo-European governments—your culture's government, give or take some ethnic flavoring, whatever your race, if you grew up in an Indo-European-language-speaking culture. Aggressive cultures always have two ruling classes: the warrior kings and the priestly advisors (what I called "royal advisors" in *The Highly Sensitive Person*).

Who are the warrior kings? The ones who want to conquer everything. Go off to war immediately. In today's corporate world, they want to expand their markets, cut costs, apply the insecticides, and cut the trees. The priestly advisors are there to put the brakes on and point out the long-term effects, which have to be considered too. They do this braking through their roles of consultants, teachers, counselors, judges, artists, historians, and scientists, as well as through their social and personal power as healers and religious authorities.

Although HSPs have probably always been found in all walks of life and classes in society, it seems obvious that where there has been a need for "priestly advisors," we HSPs have traditionally filled that niche. Our brains are designed to *enjoy* reflection. In the past we were the very essence of the ideal schoolmarm or schoolmaster, family doctor, nurse, judge, lawyer, president (think of Abe Lincoln), artist, scientist, preacher, priest, and plain old conscientious citizen.

Today, however, we HSPs are finding a hard time managing in almost all of our traditional roles. As technology increases and costs are cut in order to compete in the global economy, people who can work long hours under stress are valued more than those who cannot. But an aggressive society without sensitive counselors to temper its aggressiveness is certainly going to get into trouble. HSPs have many other qualities needed by business and government. But it will take time for the warrior kings to understand that.

Should we have a "we-them" attitude? Not permanently perhaps, but for a while you will need it. Let yourself be a little proud about your trait, just temporarily, as an antidote to past feelings of inferiority. For now it's okay to think things like, "I am just being myself and they will have to adjust." The world needs us back in our central, influential position in society. To do that, we need to value ourselves, which will help others value us as well.

In sum, as you proceed through this workbook, remember that you are not just helping yourself. Slowly, HSP by HSP, we are restoring an essential balance to the world's dominant, in all senses, culture.

Now you are ready for your first task.

Speaking Up in Defense of High Sensitivity

The purpose of this task is to develop ready answers to those criticisms of your natural, inherited HSP style that you've heard all your life. Having an answer to them is so important—for you and for all HSPs. Developing these responses will also begin to change the inner critic who developed from all the outer criticism.

1. Write in the space below, on the lines for "Mislabeling," three to five things people have said or implied about your sensitivity that you now know to be a mislabeling of your experience. If it helps, think of specific situations.

    Some typical phrases and situations might be, "Don't be so sensitive," said by your supervisor when you react to her criticisms. "What's the matter with you?" said by a doctor when you cry after a "routine" procedure. "Don't be so shy," from friends when you don't wish to meet a stranger. "Why can't you just enjoy yourself?" when others want you to join them at a movie you see as too violent. "What are you so afraid of?" "That can't possibly hurt!" And so on.

There are also the subtler hints that you are neurotic, weird, overly fearful, hypersensitive, overly sensitive, or having an abnormal reaction. The mislabels you have heard must go on the "Mislabeling" line.

2. On the "My Response" line, write down how you would like to respond to each mislabeling in the future. Keep in mind facts like how many there are of us HSPs (15–20 percent of the population), our assets (sensing subtleties, processing deeply, conscientiousness, etc.), our importance (balancing the warrior kings), and our different strategy (reflect thoroughly before acting, see page 47). Write out full sentences you can actually use.

   For example, "You're too sensitive" might be answered many ways, but if a dentist or doctor said it to me with a critical tone, I would say, "I can understand that my sensitivity may be a problem for you, but it's not for me—I like the fact I'm one of the twenty percent born with more sensitive nervous systems." Then I would suggest that the exam or procedure will be more successful if I can feel I'm in a calm, supportive atmosphere. Otherwise, I need a referral to a professional who can work better with a sensitive patient.

   If "You're too sensitive" were said to me on the job about my response to a criticism, I would say, "How is my reaction troubling you?" I'd try to find out what the person's real issue was with me, but at some point I'd also probably say something like, "I know I tend to process information deeply, which means taking criticism very seriously—probably more seriously than most people. But that's all part of my sensitivity, which also . . ." Then I would give an example of how my sensitivity is an asset in my work.

   A few one-liners are good to develop too, such as, "I may be too sensitive for you, but as for myself, I like my sensitivity just fine." Or, " 'Too' by whose standards?" Or, "Funny—most of the people I know really like my sensitivity."

3. Under "Do I say this kind of thing to myself?" note how often and in what circumstances you criticize yourself for your sensitivity—and please vow that you will in the future use the same response to that inner voice that you have rehearsed to use on others.

Mislabeling 1: _Don't be so sensitive!_

My Response: _____

_____

_____

Do I say this kind of thing to myself?

_____

_____

Mislabeling 2: _You're selfish._

My Response: _____

_____

_____

Do I say this kind of thing to myself?

_____

_____

Mislabeling 3: _____

My Response: _____

_____

_____

Do I say this kind of thing to myself?

_____

_____

Mislabeling 4: _Don't be such a crybaby!_

My Response: _Deep feelings require expression._
Tears are healing. I admire people
who aren't afraid to cry, to feel.

Do I say this kind of thing to myself?

Not usually, though I used to. I've begun
to honor my tears.

Mislabeling 5: _Don't take yourself so seriously!_

My Response: _If I don't who will? And_
besides, who are you to tell me how
to think or feel?

Do I say this kind of thing to myself?

Unconsciously, yes, particularly in
regard to my writing.

Pairs and Groups: As, Bs, and Cs. This is an excellent, must-do task. You need to brainstorm, get creative, and have some fun with this one. A group could list the mislabelings together, then work on them as a group, or go around letting each person take a turn working on their "pet peeve" with others contributing responses. Take notes!

IN CONCLUSION: Reflect on what you have learned from this task. You might want to return in a week or two to this space as well, to note how you have put your increased respect for your trait into practice. Since this is your first "In Conclusion," here is an example of what you might write:

I see that I've tended to accept some of these "mislabels" as fundamentally
true. I've worked hard to get rid of my sensitivity. It feels strange to start trying

to refute what I'd seen to be valid, helpful (although always distressing) criticisms. But I like the idea.

_____

_____

_____

_____

_____

Your Sensing Self

This task is about being aware of yourself as a sensing body. It is based on the work of people like Eugene Gendlin and Betty Winkler Keane (see Resources, page 311). Sensory awareness was, of course, an important part of the humanistic psychology of the sixties and is still important to many therapists—as important as talking. The Jungian analyst Marion Woodman, for example, has said that no insight is really integrated into our lives until we can experience it some way in the body.

I cannot teach you any method of sensory awareness or body work in one session. Indeed, it is this sort of trivializing of it that keeps causing it to be "lost" so that it needs to be "rediscovered" by another generation. It is slow work, as is psychotherapy. But it's very important work for HSPs.

We HSPs, probably more than other people, carry the effects of many, many moments of overstimulation, stress, fear, and trauma. Where do we carry them? In ourselves, of course—our organisms, our bodies, and our brains included. And sometimes we have been so sensitive we have had to cut ourselves off from our sensations in those overstimulating moments to keep from being overwhelmed. If others were the cause of our being overwhelmed, we may have used our sensitivity to tune into what they wanted, hoping to appease them, instead of attending to what we needed. Indeed, sometimes our very survival as infants and children depended on our talent for tuning in to what others wanted. Later, that effort to please and appease others may have driven us in our work or other achievements.

The point is, in all these situations we had to learn to ignore the "no" messages from our own bodies. We turned off our exquisite sensitivity to our own selves. The result of these ignored messages? Headaches, backaches, stomachaches, and heartaches.

Humans are very much self-correcting, self-healing organisms. We only have to set up the right conditions, turning our attention onto ourselves for a while instead of always onto others, noticing what's up, and attending to that aching head, back, or whatever, while resting comfortably.

Maybe you have done some kind of focusing or sensory awareness work before, or maybe you have not. But right now, try it. You will have to read these instructions to yourself if you are doing this alone. If possible, tape record them so they can guide you through the task on playback. Either way, they aren't very complicated.

1. *Be in a place where you won't be disturbed* for at least an hour (although you don't need to spend that long at this task). Turn off the phones. Put on some comfortable clothing. Take off your shoes. Lie down on the floor. *Do not use any music or sound to accompany this task.*

2. *Give your attention to the sensations.* You might want to close your eyes, but you don't have to. Give your attention over to whatever is coming to you from your body—maybe from your ears, nose, skin, muscles, stomach, or sensations in the brain, throat, heart—anywhere. If the sensations are of sounds, smells, tastes, and sensations on the skin—things "outside" of you—fine. It is still your organism's operation you are attending to. There's no right way to do this. Do not judge what you experience or try to correct it.

3. *Let your attention shift to whatever sensation is strongest in the moment.* If your attention shifts a great deal, fine. It is very important that you not give up because your "mind wanders." Where it wanders is interesting in itself to observe. If you stop observing and get lost in thought, just gently bring your attention back to your present sensory experience. If you are off into thoughts nine-tenths of the time, that's okay—it's your wound-up mind settling down into your body. Observe that too, when you are aware of it. Just stay with your sensation, as aware as you can be of what's going on in your body. If you fall asleep, that just means you are tired. So sleep. And enjoy.

4. *Let whatever you are attending to change if it wants to.* If a sensation gets stronger, let it, even if it is uncomfortable. Just let it happen. Be an alert, caring, non-judging observer.

If the sensations turn into emotions, fine. Emotions are, after all, bodily events, such as tight breathing, tense muscles, nausea, tears, lightness, laughter, liveliness, pleasurable sexual feelings, and blissful glowing throughout the body.

If the sensations turn into images, fine. Images are how the psyche uses the empty brain when you aren't thinking with words. If you'd like, try to remember the most striking images. Stop and jot them down even, if in the long run that distracts you less than trying to remember them. There are no strict rules here. Some people keep a tape recorder on record and report aloud on what they experience. You can think about these images later, as you would dream images (see Chapter 10).

5. *Spend as much time as you want at this.* Allow enough time to experience the whole range of feelings. In particular, do not stop the first time you get restless. This can be the precursor of something important. With time, you might find you would enjoy staying with this task for an hour. Like meditation or yoga, it is an excellent "downtime" activity, and as an HSP you need downtime in order to stay healthy *just as much* as you need to eat and drink fluids and sleep.

6. *When you are done, acknowledge the self-healing power you have.* You do not need anyone or anything else, including this book, as much as you need to be with yourself in this attentive way so that you can self-heal. Everything else is just frosting on the cake.

7. *Make notes below of anything you especially noticed*—for example, what emotions you felt, what part of your body/mind seemed to be hurting or healing, and anything that you learned that suggests a need to adjust your lifestyle (more exercise, change in diet, need for a massage, etc.).

Pairs and Groups: Bs and Cs. While this seems like a completely individual task, it can help to have someone else asking you to sense how you are lying, sitting, and so forth, and then after a while asking you what you sensed. A tape could do this too, of course. (Betty Winkler Keane has one you can order—see Resources, page 311.)

If you do this in a group, there should be enthusiasm by all members to do the task. And while you can discuss together your experiences if you wish to, no one should be pushed to discuss it.

IN CONCLUSION: Reflect on how you feel about your body and what you learned from it, and write some of your thoughts here.

Reframing Your Past

Now we begin on the critical task of reframing your past in the light of knowing, now, that you were highly sensitive. As I said in the Introduction, this is the essence of what this workbook is about.

This is not easy work. Reframing can be painful and more difficult than other tasks. But the results are worth it.

To begin, you will be reframing your reaction to one major change or transition in your life. You can do it for more than one if you like, but take it slow—do no more than one a day. In later chapters you will be asked to come back to these instructions to reframe your childhood, adolescence, "shy" social experiences, career choices, relationship issues, and medical experiences. Why begin with a change in your life? Because every new situation, transition, or change involves many new stimuli, and since we pick up on more stimuli because we include all the subtleties, every change is a bigger change for us than for the non-HSP. We need more time to plan the change, accept it, and process it afterward. When we don't do this, the change can be rough. But when we do, others may criticize us for being "overanxious," "indecisive," or "inflexible." Either way, we often feel long afterward that we handled the event poorly.

Don't forget any "overreactions" to good changes. Intense overarousal to a good change or surprise can be the most upsetting. So many adults have told me of lingering bad feelings about themselves because of their "wrong" reaction to a surprise birthday party in childhood. When my first and only novel was published, in England, I had to go there and enjoy my fifteen minutes of fame at parties and such. I was finally living a fantasy I had cherished for years. And I became very sick and hardly enjoyed a minute of it—which again made me feel there was something wrong with me, maybe an unconscious fear of success. Now I know it was just too much excitement.

Begin by writing down a major life change or transition that you feel you handled poorly—you think you became too stressed, made the wrong decision, reacted "abnormally." The change might be entering grade school, junior high, high school, college, getting married, landing a new job, having a child, having a child leave home, a death, menopause or other health changes, a divorce, a job loss, a move (a big one we often underestimate), a natural disaster, or a change in the life of someone close to you. It could also be a promotion or an award. It could be a change you initiated or one that just happened to you.

The life event: _____

_____

_____

_____

Now let's reframe it.

1. Recall how you responded to the event. Write here whatever you can recall about your response at the time—your mood, health, attitude, and so forth. Chances are there were signs of stress, fatigue, illness, or irritability. An example:

   When I went away to college. Very lonely. Didn't like most of the students I met. Didn't like my roommate. He drank a lot. I couldn't sleep. Couldn't concentrate. Got colitis and was sent to infirmary. Fell behind further in classes. Failing. Went home at Christmas. Couldn't make myself go back. Went to a community college, far beneath my abilities. Very depressed for rest of year.

   _____

   _____

   _____

   _____

2. Write here the feelings you still carry around about your response to the event you are trying to reframe. Continuing the example:

   I've always seen this as a big failure, a sign of my generally having something wrong with me. So did my parents. They sent me to a therapist. Didn't help much—we talked about my childhood, which made me feel bad because my parents are basically pretty great. That made me feel even more that something's the matter with me.

   _____

   _____

   _____

   _____

3. Consider your response in light of what you now know from this book, that HSPs pick up on more subtleties and process everything more deeply, and so are also more bothered by high levels of stimulation. For us, high stimulation leads to overarousal. No one feels good or performs as well when overaroused. During a change, stimulation is higher for us than others, so arousal is too. We can't expect as much of ourselves at those times.

   Use the next space to write how you understand this event in the light of HSPs' typical responses to change. What you write here is what you need to say to yourself and believe, so make it strong and kind. If it helps, imagine me saying it to you. Continuing the example:

   I was overwhelmed, overstimulated. I needed time to get used to all the new stuff—new room, people, food, college courses, keeping a checkbook. Getting sick was expectable. Back home at Christmas, of course I didn't want to go back and fail more. It was all perfectly normal, for an HSP. HSPs need to give themselves a lot of freedom to make changes slowly, not all at once. I didn't know that and nobody around me did either, so I couldn't compensate for it or get any useful help.

   _____

   _____

   _____

   _____

   _____

   _____

4. Write next how you might have been able to handle the change differently, had you known better. Do not make this a self-criticism, but a sympathetic statement of how you suffered unnecessarily because you and others did not know you were an HSP, and an acknowledgment that you are now ca-

pable of greater self-understanding and kinder self-treatment in the future. Continuing the example:

I could have gone to a local college, or to one where I knew someone. If a counselor at school had known about this trait, that would have helped a lot. Maybe I could have taken a year's leave of absence and come back into a new class, but with everything else more familiar. I'll try never to do something like that to myself again.

_____

_____

_____

_____

5. If handling it differently would have prevented your suffering or wasting a portion of your life, take time to feel whatever you feel about that. Write here what you observe. Continuing the example:

I feel lousy about this. It makes me furious. I think my life would have gone much differently if I could have stayed at that college—I would have had more self-confidence, a better education, gone to a better graduate school, had more friends who would have become high-placed contacts in my field. Knowing what I know now, I am sure I could have made it there. This will always seem like a tragedy to me. I feel like crying.

_____

_____

_____

_____

_____

6. Write a summary of your new understanding of the event and read it over often until you have absorbed the full meaning of it. Continuing the example:
   What happened does not mean I am an inherently troubled or shy person doomed to have difficulties all my life. I am a highly sensitive person, which includes being more affected by changes. I am unusually alert to subtle changes but overwhelmed by large ones. Now that I know better how to handle my reaction to change, I think I can get through any change I choose, but I'll do it at my own pace.

_____

_____

_____

_____

_____

_____

Here's a summary of the steps in reframing:
1. Recall how you responded to the event.
2. Recall how you have tended to feel about that response.
3. Consider your response in light of what you now know about your trait.
4. Think about whether the negative parts of the event might have been avoided or would have gone differently if you or others had known you were an HSP and had made adjustments for that.
5. If this knowledge would have prevented your suffering or wasting a portion of your life, take time to feel whatever you feel about that.
6. Write down your new understanding of the event and read it over often until you have absorbed the full meaning of it.

Pairs and Groups: As, Bs, and Cs.

IN CONCLUSION: In the following space you will develop a list of the experiences you have reframed, with a brief statement of that reframing. Begin with this reframing task and add to this list when you are asked to in future chapters. If you find yourself spontaneously reframing an event in terms of your sensitivity, add that to the list too. Review the list now and then to reinforce and integrate this new perspective of yourself. Here's a sample first entry, using the above experience:

1. A reaction to change—my not staying away at college. There's no reason for the shame I've felt about it. It was way too big of a change when I had no understanding of why I was so overwhelmed and no appropriate support.

1. _____

_____

2. _____

_____

etc. _____

_____

_____

_____

_____

_____

_____

_____

_____

_____

_____

_____

Your Role as a Priestly Advisor

The purpose of this task is to help you think about yourself as a priestly advisor. In the introduction to this chapter, you read that aggressive, expansive cultures always seem to have two ruling classes, the warrior kings and the priestly advisors, and the latter have probably traditionally been HSPs. In this role, the HSP teaches, counsels, advises, heals, keeps the history in words or art forms, envisions the future, thinks about the meaning of life and death, leads rituals, studies the subtleties of nature or law, and puts the brakes on the more impulsive warrior kings.

Your career may actually be in one of the above domains, or you may take the priestly advisor role in more informal ways—in your office, with clients or customers. It may also show up even more in nonwork activities—with friends, family, in the community, through a pastime, and so forth.

In the left column, list as many ways as you can think of that you function as a priestly advisor. In the right column, list as many traits as you can think of in your personality that make you seem like a priestly advisor.

Ways/Roles	*Traits*
"Open" literature	compassionate
advise	probing,
listen	synthesizing
notice	like to touch, to heal
sometimes tuned to intuitive wisdom	musical, poetic

_____   _____

_____   _____

_____   _____

_____   _____

_____   _____

Pairs and Groups: As, Bs, and Cs.

IN CONCLUSION: Take a moment to reflect and write about what you have realized
from this task.

_____

_____

_____

_____

_____

What You Don't Like About Yourself—And the Deeper Why

It's a bit bold of me to ask you to try to do this task in a workbook, but it's so important that I felt it must be included. It's walking right into the enemy camp, so to
speak—the "What's-the-matter-with-you" zone. It's the zone of all your self-criticism,
some of which may be justified but much of which is not. Sorting that out is the task.
But here more than elsewhere in this workbook, if this task isn't working for you,
leave it be, or do it with some professional help. Also, do not do this task right after
any other one. Take it on separately—perhaps when you are particularly fed up with
yourself, or with your own self-criticism. And you do not have to finish this task
now. You can return to it as you have insights later, and you will definitely be asked
to return to it at the end of the workbook.

Having made you sufficiently wary, I should also say that what you will be doing may also be all too easy—many of us do it all day! We just do it half consciously. The goal is to make it more conscious and fair.

You will be taking a close look at three aspects of yourself that you most dislike. This should not be an exercise in totally irrational self-loathing, but do allow yourself to delve into those issues that you feel are problems: The aspects that limit how much you can admire yourself. The parts of yourself that most trouble or shame you.

Begin by writing down the three aspects of yourself you do not like. Don't just call yourself bad names. "Fat," "Stupid," or "Lazy" are *not* fair or useful terms. Try to come up with more reasonable phrases, like "I can't seem to stop overeating," "I seem slow to understand," or "I wish I worked harder." List these three aspects here:

I. _____

II. _____

III. _____

Aspect I

For now, for each of the questions below, we'll just attend to Aspect I. (Later you will do Aspects II and III in the same way.)

1. *Identify specific behaviors.* Write below the specific behaviors or choices that, these days, make you feel this particular way about yourself. If Aspect I was "I wish I worked harder," you might write, "I left college without finishing" or "I can't make myself get out of bed on Saturdays to exercise."

_____

_____

_____

_____

2. *Rating of importance.* Rate this aspect on a scale of 0, "I really am not very concerned at all about this issue," to 10, "this issue creates a deep dislike of myself that is the most important influence on my life." Put your rating here: _____.

3. *Your reaction at this point.* Take a deep breath and reflect a moment. You've already done a lot. Check in with how you feel after naming these three and going into some detail about the specific behaviors involved in one of them. Scared by what you see? Disgusted? Angry with yourself? Write a little about this here:

_____

_____

_____

4. *Observations about your self-criticism.* See if you can notice a certain inner voice or part of yourself that is activated when you think about this aspect of yourself—a kind of inner critic, perhaps? Try to answer the questions below.

      a. How often do you hear this voice or think critical thoughts about this aspect of yourself? (You may have to revise your estimate upward as you become aware of how often this voice speaks to you.)

_____

_____

      b. Is the voice or critic personified or symbolized in your dreams? Perhaps it is a judge, police officer, animal trainer, teacher, cruel person, friendly advisor, competitor, or a certain friend. (This may help you answer the next question.)

_____

_____

      c. If you haven't thought of it as having a name, gender, and personality, think about that voice or figure in these ways. Is it always one gender? Different when one gender or the other? What would you name it? What kind of personality would you say it has?

_____

_____

d. Do you know when it was "born" (when it came into existence inside of you)? Did it begin as someone else's voice? If so, whose?

_____

_____

e. Do you think this voice's attitude about this aspect of you is rational and well justified by the facts, or does it come from other people's wounds and issues?

_____

_____

f. This step is important. Ask this voice what it wants. More specifically, does it want to help or hurt you? Write its answer here. (If this is difficult for you, come back to this after doing "Active Imagination" on page 61.)

_____

_____

5. *This aspect in light of your sensitivity.* Now think about anything you have learned about sensitivity that could possibly be contributing to these behaviors or choices. You will have to turn off the inner critic for this. If it would help, imagine me doing this with you.

Suppose your issue is "I can't stop overeating." Is there any way that being sensitive contributes? Do you eat when you are overstimulated or stressed? Do you feed yourself when you are anxious or depressed, and could your anxiety and depression be due to having an unhappy past that, in combination with your trait, left you vulnerable to these feelings? Is overeating really a problem (hurting your health and social life)? Or could this concern be part of a general pattern of self-criticism or even self-deprivation due to a deep sense of being flawed in a culture that does not respect sensitivity?

The point here is *not* to use sensitivity as an excuse or even an explanation for everything. We all have bad habits that we really do need to change. We're human. But I do want you to look carefully at the role of your high sensitivity in your life, particularly in those areas where you are having trouble and as a result feel bad about yourself.

Write here anything you have learned about sensitivity that could possibly be contributing to these behaviors or choices.

---

6. *A new way to approach it?* Think about how you would approach this aspect of yourself given its relationship to your sensitivity. Would you try solving it differently? Would you forgive yourself and accept it as just part of being sensitive? Would you even continue to call it a problem? Again, if it helps, imagine me doing this with you. Write down your new ideas about seeing or handling this aspect of yourself.

---

7. *What else from your past contributes to this behavior?*
   - Who in your life behaves the same way? If it's a family member, could some other inherited trait, such as a hot temper, be influencing your behavior?
   - Is this the continuation of a negative habit taught over the generations?

- Is this behavior an attempt to control anxiety or bad feelings about yourself that began in the past?
- Look back at Step 4e, where you attended to the source of the inner voice that criticizes you for this aspect of yourself. Who criticized this aspect of you? Did you hear them criticize it in others? In themselves? Do you respect their opinions on this issue?

Write here anything you know about any other sources of this disliked aspect of yourself besides your sensitivity.

_____

_____

_____

_____

_____

_____

8. *Rating now.* Try to make contact again with how much concern you have about this issue *now*, after having considered it in these ways. Rate its strength again on the 0, little, to 10, a lot, scale:_____

9. *Any change in how you feel about this aspect of yourself?* If your rating was high before, if you were full of self-loathing, has it helped at all to think about this aspect of yourself in the ways you just have, in terms of your sensitivity especially, and also in light of the other influences in your life?

_____

_____

_____

_____

Aspect II Write the issue here:_____

Now you'll do the same nine steps for Aspect II as you did for Aspect I. If you need to, look back at page 33 to get started.

1. *Identify specific behaviors.*

_____

_____

_____

_____

2. *Rating of importance.* From 0, "I really am not very concerned at all about this issue," to 10, "this issue creates a deep dislike of myself that is the most important influence on my life." Put your rating here:_____.

3. *Your reaction at this point.* How do you feel after naming these three and going into some detail about the specific behaviors involved in two of them?

_____

_____

_____

4. *Observations about your self-criticism.* See if you can notice a certain inner voice or part of yourself that is activated when you think about this aspect of yourself.
    a. How often do you hear it?

_____

_____

    b. Is it personified or symbolized in your dreams?

_____

_____

c. Is it always one gender? Different when one gender or the other? What would you name it? What kind of personality would you say it has?

_____

_____

d. Do you know when it was "born" (when it came into existence inside of you)? Did it begin as someone else's voice? If so, whose?

_____

_____

e. Do you think this voice's attitude about this aspect of you is rational and well justified by the facts, or does it come from other people's wounds and issues?

_____

_____

f. This step is important. Ask this voice what it wants. More specifically, does it want to help or hurt you?

_____

_____

5. *This aspect in light of your sensitivity.* Now think about anything you have learned about sensitivity that could possibly be contributing to these behaviors or choices.

_____

_____

_____

_____

_____

_____

6. *A new way to approach it?* Think about how you would approach this aspect of yourself given its relationship to your sensitivity. Would you try solving it differently? Would you accept it as just part of being sensitive? Would you even continue to call it a problem?

_____

_____

_____

7. *What else from your past contributes to this behavior?*
   • Who in your life behaves the same way? If it's a family member, could some other inherited trait, such as a hot temper, be influencing your behavior?
   • Is this the continuation of a negative habit taught over the generations?
   • Is this behavior an attempt to control anxiety or bad feelings about yourself that began in the past?
   • Who criticized this aspect of you? Did you hear them criticize it in others? In themselves? Do you respect their opinion?

Write here anything you know about any other sources of this disliked aspect of yourself besides your sensitivity.

_____

_____

_____

_____

_____

_____

8. *Rating now.* Rate its strength again on the 0, little, to 10, a lot, scale:_____
9. *Any change in how you feel about this aspect of yourself? If so, do you know why?*

_____

_____

_____

_____

Aspect III Write the issue: _____
Now you'll do the same nine steps for Aspect III as you did for Aspects I and II.

1. *Identify specific behaviors.*

_____

_____

_____

_____

2. *Rating of importance.* From 0, "I really am not very concerned at all about this issue" to 10, "this issue creates a deep dislike of myself that is the most important influence on my life." Put your rating here:_____.

3. *Your reaction at this point.* How do you feel after naming these three and going into some detail about the specific behaviors involved in them?

_____

_____

_____

4. *Observations about your self-criticisms.* See if you can notice a certain inner voice or part of yourself that is activated when you think about this aspect of yourself.

　　a. How often do you hear it?

_____

_____

　　b. Is it personified or symbolized in your dreams?

_____

_____

　　c. Is it always one gender? Different when one gender or the other? What would you name it? What kind of personality would you say it has?

_____

_____

　　d. Do you know when it was "born" (when it came into existence inside of you)? Did it begin as someone else's voice? If so, whose?

_____

_____

　　e. Do you think this voice's attitude about this aspect of you is rational and well justified by the facts, or does it come from other people's wounds and issues?

_____

_____

　　f. This step is important. Ask this voice what it wants. More specifically, does it want to help or hurt you?

_____

_____

5. *This aspect in light of your sensitivity.* Now think about anything you have learned about sensitivity that could possibly be contributing to these behaviors or choices.

_____

_____

_____

_____

_____

_____

6. *A new way to approach it?* Think about how you would approach this aspect of yourself given its relationship to your sensitivity. Would you try solving it differently? Would you accept it as just part of being sensitive? Would you even continue to call it a problem?

_____

_____

_____

_____

7. *What from your past contributes to this behavior?*
   - Who in your life behaves the same way? If it's a family member, could some other inherited trait, such as a hot temper, be influencing your behavior?
   - Is this the continuation of a negative habit taught over the generations?

- Is this behavior an attempt to control anxiety or bad feelings about yourself that began in the past?
- Who criticized this aspect of you? Did you hear them criticize it in others? In themselves? Do you respect their opinion?

Write here anything you know about any other sources of this disliked aspect of yourself besides your sensitivity.

_____

_____

_____

_____

_____

8. *Rating now.*_____
9. *Any change in how you feel about this aspect of yourself? If so, do you know why?*

_____

_____

_____

_____

Pairs and Groups. Cs only. Groups should not do this without an anonymous, unanimous vote. Some tips for handling this delicate material: When others are sharing their disliked aspects, you may find it quite untrue of them. Say so, but if they vehemently persist, encourage them to get help. If you recognize this aspect of them as something *you* dislike in them too, you have a chance to help, but only with great gentleness. Speak first of the positive aspects of the behavior—for example, "stubbornness" or "competitiveness" have their virtues. If you are working with a partner, suggest how you two could be closer without the behavior, and express that you'd be willing to reinforce the behavior the person wants to have instead. Lace all of this with examples of your own problem areas and how humble they make you feel!

IN CONCLUSION: Think a few minutes more, then write about what you have learned from this task.

_____

_____

_____

_____

_____

2

Going Deeper
into Who You Are

This chapter seeks to help you gain an even deeper familiarity with your body, your sensitivity, and your psyche. You will learn less about sensitivity in general, and more about you and yours in particular. It's an old cliché but true: We are each unique. While I can't write about *your* uniqueness, not knowing you, I can stir your thoughts about how you are different from others with a few more observations about how HSPs are different from others.

One way to think about the trait is to see it as a different style of being in the world, a different survival strategy. When a species has more than one innate survival strategy, there are more ways for the individuals to adapt. This makes good sense. Again, there's a reason for HSPs being around all these eons.

What's the HSP style? We are designed to consider carefully before acting so that we are rarely wrong (i.e., dead). We are designed to detect all the nuances in a situation and ponder them deeply. This strategy, when used by sensitive animals, means taking great care to avoid a predator, find the right mate, choose nutritious food and safe shelter, decide when to fight and when to run, and so forth. In humans . . . well, maybe it's not so different. We HSPs are careful about predators, mates, food, and shelter. In our hunting days, HSPs were the type who took careful aim, shot one arrow, and hit the mark.

I like to imagine that in a social group, human or animal, we would be the first ones to notice a lion in the bushes. We warn the others, and those who are better designed for fighting go to it. The group needs a few specialists in detection and the rest for carrying out the needed action. That might be why there are so many more of them than there are of us!

What is the style of the other 80 percent of the population? They like to act quickly, take more risks, and take less time to ponder. As animals, these sorts explore new territory impulsively and are quick to taste a new food or risk combat for a new mate. As hunters, they probably shot twenty arrows on the run, hoping one would hit home.

Both strategies work. Sometimes the impulsive risk taker has an advantage. In horse racing, that's when the long shot wins. Many times the careful calculator of all the conditions has the advantage. In fact, the two groups have about the same chance of doing well—but in very different ways.

To think of your trait in terms of strategy and outcome, however, is to borrow "warrior king" metaphors. HSPs also simply enjoy the subtle and deep side of life more, which is not easily observed or translated into winning or losing. In the human species, in particular, being an HSP has fresh meaning because humans seem to specialize in being aware, and HSPs are the greatest specialists in that. We are especially human in that sense. But awareness brings psychological pain, because humans appear to be the only species that anticipates loss and death, and they will kill themselves if they can find no meaning in all of this, no reason to go on in the face of eventual pain, loss, and death. Some humans manage to push the issue of loss and death out of awareness—the defense called denial. This is one reason for the unconscious. In contrast, HSPs tend to work on these issues, even before they are in their faces.

What's often observed about HSPs is our silence, our pausing, and if we say something, our "deep" or even "dark" thoughts. When we are silent and pausing, no one knows why we are pausing. Thus an observer can attribute any motive or trait to us. We have been said to be afraid, aloof, shy, inhibited, timid, arrogant, stupid, slow, deep, shallow, depressed, self-absorbed, anxious, narcissistic, and a lot of other things, too. About our deep thoughts, we are seen as pessimistic or "less capable of positive feelings." *Hmpf.*

Returning to the two-strategies-in-every-species idea, I think my favorite mislabeling of our style is from a scientific report, in which pumpkin-seed sunfish with these two survival strategies were sorted by setting out traps. It was said that the "normal" sunfish "boldly" went into the traps that the "timid" sunfish avoided. Why not speak of the "stupid" and the "smart" sunfish?

It seems to be time for us to let the rest of the world know a little more about what it's really like, from the inside, to be an HSP. And to know that, you need to explore those inner regions yourself. So let's begin.

The Adventure Party—Getting to Know Your Bodily Strengths and Weaknesses

The purpose of this task is to get to know yourself thoroughly, as an organism. The method this time will be personification and storytelling. It will be fun, but will require some work. When you are asked to write imaginatively, just make notes if you start fearing your literary skills are inadequate. Don't let issues of style get in the way of your creativity.

You will begin by thinking of your most important (to you) body parts, functions, or organ systems—nervous system, digestion, lungs, muscles, eyes, intelligence, emotions, and so forth—as a group involved in a lifelong adventure story, like the adventurers in fantasy and science fiction stories, or the characters in fairy tales or animal stories. (Tolkien's *Hobbit* stories and C. S. Lewis's *Narnia* stories are some examples.) Or you can imagine your body parts as a group on an actual expedition of exploration, like those to the Arctic and Antarctic Poles. Either way, the goal is to see them as a group of interesting characters. Some of the group's members are strong, always out in front and leading, able to carry the heaviest packs. Maybe for you, Digestive System can always be counted on. Muscles and Lungs may even be heros. Others need to be looked out for. Maybe Knees started out strong, but were injured or pushed too hard. Some—maybe for you the Immune System That Creates Allergies—have always been the weak members of the party, but are needed nevertheless.

No two adventure parties are the same. And no one knows more about yours than you do. But you need to have conscious knowledge of the group you travel with, not a vague feeling that puts too much emphasis on a single star or troublemaker.

1. *Go over your body, thinking about all the parts and functions, local and general, that you have come to be aware of at all, in any way, due to pride, illness, injury, or whatever.* These might be the muscles, hair, eyes, brain, thyroid, nervous system, immune system, skin, genitals, coordination, lung capacity, emotional responses, menopausal body, or sexual responsiveness. List these by some appropri-

ate "Adventure Party" name. Maybe you'll want to name them the way Indians name their children—with characteristics important to you, like Lungs So Much Stronger Since I Stopped Smoking or Face That Blushes Often. Or use characters from stories you like, like Eeyore for the emotions.

Make the list as long as you like. Just be sure the important ones are there. You might have someone who knows you well check to be sure you didn't forget any part important to you.

2. *In the next column, comment on the characteristic behavior of each when you are starting out on a journey or project.* (In other words, how it handles a fresh start involving change.) Examples: Strong Heart—pounding. Four Eyes (because I wear glasses)—doing fine, ready for action.

3. *In the third column, comment on each character's ability to hang in there day-to-day.* How much of a "trooper" is this character? Examples: Strong Heart—amazingly steady, thanks to daily exercise. Four Eyes—tires at the computer, likes to rest with no glasses and go walking in the woods.

4. *In the last column, comment on each character's behavior in a crisis.* You can also think how one takes over for the other. Examples: Strong Heart—does so well! But pounds of course. Four Eyes—never yet let me down; in a crisis, they help Emotions settle down by closing a moment to calm me down.

System, Body Part, or Function	*Behavior When You Start a Journey*	*Capacity to Keep Going*	*Courage Under Fire*
_____	_____	_____	_____
	_____	_____	_____
_____	_____	_____	_____
	_____	_____	_____
_____	_____	_____	_____
	_____	_____	_____
_____	_____	_____	_____

_____   _____   _____   _____

          _____   _____   _____

5. *Place a star next to the major five to ten players—the biggest heroes and trou-blemakers, those you use often, take pride in, medicate, worry about, and so forth.*

6. *Now write a fair, honest, useful description of your Adventure Party, as if it were a report for someone joining it whose life depended on it (yours does).* Make it dramatic, with plenty of interplay among the heroes, the steady ones, the ones to keep an eye on (it may help to focus on those you starred). If you are enjoying this, go on to imagine an exciting adventure they go through together—a crisis of some sort, maybe one you've actually had—and make this description into a story. Don't let the space provided here limit you—write as much as you like.

_____

_____

_____

_____

_____

_____

_____

_____

_____

_____

_____

_____

_____

_____

_____

_____

7. *In your imagination, have a talk with a few of these parts.* Maybe you want to thank one, or ask one why it keeps being a problem. You can also eavesdrop while they talk among themselves. Perhaps most important, ask each what you can do to help. And listen well to the answers. (For example, Strong Heart tells me it won't be strong forever and to have plenty of adventures while I can. Left Brain retorts that Strong Heart is such a pessimist, for all his steady pumping. And Strong Heart says Left Brain is a cheerful fool, always in denial about death and other limits. They could fight all day.) Make notes of what you learn here.

_____

_____

_____

_____

_____

Pairs and Groups: Bs and Cs.

IN CONCLUSION: Use the lines below to summarize your insights from spending this time with your bodily aspects/characters.

_____

_____

_____

_____

_____

A Self-Assessment to Discover Your Style of Sensitivity

The following questions are mostly from a research questionnaire I have given to at least a thousand people. A few are based on research by others. After you have answered them, you will read what I know about HSPs who say yes or no to each.

1. Do you love trying new things (if they are not going to be too overwhelming)? Yes No (Circle one.)
2. Are you easily bored? Yes No
3. Would you eventually be restless living a quiet, secluded, regulated life, like in a monastery or running a lighthouse? Yes No
4. Do you usually not want to see a movie twice, even if you enjoyed it the first time? Yes No
5. Do you enjoy trying new things? Yes No
6. Do you like having just a few close friends (as opposed to a large circle of friends)? Yes No
7. Do you prefer to go out with one or two friends (versus in a large group)? Yes No
8. Are you a tense or worried person by nature? Yes No
9. Are you prone to fears? Yes No
10. Do you cry easily? Yes No
11. Are you prone to depression? Yes No
12. Were you close to your father? Yes No
13. Was your father involved in your family during your childhood? Yes No
14. Were you close to your mother? Yes No
15. Was your mother fond of infants and small children (liking to hold and cuddle them, having them around her)? Yes No
16. Was alcoholism a problem in your immediate family while you were growing up? Yes No

17. Was mental illness a problem in your immediate family while you were growing up? Yes No

18. Do you consider yourself to be a shy person? Yes No

19. Are you a "morning person" (liking to go to bed early and get up early, working best in the morning, tiring most in late afternoon and evening)? Yes No

20. Are you particularly sensitive to the effects of caffeine? Yes No

21. Are you ambitious? Yes No

22. Do you avoid angry confrontations? Yes No

Reviewing the Self-Assessment of Your Style of Sensitivity

Sensitivity comes in many "flavors." This may be because there are several genes controlling it, or it may be due to its interaction with other genetic traits. In some cases, as I will explain, life experiences are the best explanation for the variations. I have researched only a few of these flavors, but here are the ones I know about so far.

HSPs High and Low on Curiosity (Questions 1–5)

These questions explore how much, in spite of your sensitivity, you seek new stimulation. Research suggests that there are two brain systems that control our impulses to act. We all have both, and everyone varies in how active the two systems are. One, called the Behavioral Inhibition System or BIS, causes us to pause and check before acting. This system is thought to be strong in all HSPs. The other is called the Behavioral Activation System or BAS. It causes us to seek rewards and be curious, active, and easily bored. People high in the BAS are called "sensation seekers." HSPs can be either high or low on this one, making two types of HSPs. HSPs high in both systems are going to find it hard to stay in their optimal level of arousal. They can easily slip into boredom on the one hand or into overarousal on the other. Many HSPs of this sort wonder how they can be HSPs at all when they compare themselves to those HSPs who love quiet, reclusive lives and are never bored. But these are two distinct types of HSPs (and of course, many fall in the middle).

The first five questions roughly measure curiosity, sensation seeking, or the strength of the BAS. A yes to four or five of these questions would definitely make you a sensation-seeking HSP. A yes to three would put you comfortably in the middle. A yes to none, one, or two means you have the thoughtful, calm-loving style of a pure HSP.

Introverted and Extroverted HSPs (Questions 6 and 7)

About 70 percent of HSPs are introverts, meaning they need and like people, but prefer to have a few close friends and to be with one or two of them rather than in a large group. Like sensation-seeking HSPs, many extroverted HSPs wonder if they are HSPs at all because they are so different from introverted HSPs. But if you prefer to "recharge your batteries" alone (or in silence with a friend), and if you like to take your time making decisions, then you are still an HSP. The non-HSP extroverts can hardly settle down without some people in the vicinity, and they tend to be impulsive decision makers.

How do HSPs become extroverted? Usually from growing up in an extroverted family, neighborhood, or community, where there were lots of people coming and going and everyone enjoyed that. It became familiar, safe. Some HSPs may also be forced into extroversion to please an extroverted family or to compensate for or hide their sensitivity.

A yes on both 6 and 7 indicates introversion. For an HSP, a no on either one (or both) would indicate a fair amount of extroversion.

Troubled and Untroubled HSPs (Questions 8–17)

When I began my research, I asked questions 8 through 11 (about depression, anxiety, worry, etc.) to see the relation of anxiety and depression to sensitivity, and I found two rather distinct types of HSPs. About a third answered yes to these questions—they seemed to be anxious and depressed. The rest did not. At first I thought there might be two kinds of sensitivity being inherited—one that has an element of anxiety and depression and one that does not. Then I looked at the data on questions 12 through 17, on childhood home environment. The more of these that HSPs answered in a way that suggested a bad home environment during childhood, the more likely it was that those people answered yes to questions 8 through 11.

To put it another way, HSPs without a troubled childhood home were not anxious or depressed; non-HSPs with a troubled childhood home were somewhat anxious and depressed, but not as much as HSPs with a bad childhood home life. This makes sense, for three reasons. First, as children we HSPs are more aware of what is happening and feel it more deeply. Second, we need wise guidance in handling novel situations and overwhelming emotions, which stressed parents can't supply, so their sensitive children grow up without the skills for handling their fears and sadness. Third, childhood home environment affects the brain physiology (although this is not necessarily irreversible). One study found that monkeys separated from their mothers when young were fine as adults until under stress—then they became more distressed and anxious than monkeys never separated from their mothers when young.

A yes to any of questions 8 through 11—about anxiety, depression, and worry— suggests some personal troubles (although crying easily is not as clear a sign as the others). This is probably no surprise to you if you answered yes to them. Answers of no on 12 through 15 and yes on 16 and 17 (about your parents, and on mental ill- ness and alcoholism in your family) are some indications of a difficult home envi- ronment in your childhood.

Again, adult depression and anxiety *tend* to go hand in hand with a negative childhood home life. But "tend" is an important qualifier here because you may have enjoyed some compensating circumstances, such as wonderful grandparents. And my questions about childhood stressors are not complete, although they were certainly enough to show the connection statistically in my research. But rather than list all the possibilities here, and still perhaps miss the one most important for you, please think for yourself about whether your childhood was unusually stressful (or for a longer list to jog your memory, turn to page 201). If you have some difficulties with anxiety and depression, now you know why. We'll return to these topics in chapters 4 and 8.

Shyness (Question 18)

Did you say yes, you consider yourself to be a shy person? In my research, I found the relationship between shyness and sensitivity was the same as that be- tween anxiety/depression and sensitivity: While there are many shy people who are not HSPs, those who are HSPs and shy tend to be those whose answers to questions 12 through 17 indicated a negative childhood home environment. So we are not born shy, just sensitive, but a hostile or insensitive home can and often does lead to shyness.

Miscellaneous but Important Differences (Questions 19–22)

Questions 19 and 20, on being a morning person and on caffeine sensitivity, are important because if you realize these are true for you, you will be better able to maintain your optimal level of arousal. If you are a morning person (many HSPs are, but not all by any means), you are probably more easily overaroused in the morning, even if you don't notice the effects until the end of the day. Make good use of your fresh energy in the mornings and don't push yourself in the afternoon. Evenings are your time to recuperate and go to bed early. Being a morning person puts you out of synch with night people, of course, but also with most non-HSPs, who can usually keep going in the evening whether they are morning or night people.

HSPs who are not morning people, however, often sing the praises of their lifestyle. It's so quiet at night after everyone has gone to bed. Indeed, one HSP told me her life was much happier once she took the evening shift at her job, working 4 to 11 P.M. She could sleep in every morning, commute at quiet times, and encounter fewer problems and people to deal with on the job. Clearly, this is something to consider.

Most HSPs are sensitive to caffeine. Even if you are used to caffeine, you will probably have a strong reaction if you take more than your usual amount. If you are not used to it, use it cautiously, especially if you are a morning person not used to caffeine and decide to drink coffee one morning to perform better. That could be a mistake, making you overaroused.

Question 21 (ambitiousness) is not related one way or the other to being an HSP, although in my research very introverted HSPs were definitely less ambitious. Those HSPs who were ambitious saw the trait as an advantage—which is a good thing for anyone, but especially if an HSP plans to go places.

A yes on question 22 (avoiding anger) is only very slightly more common among HSPs, and mainly, again, if you are very introverted. I find that HSPs who can get angry seem to have a little easier life—they are quicker to say "enough!"

Putting It All Together

I think you can see that an introverted, sensation-seeking HSP with a troubled childhood would be quite different from an extroverted, easily contented HSP with a good childhood. Add a dash of ambition or anger, and the mixture gets even more interesting. And we haven't touched on other differences, such as your special abilities—cognitive, musical, artistic, athletic, and so on. So you are quite unique after all.

Pairs and Groups: As, Bs, and Cs. You can certainly discuss your results, but probably this is mostly an individual task.

IN CONCLUSION: Any reactions to what you have learned? Write them down here.

Some of these were hard to answer. I don't like thinking that I had a "troubled" child-

work. Heavy denial arises — I want to defend my points!

Summarizing You

Having explored yourself so deeply, write below a brief description of the *unique* HSP you are. *Start your description with this qualification:* "At this point in my life I am . . ." Because, of course, change is not only possible but desirable and inevitable. Include in your statement whatever you learned from the "Adventure Party" task and whatever you learned from the self-assessment I just discussed. Start with the characteristics or experiences that seem most important, then add anything else that stands out and would be necessary to give an accurate brief description.

This statement will be like no one else's. It will be yours. However, here are some examples to give you an idea. One HSP I know could have written this:

> *At this point in my life I am an extroverted, emotional HSP, an executive (male) who makes use of these traits to enjoy considerable success, controlling my reactions when I have to, but also using them when they are an asset. I had a happy, healthy childhood except for many allergies. As an adult I suffer from terrible headaches, but have a strong stomach (I can eat anything), generally sleep like a bear in winter, and will happily tell people off when they do not leave me alone to get some rest.*

Another would write:

> *At this point in my life I am an introverted, gifted, ambitious woman with many health problems, a morning person who drives herself all day long and halfway into the night, so that I rarely get a good night's sleep and often fall into deep depressions. Still, I have to try new things (if I can stand them), and want to actualize as many of my ideas as possible, so life is generally good, if I can just make myself get some decent rest now and then.*

Still another would write:

> *At this point in my life I am a very introverted morning person, a male HSP who has always cried easily, been prone to fears, and otherwise been very emotional. This has made it difficult for me in this culture to find the right job or relationships, but none of this bothers me as I grow older. I am a deeply spir-*

itual person—that is what matters now. In most ways, I must admit, I am happy and healthy.

At this point in my life, I am

extremely introverted although — in controlled ways, like teaching — I can be extroverted. I don't really know if I'm a morning person — my natural pattern always seemed the opposite — but I am doing my best work (teaching) in the early morning now, though the demands of my schedule leave me exhausted. I thirst for time alone, am not taking good care of myself, drinking too much, often feel over-whelmed. I am also deeply afraid. I want to be left alone. I feel somehow that I could heal if I had big stretches of alone-time.

Pairs and Groups: As, Bs, and Cs. But it depends on the content of the statement. Do not read it to any-one else before you feel you are ready.

In groups, be sure to keep the paragraphs as short as the examples, about eighty words.

IN CONCLUSION: Reread your self-description, see how it feels, and then write a few sentences to yourself about your reactions to who you are right now.

I am concerned. Much of my behavior is self destructive. I need to know where the *fear is really coming from — or I need to know myself — and to heal.*

Active Imagination: Inviting the Neglected, Dangerous, and Despised

This next task needs some introduction, so relax and read on. Humans have a divided psyche—a conscious and an unconscious mind. It has become increasingly clear from recent psychological research that the unconscious part determines much of what we feel and do, with the conscious mind often just taking note and rationalizing after the fact. I think it is extremely important for all humans to strive to make more of their unconscious mind conscious. To give just one important reason, prejudice is rooted in the unconscious, in very early learned reactions. If we want to be just, we must strive to be aware of our prejudices and compensate for them consciously.

Although the two parts of the psyche seem to be forever separated, I think we can safely say, given certain spiritual and psychological pursuits of our species, that we seem to long for a wholeness of consciousness. It is also clear that some people have at the outset, or develop, a greater awareness of what is usually unconscious. The door between is not locked, but swings a bit, and you get glimpses when it does.

HSPs seem to have such a doorway (something to remember next time you think you are "coming unhinged"). We have more vivid dreams, more unusual states of consciousness, and more difficulty denying and repressing what's been put out of consciousness. Indeed, it is my experience that for some HSPs inner work with the unconscious is not just a luxury or a way to learn more. It is necessary. For many of us, if we do not meet this force halfway, it can threaten to flood us. You cannot get rid of the unconscious mind, and if you are born with a somewhat freely swinging door between the conscious and unconscious minds, your only hope is to work *with* what comes through from the unconscious. You must learn to trust what comes as part of a *process*. If you have a nightmare, this process does not mean to be unkind or scary, any more than the weather means to be. It just is. What matters is what you are able to grow thanks to the weather brought by the seasons of your inner process.

So let's get down to the work of increasing wholeness—*our* sort of work.

How the Two Parts of the Psyche Communicate with Each Other

The unconscious part of the psyche includes automatic knowledge and skills that we are lucky we don't have to think about, like how to stand up and walk across a room. It also includes deeper matters—feelings and memories we have repressed, parts of ourselves that have been banished as too "unimportant" to develop, too distasteful or seemingly shameful to be looked at, or too seemingly dangerous to the conscious mind's stability for it even to admit that these parts exist (traumas are examples). It also contains the instincts and archetypes—culturally broad tendencies to view the world in certain ways, which surface as symbols and instinctual responses. All of this means there's some useful information and energy in there, if we could just access it.

It is my experience that the psyche wants us to have all of the energy and information locked up in its deeply unconscious part. It does not try to be obscure. But you have to be ready developmentally and situationally, and then the psyche has to find a way to get around your having forgotten; it needs a way to get your attention. One way it does this is through the dreams you remember. Another is through things you do that seem odd—not how you usually behave. For example, you think you are feeling nothing throughout a doctor's exam, then are left alone to change your clothes and burst into tears. Something is clearly wrong. Odd behavior is usually a sign of a less conscious part taking over.

Yet another way the unconscious can reach consciousness is through bodily symptoms. For example, chronic neck problems due to muscle tension can be due to an unconscious attempt to shut off the connection between mind and body.

How does the psyche communicate unconscious material to the conscious mind? Always symbolically or metaphorically—through metaphors, images, symbols, plays on words, or plays on parts of the body that are being affected, such as in the cases of people going functionally blind because of not wanting to "see" (be conscious of) something they had once witnessed, or mute because of being afraid they would tell something they think must be kept secret. We'll return to symbolism in Chapter 10 when we talk about dreams.

Active Imagination—An Inner Walkabout

If messages from the unconscious are so important, naturally we HSPs would look for ways to receive them without waiting for a dream or bodily symptoms or unusual inclinations. Actually, more than one HSP has found such a way. The method I will discuss here is Carl Jung's "active imagination" (Jung was clearly an

HSP, and even discussed it in volume four of his *Collected Works*). For a more complete but simple description of active imagination, you can read Robert Johnson's *Inner Work*. (See Resources, page 311.)

Active imagination is a way both to work with your dreams and to do inner work without a dream. Indeed, some people find that the more active imagination they do, the less they dream. You may especially notice you have fewer recurring or upsetting dreams—your unconscious psyche no longer needs to get your attention in these dramatic ways. You might say that active imagination is a way of giving your psyche the attention it deserves. Or you might call it an inner walkabout.

In simplest terms, active imagination involves turning your attention inward and inviting what wants to be known. It is active in that the conscious mind is engaged as an equal in the dialogue. The conscious mind is neither passive, as in daydreaming, nor in charge, as in "guided imagery," where you consciously create the image of a beautiful day or a safe place or a happy self.

One does not dialogue with the whole unconscious at once, of course, but with some aspect, some inner figure or energy. If one is going to be active and choose who or what that inner figure or energy should be, one needs to begin with that very question of . . .

Who? What?

An obvious choice to dialogue with would be a dream figure—someone from a recurring dream, a distressing dream, or a very recent dream. In this case, I need to say a little something here about dreams, particularly about people or animals who appear in dreams. (You can also turn ahead to Chapter 10 for more on dreams.)

Sometimes when you dream about people, it makes the most sense to think that the dream is providing fresh information about those people and your relationships with them. A dream about your mother being lonely may mean you need to give her a call. Indeed, dreams can bring to dream-life persons important to you, living or dead, in your life now or not, such as a lover, therapist, or brother. The relationship goes on in the dream, teaching you more about it and yourself.

More often, however, a person in a dream, even a familiar person, stands for a part of yourself. An old elementary school friend who gossiped a lot may represent the gossipy part of yourself. A dream figure can also be revealing aspects of natural, cultural, religious, and mythological archetypes such as the Tiger, Aphrodite, the Patriarchal Father, or the Witch.

How do you know the correct interpretation? You get a strong feeling of "Ah ha, that's it." But it may also be that more than one interpretation is correct—dreams can pack many messages into one figure. For example, let's say you had a beloved dog, lost to you years ago. The psyche chooses that dog to take you, in a dream, to see something upsetting that you can hardly believe. The psyche knows you will only believe it because you trust your dog, and your dog's presence will comfort you. But you might also ask yourself, what does Dog (the instincts of that species) have to teach me about this situation it has shown me? You may find that Dog's instincts or perspectives—maybe Dog's loyalty, or acute senses, or "doggedness"—are exactly what you need to master this situation shown in your dreams (perhaps as a metaphor) that was once too frightening to allow into consciousness.

In active imagination, you can talk with your beloved dog. Or to Dog. Or both. Or you can talk to the part of yourself still in grief about losing your dog or to the part of yourself that is so upset by the situation you are being shown.

But Please

You must always proceed with great respect and caution when entering the psyche's realm, especially when you are not in psychotherapy. Very intense reactions can occur, and that process may need more containment or guidance. More often, there is such resistance from the conscious mind that little or nothing happens without such containment. But should your psyche jump at the chance to be heard and overwhelm you with instinctual and symbolic material, do seek help from a Jungian analyst or therapist or even a layperson very experienced with active imagination.

Before we begin, some practical points: When you are doing Step II, the active imagination itself, it helps to write down what is happening while it happens or at frequent pauses. Some Jungians feel writing down active imagination while doing it is essential to prevent mere daydreaming. But you may prefer to stay in a deeper state and do your writing afterward. Whenever you do the writing, writing does honor the experience and lift it above the category of daydreaming, so consider having a paper and pen handy, or a word processor.

As always, you can do as you please, however, and not write anything at all, during or after the task. I know one tidy person who simply devotes the first half hour of her day, before she leaves her bed, to doing active imagination based on her dreams of that night. After that, she plans any action she's going to take as a result of this inner work, and then the night's dreams and morning's active imagination are forgotten, taken care of.

Step I: Emptying the Conscious Mind, Going In, and Inviting the Unconscious

Read these Step I instructions before going ahead. The first step of active imagination is entering into a receptive state of mind. You want to be in a protected, quiet place—no phones, no one around who will interrupt. And maybe there are objects you can have around you that further make you feel you are in a safe or even sacred place—a candle, photo, sculpture, flowers, a certain view out of a window. But it's the inner state that matters most. To have that, you may want to meditate (see Resources, page 311); practice abdominal breathing, as discussed on page 84, attend to your body's inner state as discussed on page 22, or do whatever else you do to move inward, to come closer to your instinctive, spiritual self.

When you feel ready, invite the deep psyche to speak.

One possibility is that you already have something or someone in mind whom you want to meet in active imagination—the "who" or "what" we explored earlier, perhaps a dream figure. Or you may want to begin where a dream left off. Some dreams just seem to beg for this, as when a dream ends with someone about to be introduced to you, to embrace you, to rob you. Or maybe you woke up just as you were about to be awarded a prize or sail away in a ship. Dreams with figures who are hard to see or that are taking place at night seem to be especially important subjects of active imagination—for me, as least, they signal something coming out of the unconscious for the first time.

The second possibility is that you want to invite whatever wants to come—any thought, feeling, sensation, or image wanting to be present. Or you can think of a problem and wait for the image or personification of that issue to appear in that space.

Or you can prime the pump a bit more. You can imagine a situation where something is about to happen—for example, going out into the forest and asking an animal spirit to come to your aid. You hear something approaching through the underbrush, see its eyes in the darkness, and then . . . you stop and let your psyche provide the animal.

Step II: Your Experience or Dialogue

The second step, the inner experience itself, flows naturally from the first step, of invitation: You have invited, and the response is a voice, figure, or scene in imagination. Now you can speak back or take action. Just be certain that your interaction stays fifty-fifty—you act, and then from the unconscious side of the psyche there's action or speech that you do not consciously determine. Please note again that this is quite different from guided imagination, in which you or someone else dictates all of the action, and different also from setting out to visualize a goal or end state such as high self-esteem or prosperity or health.

Here's an example. In a dream, a tough-looking young woman taunts me for not going on a roller coaster and goes off with all my friends, leaving me alone and feeling bad. In active imagination I stop her, asking, "Why are you being so mean to me?"

She answers, YOU DISGUST ME. (For easy typing, I suggest you just tap the shift key to distinguish the second voice with upper case type, as I have done here.)

Just because I don't like roller coasters?

THAT'S RIGHT. EVERYONE'S GOING BUT YOU.

You want me to be like everyone else?

YES, I DO. EVERYONE LOVES IT BUT YOU. WHAT A VIEW FROM UP THERE. WHAT A THRILL, HANGING UPSIDE DOWN.

Yeah, what a thrill. If I don't go, I guess you don't get to go.

She gets very angry: I CAN DO WHATEVER I WANT. YOU CAN'T STOP ME.

You are right, sometimes I can't stop you. I couldn't when I was twelve and went on a roller coaster and got very sick. I couldn't seem to stop you yesterday either, when you took me to that movie I hated, just because everyone else wanted to go and said it was so great. You make me miserable.

SO WHAT? I HATE YOU AND YOUR WEAK, PRISSY SENSITIVITY.

I hate you and your having to go along with the crowd, your having to prove I'm okay, "normal." I really, really don't like your secret view of me as weak.

BOO HOO.

So what do we do now? We are stuck with each other. I can't stop you, but you can't get away from me, much as you want to. This is a sensitive body we are in.

I HATE THAT BODY TOO. I WANT TO LEAVE.

You are pretty unhappy, I guess.

VERY. (She pouts.)

Is there anything you would like to do that I might like to do too?

TRAVEL.

You know I don't like to travel. It's expensive and a lot of stress.

YOU ASKED. THEN HOW ABOUT HANG GLIDING LESSONS?

Where do you want to travel?

SOMEWHERE REALLY DIFFERENT. HOW ABOUT BALI?

Nothing "Third World"—you know I get dysentery if I just look at a glass of tap water. How about Ireland?

BOOOORING. TOO GREEN, TOO ENGLISH. LET'S GO TO TURKEY.

On a tour. Only on a tour.

GREECE, NOT ON A TOUR.

Deal.

AND YOU BETTER STICK TO IT.

If your mind wanders during active imagination, just bring it gently back. This is easier when you write it down as it happens. But be aware that writing can make the experience feel less deep, so that it may seem you are just writing from an "ordinary" state. This is rarely the case, but this devaluing of your work and the problem of the wandering mind do bring up an important issue . . .

Resistance

During or after active imagination it is common to have an acute attack of thinking "I'm just making all of this up." Of course sometimes active imagination is pervaded by a powerful, inevitable sense of reality, as though you were speaking directly with another entity or have entered into another world. But just as often it seems "stupid" or "meaningless." I recall an experience when a therapist was helping me with some active imagination. During every second of it I was sure nothing was happening and I should have been discussing what I had originally planned for that session. In fact, I know now that I was doing one of the most crucial pieces of inner work of my entire life. My divided mind that day was a classic example of resistance. My conscious mind was in a state of sheer panic and trying to distract me. It does that.

When resistance arises as doubt, it helps to remember that no matter how shallow the thing you have "made up" seems to be, it is at least some clue into the rest of who you are. Someone else would have "just made up" something very different. Further, what seems shallow today may seem profound when this resistance wears off. *Don't judge* your active imagination. Or yourself for your resistance. Resistance to active imagination happens even in those who think they are very dedicated to such things.

The conscious mind probably puts up all this resistance because it fears being usurped or overwhelmed. Even though a dialogue with the unconscious parts of the psyche might actually give the conscious mind more power in the relationship, it still seems to dread it, just as we dread going to the boss to ask for a raise. In the same way, we delay any real contact with the unconscious psyche, day after day "forgetting" or being "too busy." Since these "ego defenses" serve a purpose, you will have to sense whether to force the issue or not. Perhaps ask your ego, which is also just another part of yourself!

Step III: Conscious Honoring of What Has Happened

Leave out this last step and "all is lost." This step requires taking some conscious action based on what you have learned. Think of this as a sacred and essential ritual. And often, performing a ritual or symbolic act is exactly the right action to take. If you have learned through active imagination that you must contact your father, but he has died, write a letter to him and send it up in flames, out to sea, or whatever is appropriate. The psyche-logical goal has been accomplished.

Sometimes, however, you will know that you are being shown that you need to make major life changes. Or at least take an action that is more than symbolic. Perhaps you need to apologize to someone or reread a book or look up the mythological meaning of a symbol. An artistic act can give you a concrete object as a reminder—perhaps you need to draw or paint something from the active imagination. And of course, HSPs may frequently learn that they need to restore balance, take some downtime.

After your active imagination experience, you should have a sense of what needs to be done. And if your relationship with the deeper psyche has some good level of integrity—that is, you listen to each other respectfully—then if you have not taken the right action, a dream or symptom will usually let you know soon enough.

This last step of honoring and taking action definitely does not mean just doing whatever an inner figure said. The deep psyche is like a force of nature, powerful and somewhat impersonal. The conscious mind is small in comparison, but equally important. Consciousness is that special human accomplishment. Your conscious mind can and should weigh fairly its own interests and the interests of those around you against the requests of any inner figure. If I would need to go seriously into debt to make the trip to Greece decided on in Step II, that also needs to be discussed with Her Royal Toughness in active imagination. Don't assume these inner parts know about each other or what's going on out in the world.

During an active imagination a woman I know had a powerful male inner voice tell her to leave home, family, and all commitments behind, immediately, and go across the country to a certain city and wait for further instructions. She was sure it was God and was so upset that she did not have the courage to follow these instructions that very night. The next night when she looked for more inner instruction, another, softer, feminine voice approved of her not leaving husband and home, comforting her with the words, "There's always another train leaving the station—there's always another way." She said, "But I disobeyed God." And the feminine voice answered, "But how do you know I am not also God?"

So one guideline is to wait before acting. Another guideline is not to wait. How easily a postponement turns into never acting at all. And if you fail to honor a message from the deep psyche through some kind of action, even if it is a small symbolic act, it will turn its back on you (for a while), or make even more strident demands. You are negotiating with a formidable force. However, you do have equal rights in these negotiations. There's always the possibility of compromise—instead of leaving her family forever, the woman with the commanding inner voice learned to take weekend retreats alone at a monastery, leaving her family behind. That in itself was something she probably would not have done without the intense demand of that inner figure.

One famous Jungian analyst is said to have greeted her analysands at each session by asking if they had done whatever she and they had decided in the last session would be appropriate for honoring a dream or active imagination experience. If an analysand had not, she would not see the person for that session. Maybe every active imagination should end with imagining having to report to her. I leave her for you as a guide, with my best wishes for a good inner walkabout.

Back to "Who" Again, and Actually Doing It

I introduced active imagination early in this workbook because I wanted it to be available to you as you proceeded. So after this section, you will find a blank page. I think of that page as a symbolic invitation, as the place I have prepared for you to meet with your neglected parts. Whether you actually write there or turn to a computer or journal, I hope this space seems safe and inviting. To review the steps:

I. *Set yourself up comfortably and invite your psyche to speak.* Be organized to write during or after your meeting. Go inward, through meditation or whatever means you prefer. Then invite who or what you wish to dialogue with or have unfold, or the scene, such as the end of a dream, that you want to unfold. Some possible inner figures who may have surfaced as you have worked with this book:

- Whoever makes you feel you should *not* do this workbook or some part of it.
- The inner critic you met in "What You Don't Like About Yourself—And the Deeper Why" (see page 32).
- Whomever you have dreamed about since beginning this workbook—for example, whoever appeared last night.
- Any of the parts of your body you got to know in the "Adventure Party."

II. *Let the experience happen.* You should act neither as the one in charge nor as a passive witness. Be alert to what comes and then respond. You are a cocreator with your unconscious psyche. When your mind wanders or you think "this is dumb," understand it as resistance and continue as you are able.

III. *Honor what has happened* by deciding what wisdom you have gained and what action (or nonaction) you need to take.

Here is the space welcoming you to write your active imagination experience.

_____

_____

_____

_____

_____

_____

_____

_____

_____

_____

_____

_____

_____

_____

Pairs and Groups. Cs only. This is very personal work. I do not suggest doing active imagination itself in a group, but you might share the results there. In pairs, there is a variant of active imagination, called voice dialogue, that is best facilitated by another person with some experience with active imagination or similar methods. See *Embracing Ourselves* by Hal Stone and Sidra Winkelman (see Resources, page 311).

IN CONCLUSION: Use these few lines to reflect on how you feel about active imagination in general or about the one you have just done in particular.

3

Taking Care of
Your Sensitive Self

It can be miserably difficult to conduct life in a way that is appropriate, healthy, and happy for an HSP. There are life's pressures and there is the fact that 80 percent of the people around you are not HSPs and can live their lives differently. But if you conform to their style and rebel against your sensitivity, you are always brought back to square one: If you don't do it the sensitive way, you suffer.

As I said in the introduction to Chapter 1, overstimulation leads to a physical state of overarousal that is uncomfortable and can cause anyone to perform worse professionally, socially, athletically, mentally, sexually, financially—you name it. Overarousal also affects one's simple ability to enjoy what's happening. Because HSPs pick up on subtleties and process things so deeply, it has to be the case that we are more easily overaroused in a given situation. Overarousal is our Achilles' heel, so we need to be experts on avoiding, surviving, and recovering from it.

Let's compare sudden overarousal and chronic overarousal. The sudden kind usually involves a startle response, a rush of adrenaline that makes the heart pound, the muscles tense, and the whole body prepare for fight, flight, or freeze. If the initial startling experience is judged by you to be a threat, your body next produces cortisol, the "stress" hormone designed to further help the body in its fight, flight, or freeze. Cortisol shuts down digestion and other maintenance functions, diverting everything to emergency needs. Cortisol and adrenaline can both be present, creating an intense "flooded" feeling, even panic. But let's focus on cortisol now, as it is always present in chronic overarousal.

Cortisol stays in the body longer than adrenaline, at least twenty minutes, and can be around for hours, days, months, or years. It's not good to have cortisol pumping around in you that much. For example, it can interfere with digestion and suppress the immune system so that tumors grow faster. We may be exhausted when we go to sleep after a cortisol-filled day, but the cortisol will recycle in the night and wake us, or wake us too early in the morning. Cortisol can produce a fearful, threatened mood in which we entertain all kinds of worries. Lack of sleep and all this hypervigilance all day can lead to lower serotonin levels in the brain, and low serotonin means depression is likely to follow eventually. Sorry to scare you, but you need to know about the effects of chronic overarousal.

To make you an expert on brief and chronic overarousal, here are some of the indicators: A brief state of overarousal can lead to feeling overwhelmed or anxious; blushing or flushing; having a pounding heart, churning stomach, or tight muscles, especially in the neck or jaw; breaking out in a sweat; not being able to remember well or concentrate; being shaky or having poor coordination; and feeling angry or "ready to snap." Chronic overarousal may be noticed as, again, feeling overwhelmed, vaguely anxious, or anxious about getting everything done; having unexplained heart palpitations or a "nervous stomach"; driving too fast; being short-tempered with anyone who slows you down for a moment; going to bed tired and then lying there wide awake; or waking in the middle of the night or too early in the morning; chronic, unexplained muscle aches, pains, or tightness; chronic headaches; feeling hopeless or helpless; crying more often than usual or over "nothing"; feeling numb; or feeling just plain exhausted. All of these signs of brief and chronic overarousal vary greatly from person to person (and even from situation to situation), so you need to know your particular signs.

Clearly, chronic overarousal is a serious problem. Frequent episodes of overstimulation, even pleasant overstimulation, is one way to find yourself in a chronic cortisol-induced state. This chapter is designed to help you in coping with the stimulation coming in from the world and up from within ourselves, and the brief and then chronic overarousal that can result. I wish I could offer even more help for coping with that not-so-sensitive world out there, but each individual's situation varies so much that it's hard to give one-size-fits-all advice. We each have to be inventive, then share our solutions with HSPs in situations similar to our own. It helps to practice being mindful of your trait, as you will do in this chapter. And it helps to have the paradoxical attitude of accepting that where you are today is the time and place you were given to cope with (to shoulder today's burden bravely), along with an active refusal to accept being the victim of conditions optimal for others but not for you.

An Inventory and Celebration of the Ways You Cope with Overarousal

Overstimulation, overarousal, and the resulting stress are the downside of being highly sensitive. All HSPs develop ways of coping with this tendency to reach overarousal more easily than others. Your first task is to take notice of what you already do to handle overarousal by making a list of your especially brilliant coping strategies.

Purely as examples to warm you to the subject, here are five of my own.

- If I'm being overstimulated by a situation, I leave! I've learned I'm not irreplaceable. I can always apologize later.
- I try not to say yes to a request for my time without reflecting on it—saying, "Let me get back to you on that."
- I block off rest time in my date book, and set aside even more time after a day that will be highly stimulating, and keep that sacred.
- I take a walk when things get intense, preferably in the woods or near water.
- I take ten breaths from the abdomen (see page 84).

Now make your own list:

_____

_____

_____

_____

_____

Now, review your list, and please acknowledge how much you already do right. The rest of this chapter tries to improve upon all of this—that's the point of a workbook. But it's just as important to remind yourself of the skills you have already developed to help you manage.

Pairs and Groups: As, Bs, and Cs.

In Conclusion: Use this space to comment on the breadth and flavor of your coping skills and anything else you have learned from making this list.

Your Optimal Level of Arousal

I have already mentioned several times the importance for all organisms of staying in their optimal level of arousal by regulating the amount of stimulation being experienced. No one is comfortable or performs well when understimulated and bored, or when overstimulated and agitated. We all need to stay in the middle. But again, this is more difficult for HSPs because we need less stimulation than those around us to stay in that optimal range. So we frequently slip into being "too out," too exposed to stimulation, acting in ways more appropriate to non-HSPs. We take on more responsibilities or pleasures than we can handle. (On page 74 I described some signs of being briefly and chronically overaroused, so please refer to them if you need a reminder.)

We HSPs can also slip into being "too in," dreading overarousal and trying to protect ourselves so much that we are actually uncomfortable, physically and psychologically, due to underarousal. We say no to too much. We may fail to have hopes or make plans, meet new people, travel, or expose ourselves to new ideas. A few signs of underarousal (as with overarousal, they vary greatly) are feeling bored, restless, hungry when there's no real need for food, sleeping more than you need, drinking or taking recreational drugs or engaging in sexual activities out of boredom, acting like a pest or causing trouble for those around you, becoming preoccupied with daydreams, or feeling dissatisfied with your life or yourself or envious of those doing more.

This next task is to keep a record of how many times you feel overaroused or underaroused during the day. This kind of self-monitoring is always the first step in making changes. Your record keeping doesn't have to be perfect. You can do it before going to bed and rely on your memory of the ups and downs of the day, helped by your intention to keep this record. Make three to six natural divisions of your day. On a typical workday they might be these six: getting ready to go to work and getting there, the morning at work, midday at work, the last two hours of work and getting home, the early evening, the later evening. On a day off when you sleep late you might make a different division: getting up and having breakfast, going out in early afternoon for a hike, shopping in the late afternoon, going out to dinner with friends, and your last hour or two before bed.

For each division of the day, use a minus sign to indicate that during this period you were mostly in a state of underarousal, a zero for optimal arousal, and a plus sign for overarousal. If it helps (it does for me), use double minuses or double pluses for extreme states and the single minus and plus for moderate states. Consider the sample two days above. For the first day, you might put a ++ for getting ready and going to work, 0 for the morning at work, + for midday, ++ for last two hours and getting home, – – for early evening, 0 for late evening. For the day off example, 0 for the late morning, 0 for the hike, ++ for the shopping, + for being with friends, 0 for late evening.

At the end of the day you can figure an average for the day. You add up the number of pluses, subtract the number of minuses, and then divide by the number of divisions of the day. In the work day example above, there are 5 pluses and 2 minuses, making a sum of plus 3. When you divide that by the 6 divisions, this gives you an average of plus $1/2$. For the day off, there are 3 pluses and 0 minuses, and 5 divisions. This means the average in that example is 3 divided by 5, or .6 in the overaroused direction.

When thinking about underarousal, do not count times you were meditating or sleepy due to not having had enough rest as periods of underarousal. Only record times when you were uncomfortably underaroused—bored, restless, listless, dissatisfied with how little you get out and socialize or try new things, or drowsy even after having a good night's sleep. When rating for overarousal, you can look back at page 74. Or you may recall overarousal better as certain events—times you were feeling pressured to make a quick decision, nervous while being observed, or crying. Don't forget the instances of positive overarousal, like being praised publicly or receiving a pleasant surprise. These you may recall only as positive excitement, or as numbness when you ought to have been happy. These are still taxing.

After rating the divisions of the day and figuring the average, in the last column below, use the same plus and minus system to rate your state as you go to bed. You may need to revise this rating in the morning, after you see how well you slept—a poor night's sleep often being an indicator of over- or underarousal at bedtime. Signs of overarousal as you go to bed are a feeling of exhaustion that is not just from muscle fatigue or sleepiness, noticing your stress signs flaring up (poor digestion, diarrhea, muscle tension, etc.), or feeling "wired," frazzled, too tired to sleep, hopeless, anxious, or depressed about tomorrow or the future. Signs of underarousal might be trying to go to sleep but feeling physically restless, inclined to stay up too late, or unhappy with yourself for not having done much or enjoyed the day. This before-bed rating is important because sleep, like everything else, requires an optimal level of arousal.

Example:

Date	*Ratings for divisions of day (-, 0, +)*						*Average*	*Overall at Bedtime*
Day 1	++	0	+	++	--	0	.5	-
Day 2	0	0	++	+	0	–	.6	0

Ratings of your own days:

	Up	Arr	Ph	EVE	Night	Slep		
R Day 1	0	++	+	+	–	too little	.8	--
F 2	+	0	–	0	0	11	0	→
S 3	0	0	+	0				

After about a week of recording your daily and bedtime levels of arousal, find your overall average of the daily averages and also the bedtime average. (For the overall average, add up the daily averages—being sure to add the plus averages and sub-tract the minus averages—and divide by the number of days. For the overall bedtime average, add the number of pluses, subtract the number of minuses, and divide by the number of days.) Also note how wide your range of arousal is, since a row of 0s is easier on your body than a daily average of 0 that results from an equal number of double minuses and double pluses.

A note about bedtime arousal, as we will not come back to that specifically: If your average at bedtime is over 0, then you need to spend more time protecting your sleep time by surrounding it with calm. This means calming yourself before bed—even with some "minus" or underaroused time by sticking to routines and reading settling or repetitive material (I use the latest *National Geographic,* followed by a few Psalms). Make waking up calm too. Ideally, I go to bed early enough to have enough sleep even if I "waste" some time falling asleep slowly or awakening in the night, *and* enough sleep to wake up naturally, before an alarm if I must set one. This sleep routine is something to aim for, even if circumstances now make it diffi-cult. Think of it as living gracefully.

Pairs and Groups: As, Bs, and Cs. This task is a good one to discuss.

In Conclusion: Look again at your averages, and also your variations within and between days. Reflect for a few minutes, then express your thoughts about your op-timal level of arousal.

_____

_____

_____

_____

_____

Spending More Time in Your Optimal Range of Arousal

Your next task is just to read one or both of the following lists, depending on which you feel you need help with right now: "Ideas for Getting Yourself Out More" and "Ideas for Getting Yourself Some Rest." If according to the previous task your state of arousal was often not optimal, then I am warning you that at the end of this task I will ask you to commit yourself to applying some of these ideas. If you are doing well in maintaining your optimal level of arousal, just read the lists, or the one more useful to you, as a refresher.

Staying within your optimal range of arousal, not too underaroused and not too overaroused, is not a trivial matter. Nor is it a selfish goal. It will give you a comfortable nervous system, and this affects the very core of all your experiences, determining much of your health and happiness and your impact on everyone around you. So take it very seriously.

Ideas for Getting Yourself Out More

- Call a friend or someone you would like to get to know better and arrange to see him or her soon.
- If you are avoiding a situation or action that you would like to work your way through, have someone you trust go through it with you the first few times.
- If you have a special fear or problem that keeps you from going out, join a support group or treatment group—for example, for agoraphobia (the fear of going out to places where you believe it will be difficult or embarrassing to leave) or any other phobia or fear, such as fear of driving, that keeps you from going out. You can call the Anxiety Association of America, a nonprofit organization created by leaders in the field. (See Resources, page 311.)
- This is a big ongoing task, but an important one: Decide what you want out of life—what you don't want to die not having done. If you have been thinking that your goal is unattainable because of your sensitivity, try accepting your sensitivity as a given and creatively working around it. Decide what the first step is *for an HSP* to achieve your goal. For example, an HSP might choose to write or e-mail for information rather than call, and obtain quite a bit of information before deciding for certain on a plan. Now, take that first step.
- Discuss with someone you trust your reasons for not doing what you want

to be doing. Ask the person simply to listen and reflect back your feelings to you, not advise. (See page 166 for how the person can do reflective listening for you.)

- Take a trip—for a few hours, a few days. Or plan something much longer, and do it, soon.
- Overcome any transportation obstacles. If you don't know how to drive (many HSPs don't), consider learning. If you drive but don't own a car, rent one now and then. Get used to taking taxis in case you ever need to. Master the public transportation system in a strange city so you know you can. Take a plane flight if that seems daunting. Do these things until they are easy for you, even when you don't have to, so that they are not additional sources of arousal when you are going someplace new. Besides, the process of mastering them can give you an exhilarating sense of freedom and present other new opportunities, like exploring new neighborhoods or having conversations with interesting, kind strangers. Note that any amount of travel is no small matter for many HSPs—we don't like leaving our safe "hobbit hole" of home. Expect just before you go to wish you weren't. Expect to worry that you have forgotten something, will lose something, will do something wrong. Expect to be easily overaroused by the unfamiliarity of the changing scene, the subtle sense of the dangers and the unnaturalness of rapid movement. I know about all of these, and although they remain sources of strong stimulation, I have licked the dread of each by simply doing them enough. Trust me—you can too.
- Stimulation does not always require going out—read, enjoy some non-deadening TV or radio (for me, NPR or PBS), get onto the Internet, use the phone, pick up this workbook.

On the following lines, list your fears (one per line) surrounding something that would get you out more, especially the "silly fears." Then imagine a wise inner parent, who is skilled in dealing with a sensitive child, honoring each fear and helping with it. Next to each fear, write one thing this wise parent might say about your fear.

_____

_____

_____

_____

_____

Plan how to get yourself out gradually—step-by-step. Write the steps on the lines below. Make them very small steps, and with plenty of time for getting used to each step. But do that first step today.

_____   _____

_____   _____

_____   _____

_____   _____

_____   _____

Ideas for Getting Yourself Some Rest

- Aspire to put into practice the following formula (parents and others who *just can't* are excused, for now):

  a. 8–10 hours in bed per day, sleeping or not, plus 2 hours additional downtime to meditate, contemplate, putter, etc. (if necessary, this *can* be during driving or daily chores if you remain in silence), plus 1 hour for outdoor exercise.

  b. One day per week completely off—no errands, no working at home.

  c. The equivalent of one month per year off; preferably, this time will be scattered through the year. Appreciate the fact that nothing less is likely to work for an HSP.

- Get out your date book. Block off the schedule given above. If in a particular week you can't follow it, make it up the next week. Take extra time after anything demanding like a public presentation or air travel.

- While you have out the date book, plan a vacation, preferably for two weeks, that will allow you to sleep as much as you want. Nothing else should come ahead of sleeping. Second priority should be whatever else pleases you: a spiritual program, sightseeing, nice restaurants, nice places in nature to walk, opportunities to hear music or see art. These sorts of vacations can be cheap—you just need a quiet house or an off-season hotel. But you will probably have to get away from home.

- Consider what sorts of spiritual experiences uplift you and plan these into your daily, weekly, and quarterly schedule. If you aren't sure what these experiences might be, devote some time to exploring this topic.

- Learn to meditate and do it daily. I like Transcendental Meditation (see Resources, page 311), but to each his or her own.

- Practice abdominal breathing. Shallow breaths from the upper chest are associated with tension, and unless you are breathing fast, they don't bring in enough oxygen. If you are breathing from the abdomen, you just can't stay tense. Abdominal breathing doesn't mean deep breaths—that would make you dizzy with too much oxygen—but your breathing should be slow. To be sure you are breathing abdominally, take a normal but slow breath in through your nose, then breathe slowly out through your mouth as if you are blowing out a candle. This automatically makes your next breath come from the abdomen. The point is not to breathe out through your mouth *all* the time, but to do this occasionally to reestablish abdominal breathing. Try ten of these carefully counted "candle blowings" anytime, anywhere, for a quick calming down.

- Create a secure, pleasing place in your house, just for meditation, prayer, reading, and other kinds of private downtime. Make it beautiful but keep it simple. Bring in flowers, a candle, incense, or essential oils to give it a soothing scent. You may want to buy the innards of a fountain from a craft store and make a fountain with rocks you have found. Keep a goldfish in a bowl. Buy a piece of silk or a blanket of natural materials that you can wrap around yourself or sit on. Take in your favorite tea or other drink to sip. That is, please all the senses.

- Keep a journal to encourage reflection and a larger perspective on what you are doing with your time.

- Form a group to share journal entries and life experiences. Let the group help you with your difficulty finding balance in your life.

- Discuss with a trusted friend your difficulty finding balance in your life.

- Always keep a protein snack with you—perhaps string cheese, a hard-boiled egg, a protein bar, a can of tuna, some nuts, or a snack-sized package of cottage cheese. (You can keep a cold pack in your freezer and put it and the food into an insulated bag for the day.) Being overaroused can deplete your blood sugar, and low blood sugar leads to being more easily overaroused. A hurried life can make it difficult to find appropriate food or any at all. Once your body chemistry is off, you will definitely make poorer choices for maintaining an optimal level of arousal and are likely to get into more and more trouble. This gets even more true after age thirty. Trust me—I've been there.

- Learn about nutrition and the dietary supplements you may need. There are a zillion books and newsletters on the topic. Be sure what you do is well supported by recent research and avoid sudden changes or extremes of any kind. Then *take* those pills. Don't forget them.
- Keep earplugs with you for those occasions when you are exposed to loud noise.
- Keep an inspirational book with you. I like poetry myself. It helps keep the demands on you in better perspective.
- Get a weekly massage. If you can't afford that, you and a close friend can read a book or take a course on giving massages and give them to each other.
- Use aromatherapy. It is just right for HSPs. Many scents, such as lavender, actually lower the arousal level. Further, once you associate a scent with peace of mind, it will lower your level of arousal the moment you smell it.
- Spend regular time with animals and plants, and near water or forests.
- Let music or other sounds soothe you.
- Consider what touches your skin—clothing, sheets, soaps, lotions, and so forth—and upgrade any that are irritants until you find what makes you truly comfortable.
- Think of the relationship causing you the most stress in your life. Can it be altered so that it is less stressful for you by setting clearer boundaries, expressing your needs, the two of you going to a mediator or counselor, spending less time with the person, having others present, or even ending the relationship? Or read a book on dealing with difficult people. (See Resources, pages 311–12.)

Pairs and Groups: As, Bs, and Cs could discuss this task.

IN CONCLUSION: Look back at your average optimal level of arousal and bedtime average level of arousal from the previous task. If these were about 0 or optimal, use the space below to reflect on the lists you just read and how your methods are similar or different. If your levels of arousal were often higher or lower than optimal (0), list here what you are going to do about that and *when,* referring as appropriate to the specific ideas in the two lists above.

_____

_____

_____

_____

_____

If You Still Are Not Doing What You Need to Do

If you are often very much too "out" or "in" and you did not decide to do more than one or two items on the lists provided (or others you thought of on your own), think seriously about why. I realize some people have responsibilities to others that simply must be met, or cannot support themselves without working long hours. But you must think very carefully about whether that is really the situation. Do some active imagination (see page 65) with whatever part of you decides not to do more to keep you in the optimal range. Ask that part *why?* If you don't think the answer you get is legitimate, then ask again why this part of you drives you and won't let you rest enough, or why it keeps you underaroused and a spectator of life.

Even if this part of you that resists change has reasons that seem realistic—"I just don't have time"—you must confront this part with the truth: You are jeopardizing your health as well as your potential for happiness, and this affects those around you as well. No time? Once you are sick or laid up from an accident due to your operating too far out of your optimal level of arousal, you will have plenty of time.

If this inner work does not give you any insight into what you realize to be totally irrational behavior (that is, driven by unconscious needs), then you should consider some psychotherapy to help you answer the why and change your ways. See page

196 for help with choosing a therapist you can afford, but you must also think of changing your behavior as an investment in yourself. You'll be smarter, more productive, more energetic, and healthier when you are operating more often within your optimal level of arousal.

It always helps just to stop denying what's going on, so on these lines write *why* you are not changing.

_____

_____

_____

_____

Pairs and Groups: As, Bs, and Cs. Those "out" and those "in" too much may find each other too different to empathize fully or offer help to each other. In a group, perhaps those with similar problems should talk with each other while the others just listen, then vice versa.

The Umbrella Walk

This task evolved from the many HSPs who asked me how to keep from being affected by the moods of strangers or others they do not wish to attend to. We HSPs are built to be receivers, "designed to detect," quick to process to deep levels every little message. We know all too well what is meant by "subtle energy" and "vibrations." So how do we protect ourselves?

Paul Radde, an HSP, therapist, and motivational speaker in Washington, D.C., gave me the idea for this task. In dealing with this problem, he uses the analogy of an umbrella. An umbrella down and closed gathers a lot of water into every crease and fold, but when it is up and out, it sheds water like a duck's back. Likewise, when you are "up," you can better shed the stuff coming at you. By "up" I definitely do not mean cheerful (although being cheerful can help, it is even more important to be able to keep your umbrella up when you are not feeling so great). By "up" I mean that you are broadcasting rather than receiving. Whether you say it or not, the message is, "Hello, good day, I'm busy." Or just, "I'm busy." You are broadcasting that, constantly. You are *not* receiving right now.

When your umbrella is up, you have your own purpose foremost on your mind. You are on the way to the post office. You are heading for the produce section of the store. You are not coming through the store to know what's going on with everyone around you. Don't go out without a purpose unless you *want* to receive.

Everyone wants our attention, or gets it because we HSPs are naturally curious. But the HSP's attention is a precious commodity, easily squandered. Decide who gets it. Don't leave it to chance or let someone else decide.

A homeless person asking for spare change? They usually touch us deeply. Decide your attitude toward the homeless and stick to it: Silence if you want—that's your right. "No" if you want. Or keep a pocketful of change and take an attitude of "Yes." Then you can simply say "Have a nice day" and move on.

People selling or advertising? If your purpose today is not shopping, you are not receiving. Period. Don't get pulled into a sales attempt. Don't even read advertising signs. They will wear you out.

Interesting people to look at? Fine, look at them if that's how you want to use your energy today. Otherwise, don't look at people. Keep your eyes ahead on your destination.

A word about mindfulness and meditation. You may have taught yourself to "smell the flowers" or be mindful, so that a task about shutting out the world feels strange or wrong. But being mindful of your body's arousal level and protecting that by being mindful of your goal is also a kind of mindfulness.

Try the following exercises to keep yourself broadcasting and not receiving.

1. Now, or the next time you are going out among people, take a deliberate "Umbrella Walk." Go out with a purpose and a brisk stride. Think about where you are going and what you are going to do there. Have a pleasant but I'm-busy attitude toward others. You can even say *silently*, "Sorry, I'm not receiving today."

2. Looking back on your first "Umbrella Walk," rate it on a scale of 1, easy, to 10, impossible. How hard was it? _____ Record your observations about this first try here:

_____

_____

If it was harder than a 3 rating, do it again and rate it again.

3. If you feel ready to try the "Umbrella Walk" in a new setting, do it at work when you are headed somewhere and don't want to be stopped, or do it when seated rather than walking. Rate this attempt from 1, easy, to 10, impossible, and record your observations about the attempt here.

4. Use the "Umbrella Walk" as often as you can for a few weeks, to develop the skill and the habit. In time it will become automatic and you can forget about the umbrella imagery.

Pairs and Groups: As, Bs, and Cs. You can try walking silently with another person, both doing the "Umbrella Walk," and discussing your experiences together afterward. In a group, you can discuss your experiences.

IN CONCLUSION: Reflect on what you have observed about yourself while trying this task and write your observations here.

_____

_____

_____

_____

_____

Shutting Out Sound

Noise! It's the bane of our existence, isn't it? We are more sensitive to it, plain and simple. It's not that our hearing is better, but research shows that even on the way to the brain, the auditory input of HSPs is being "augmented." And unlike light waves, sound waves travel through walls. Since we have no "earlids," what do we do? I've gleaned suggestions from everyone I could, including an acoustical engineer.

- *Use earplugs*—for sleeping, in subways, where there's loud music. And yes, dear cautious HSP, you will probably hear a smoke alarm through earplugs (although I am not guaranteeing it). You can buy them in drugstores—buy the type for blocking sound, not water. I like the foam type that you roll in your fingers and squash into your ear, where they expand. Follow the directions, change to fresh ones often, and check with a doctor if anything unusual is going on in your ears. For even more quiet when sleeping, use earplugs plus a very light pillow over your "up" ear (if you sleep on your side). You just have to get used to moving it when you turn over.

- *Shop for quiet.* Buy quiet appliances, especially a quiet refrigerator, and a phone with a ringer that can be turned off. Digital answering machines are quieter than clicking tape machines. Or put your answering machine in a drawer.

- *Know your local noise ordinances.* Quiet hours are often the law. Building codes often dictate that structures near noise sources like freeways are supposed to be built to be especially quiet. If sound travels with absurd ease in the building where you live, so that you know more than you ever wanted to about your neighbor's lifestyle, the building may be in violation of the law. Find out if where you live meets the legal requirements for soundproofing, and who to complain to if it doesn't, by consulting an acoustical engineer, listed in the Yellow Pages.

- *Consider soundproofing your residence*, whether you are a home owner or a renter with a sympathetic landlord (the following suggestions do increase the value of a dwelling). If the source of your noise is outside, the noise is airborne and the strategies are similar to keeping out drafts. For example, put in a second pane of glass in the window nearest the noise. Make sure the glass is at least a quarter-inch thick, with as much space as possible between the existing and new panes and nothing touching between them. Caulk and seal along the walls and make the window unopenable. But you only need to do this on the side nearest the noise, so you can open other windows for air or as emergency exits. Any doors on the noise side should be thick and tight-fitting.

  Noise coming from inside is at least partly structure-borne—the walls, floors, and ceilings act as conductors. You can build a whole new wall on the noisy side, completely structurally separate from the old wall. This should be a double wall itself, with fiberglass in between and with the side toward you made of Sheetrock a half inch or thicker. Nails connecting it to the building should be set into "resilient channels" to absorb energy. Again, an acoustic engineer can give you advice.

- *At work, find out if others are bothered by the noise.* Especially if you are not alone, you can argue that productivity is being affected. If it's just you, you have to have enough "Brownie points" to be able to ask for special treatment. If you are the only one in your group who can solve certain problems, you are in a better position to say, "Sure, as soon as you turn off the radio." But leave at home any fantasies that the organization will take care of you unless your problem affects the bottom line or your immediate supervisor's position. So you may have to just change jobs, or wear those earplugs, or use a Walkman with soothing tapes.

- *Use "noise busters,"* gadgets that delete only certain annoying frequencies (see Resources, page 312). You wear them like earphones.
- *Use noise generators that create white noise, the sound of rain, or other sounds you choose,* but at frequencies that interfere with sounds like snoring, passing cars, voices, or barking dogs. As the sounds become associated with rest, they really help (see Resources, page 312).
- *Ask for a quiet corner* when entering noisy restaurants, hair salons, or other places that ought to be relaxing. The staff usually knows where one is, and some restaurants are designing quiet sections. As with smoking, the times are changing: In San Francisco, where I live, restaurant reviewers now rate the decibel level with little bell icons. With movies, consider complaining when the sound is too loud. Or rent a video and control the sound yourself.
- *Reframe your thoughts about the source of the noise.* Why are drips annoying while rain is soothing? Mostly it's in the head. The perfect way for me to be tortured by noise is to feel victimized, as when I ask for quiet and get no respect. If I wanted the noise—say, I wanted the pot holes on my street fixed and the crews had finally come with their jack hammers—I would welcome the racket. So get creative. Get to know and love those neighborhood dogs that bark and the kids that shout. Or fall back on the advice about noise that a meditation teacher gave me: "The ocean cannot escape its waves." That is, we are not anywhere entirely by chance, and the jack hammers are your waves, a part of your fate. They are your teachers today, hammering home your need to be more patient.
- *Develop the ability to shut out sound.* This is *not* easy. It is definitely much harder than the "Umbrella Walk." Yet I have met people who can do this completely, others who can do it partially, and they all say it is a learned ability, although only the real pros find it as good as actual quiet—there's still some cost to them in energy.

  Here's what you can do to practice. Go sit where other people are talking, perhaps in a waiting room, and experiment with ways not to hear them. For example, decide you will hear their words but their meaning will not penetrate into your deeper mind. Or distract yourself with other thoughts. Or put an imaginary force field around yourself.

Pairs and Groups: As, Bs, and Cs. Share methods with each other.

IN CONCLUSION: Write here what you will do to reduce the noise in your life, but also reflect on the meaning of noise for you and what you can learn about yourself from your struggle with it.

4

Your Childhood
and Your Sensitivity

Psychology has trained us to think of our personalities as the product of our childhood and of the learning experiences and traumas in our lives. But prior to psychology, people thought personality was largely determined by inheritance or "good breeding." That old view is returning with the discovery that many personality traits, including high sensitivity, are partly genetically determined. How should you think about the forces shaping your life, now that you know an inherited trait has affected you so much?

The idea of any inherited trait being very influential in one's life can sometimes be a little disturbing. We all like to think that we can change and improve our personalities. An important inherited trait could seem to imply that everything is set in stone. Indeed, those studying problems like depression, anxiety, and shyness divide into two hostile camps on the issue of whether these are inherited or learned. In spite of my interest in inherited temperament, the all-personality-is-inherited camp was never one I wanted to support. While genes clearly play a role in personality and mental health, any psychotherapist willing to listen to a life history will find equal or stronger connections between an adult's personality and mental health and certain quite obvious objective life experiences, often occurring in childhood. To put it simply, lousy families produce unhappy children and distressed adults. But I can't join the all-personality-is-childhood camp either, because we've all seen the evidence for inherited differences—for example, in the way that two children in the same family can be so different, from the moment of birth, before any experiences have made them different. Thus, it seems perfectly obvious that the truth lies in between, in the interaction of inherited temperament and childhood environment. Alas, there's been little research on the point because of this division among the researchers. There are a few pioneers, however, and some of their research is worth describing because it is so directly relevant to your life.

Megan Gunnar has found that even nine-month-olds are aware of whether they are with a supportive, caring person, and this affects how stressed they become when separated from their mothers. It is only when left with a nonresponsive, indifferent-seeming babysitter that children show in their saliva higher levels of cortisol, the stress hormone. This effect, according to Gunnar, is even stronger for sensitive children.

More important to your own life, Gunnar's colleagues have looked at the support sensitive children experience from their own mothers, which affects daily life so much. Sensitive eighteen-month-olds with secure or insecure attachments to their mothers were compared when they were introduced to four different, highly stimulating, novel situations (a live clown, a clown robot, a puppet show, etc.). The researchers measured both adrenaline (the sudden startle hormone, expected in any sensitive child in a new situation) and cortisol (indicating stress and a sense of threat). You can guess the results, but it's more powerful if you first understand attachment style and think of your own relation to your caretakers.

Attachment style in children is easily measured by observing infants and their "primary caretakers," generally their mothers, for a short time. Some mothers seem in tune with their children while others seem to be inconsistent, distracted, or uncaring, putting their own needs ahead of the child's. What matters for us as adults is that attachment styles are very resistant to change—they get wired in during childhood as the safest way to behave in a close relationship, and they remain in adulthood too unless other relationships disprove the basic assumption about the people you can count on.

A secure attachment means having a sense of a safe home base from which to explore. Your needs came first, not your caretaker's. If you needed to explore, that was fine. If you needed to be close in order to feel safe and comforted, fine. Adults with a secure attachment style in their close adult relationships tend to agree with the following: I find it relatively easy to get close to others and am comfortable depending on them and having them depend on me. I don't often worry about being abandoned or about someone getting too close to me.

Insecure attachment comes in two "flavors." Anxious ambivalent attachment results from the caretaker being inconsistent about support and anxious about the child's explorations, so the child's best strategy is to stay close. Adults with this attachment style tend to agree with the following: Others do not seem to want to be as close as I would like. I tend to worry that my partner won't stay with me or doesn't really love me. I would like to be very close to someone, even merge with someone, and this seems to make others uncomfortable with me.

Avoidant attachment results from the caretaker being too busy for the child—too stressed, ill, absent, neglectful, or dangerous, so the child's best strategy was to stay at a distance and avoid needing or bothering this person. Adults with an avoidant attachment style tend to agree with these statements: I am a little uneasy being close to others. I prefer not to depend on others. Others sometimes want me to be more loving and open than I want to be.

Back to the infants in the playroom. The sensitive children facing the highly stimulating situations with a mother with whom they had a secure attachment did have an adrenaline response, but no cortisol response. Those with insecure attachments had an adrenaline response and then the cortisol response too.

Since only about 50 to 60 percent of children, sensitive or not, are securely attached to their primary caretaker, you can see that almost half of you reading this book grew up without the emotional social support you needed to learn to enjoy and explore new situations. Instead, you felt afraid because you could not count on your caretaker. Physically, your body was being flooded with cortisol in every new situation, which means your nervous system and whole body were developing under less than optimal conditions. This has to affect how you view people, and the whole world.

My own research has repeatedly found this same sort of interaction of temperament and environment. Sensitive children seem to do fine or even unusually well in good circumstances, unusually poorly in bad ones.

The bottom line here is very important: To understand what's going on for you as an HSP, you absolutely must have insight into your childhood. Your assets and your problems are not all due to being highly sensitive, and neither are they all due to your upbringing. They worked together. Sorting out what's what is not easy, but very worth the effort. By becoming clear about this interaction of temperament and life experiences, HSPs with and without troubled pasts will be better able to resist negative labels of us as innately "inhibited," "fearful," "reactive," "negative," and "vulnerable to mental illness." We are much more than that. And those HSPs with troubled childhoods will be able to have more sympathy for themselves, more permission to seek the help that's out there. There will be no more bowing your head in shame when you hear about others (non-HSPs) who had a bad or worse childhood than you and are "just fine" or all fixed up in ten psychotherapy sessions.

Assessing Your Early Childhood Attachment Style

To begin this process of sorting out the effect of your temperament and your attachment style on you as an adult, you can rate your caretaker's (probably your mother's) child-rearing style with you on the three statements below. Use a 9-point scale from 1, "not at all like my parent," to 9, "very much like my parent."

___4___ She/he was generally loving and aware of my needs, sensitive to when I needed help and when I would prefer to do things for myself. It was a comfortable relationship—basically warm and responsive. I feel good when I think about it.

___9___ She/he could vary a lot in how he/she treated me. I think his/her needs tended to come ahead of mine. Sometimes I could count on her/him, sometimes not. I felt loved, but I couldn't trust how it would be expressed.

___4___ She/he was generally not warm toward me. I felt unnoticed, sometimes even rejected. She/he put his/her needs first almost always. I sometimes wonder if she/he even wished I hadn't been born.

If you rated the first statement the highest, this suggests that in childhood you probably had a secure relationship. Rating the second statement highest suggests an anxious ambivalent attachment, and the third, an avoidant attachment style. But these statements only begin to explore the issue and certainly miss many nuances. Write a bit more here about what you suspect your attachment to your caretaker was like in early childhood.

_____

_____

When the time is right, use active imagination as described in Chapter 2 to invite into your awareness this young child who lived in the situation you have just described. Ask him or her how it was, how he or she feels now, what you can do to help if help is needed. Like all active imagination, this is not to be done lightly. But when you do find yourself ready to do it, use this space for the dialogue or to write what you learned from it.

Pairs and Groups: Bs and Cs could discuss this task.

In Conclusion: The role of the early years is often underestimated. Take time now to reflect on your own early years, their impact on you now, and how you have or plan to take greatest advantage of this force that has shaped your life. (I know that if your early childhood seems to have been difficult, it is hard to imagine turning that into an advantage, but research on what are called "earned secures," or those who became secure as adults, shows them to be unusually aware, interesting people. And at least avoidants can handle solitude, while anxious ambivalents can truly appreciate another's consistent caring.)

Reframing Childhood Events

So much of our current self-concept is the product of how we and others interpreted our behavior in childhood, and the negative parts of our self-concept are the product of what we or others saw to be our childhood failures, humiliating moments, or times when we received the most painful criticism. Your trait of high sensitivity was almost always involved in some way in these events. Reframing them is essential.

Take your time, however. Don't try to reframe more than one in a given day. Indeed, if you plan to reframe something exceptionally traumatic, such as your reaction to a sexual violation (a fact in the lives of one in three women, according to some sources), and you have never worked with these memories before, please do *not* try to reframe such an event without professional help.

Below are the familiar steps you learned in "Reframing Your Past" (page 24). Choose a childhood experience that seems to stand out as decisive in developing whatever low points you have in your self-esteem. This might be a single moment that has deeply shaped who you are, such as being overwhelmed by your first day of kindergarten, or a whole category of events, such as trying to succeed in Little League. Remember that it could have been in some sense a very positive moment, like a surprise birthday party or your first horseback ride, but if you have always disliked how you reacted, it needs reframing.

The experience needs to be one that you can eventually see in a new light, knowing about your trait. But don't consider that too much at first—just think about the most decisively upsetting event. Chances are it was related to your sensitivity, because you were probably overaroused.

Write here the childhood event or category of events you wish to reframe.

Now let's reframe it. Each step is numbered, has an example beneath it, and then space for your own work.

1. Recall how you responded to the event—as many emotions, behaviors, images as you can bring up.

    Example: *I loved the water but couldn't learn to swim. For me—only for me—the classes were humiliating. I always fell behind when I couldn't put my face under. Practiced at home in the sink for hours. Couldn't put my face under. As other children could, they moved to another group. Eventually I'd be alone. Then someone would suggest I quit the class. I usually knew the other kids and felt this added to their ideas of me as strange and someone to be avoided.*

    _____

    _____

    _____

    _____

    _____

2. Recall how you have always tended to feel about that response.

    It was just one more demonstration that I was defective. It was my fault—I was a coward—but I was powerless to change. That's what made it a defect.

    _____

    _____

    _____

    _____

3. Consider your response in light of what you now know about how your trait (or imagine me explaining it to you).

It was all due to my sensitivity. For example, I hated water in my eyes, ears, and nose. (When I finally learned, with a private teacher, she gave me ear and nose plugs.) I was afraid of water because I'd picked up from my parents their fear that I would drown. I was overaroused by the presence of the class. I hated the noise and splashing, and the cold water made me tenser than others. The teacher's impatience was the last straw. Learning in a class was impossible for me.

4. Think about whether the negative parts of the event might have been avoided or would have gone differently if you or others had known you were an HSP and had made adjustments for that.

It all could have been avoided, because when I was thirteen it finally was. An intelligent young woman gave me private lessons. She quietly taught diving to one student at the deep end of the pool, leaving me alone at the shallow end to pick up rocks off the bottom. She never shamed me, only praised me when I succeeded. Then she put the rocks in deeper water and my body would lift when I reached down and I was floating. I taught my sensitive son the same way, after one try at group lessons for him. Lucky kid.

_____

_____

_____

_____

5. If this knowledge would have prevented your suffering or wasting a portion of your life, take time to feel whatever you feel about that.

It's hard to let in the feelings—she seems like another person, that terrified, humiliated little girl who never expressed any of those feelings out loud. But it was just terrible, every summer. I remember the sick feeling in my stomach and what I now know was constant depression and anxiety due to this and similar events.

_____

_____

_____

_____

6. Write down your new understanding of the event and read it over often until you have absorbed the full meaning of it.

There was nothing wrong with me. There is nothing wrong with me. I am just different, a rare type, with wonderful, interesting qualities as a result, including an archetypal passion for being in water (I swim as often as I can, even in the San Francisco Bay in winter). I needed to be raised with special care, but no one knew that. Above all, I needed to have successful experiences and never be shamed for my more sensitive reactions. A lot of pain could have been prevented if my parents had known, but at least I am a more compassionate person because of it.

_____

_____

_____

_____

_____

_____

_____

Pairs and Groups: Bs and Cs. Groups using Chapter 11 will do this in their fifth session (page 300).

IN CONCLUSION: Reflect on what you have learned about yourself and summarize this on page 30 of Chapter 1.

Reframing Adolescence

Now reframe your most painful, life-altering moments in adolescence (with the same caveat that you not take on your sensitive reactions to deeply traumatic events for the first time without professional help). My research shows that adolescence can be the most trying time for HSPs, so it deserves special attention. Research by others finds this is the period when shyness often begins.

Write here the event or category of events you wish to reframe.

Example: *My general reaction to realizing that being a "successful" teenager meant liking sexual experimentation with lots of different boys, and that I couldn't do that.*

_____

_____

_____

_____

Now let's reframe it.

1. Recall how you responded to the event—as many emotions, behaviors, and images as you can bring up.

   First party where there were kissing games. I'd forgotten it. A childhood friend reminded me I'd left, and then I realized it was because I'd known I could not do that. *At that party, I had instantly seen all of adolescence as boys wanting to kiss, me being expected to like it and also stop it, never sure of when to do which, and pregnancy in those days looming as something worse than death. Soon after that, at thirteen, I got a boyfriend—a much older, skinny boy, someone whom I thought no one else would want. A safe protector I stayed with and eventually even married, just to avoid all that sexual stuff with strangers that had terrified me.*

   _____

   _____

   _____

   _____

   _____

2. Recall how you have always tended to feel about that response.

   I never understood my first marriage or that long relationship with him before it. I took it as more proof that something was wrong with me—this time my low self-esteem. I had assumed I'd stayed with him because I thought no one else would want me.

   _____

   _____

   _____

   _____

3. Consider your response in light of what you now know about your trait.

Being sensitive, I guess I've always seen sexuality as deep, mysterious, powerful—maybe much more so than people like the kids at that party. My sensitivity also tuned me in to the predatory side of sex, the unkind stuff about boys wanting to "score." I could not trust their motives, but feared hurting their feelings by rejecting them, so my only safe course was the one I took.

_____

_____

_____

_____

_____

_____

4. Think about whether the negative parts of the event might have been avoided or would have gone differently if you or others had known you were an HSP and had made adjustments for that.

I don't know. If someone had understood me, helped me meet boys like me, and if sex had been openly discussed and permission given to do very little without feeling like a chicken—maybe.

_____

_____

_____

_____

_____

_____

5. If this knowledge would have prevented your suffering or wasting a portion of your life, take time to feel whatever you feel about that.

   In some ways it worked out well—my initiation into sexuality was at my own pace. But the marriage turned out very badly and I deeply wish it hadn't happened to both of us. I feel sad for him, as I hurt him deeply in the end.

   _____

   _____

   _____

   _____

6. Write down your new understanding of the event and read it over often until you have absorbed the full meaning of it.

   My sensitivity had to affect my sexuality, making me afraid and rushing me into a safe solution. I had no one to help me with the sensitivity or the sexuality, so I did the best I could. I'm not disturbed, sexually odd, or even unattractive. I am simply highly sensitive. That's it.

   _____

   _____

   _____

   _____

   _____

   _____

   _____

Pairs and Groups: Bs and Cs only.

IN CONCLUSION: Reflect on what you have learned about yourself at this stage of life and summarize your thoughts on page 30.

The Lessons Learned from Your Parents

Your style of approaching new situations and life in general has been deeply affected by your temperament, but your specific methods of dealing with new situations and handling your temperament have been largely learned from your parents. If you are mostly happy with how you learned to face life's challenges, then it is good to acknowledge the source of your strengths. If you want to change, it helps to know that your behaviors came from elsewhere. You can then see clearly that these behaviors do not belong to you, and you can be fully committed to changing.

On the following pages you'll see the same two sets of questions repeated three times, so you can do this task three times, about three different areas of your life. The first set of questions always asks about what your parents (or whoever was most influential in your life in this area) said or did when you were facing a challenge in that aspect of your life. The second set is about what you do or tell yourself when facing a challenge in that same aspect of life. At the end you are asked to compare these. It is better to do the first set of questions for all three areas of life on one day, the second set and making the comparison on another day. (You'll be reminded of this throughout.)

First Area of Life

1. After reading the following list, write on the line at the bottom of the list the area of life you want to explore. You will look at three areas (later you can do more if you want), choosing from those listed, or investigate any other area of life you wish.
    - Physical skills and risks, such as learning to ride a bike or drive a car.
    - "Stranger" skills and risks, such as dealing with strangers, traveling alone, or going beyond your neighborhood.
    - School or work life, such as choosing what you want to study or pursue as a career, committing yourself to that, finishing assignments, accepting new responsibilities, and not working too little or too much.
    - Dealing with teachers and other authorities, reacting to feedback, speaking up for yourself.
    - Social activities, such as joining clubs, playing sports with others, going to parties, and feeling accepted by a group of friends you like.

- Social leadership, such as public speaking, performing, and running for office.
- Sexuality and romantic relationships, such as how you handle dating and sexual advances, understand your sexual impulses, and react to sex in the media.
- Deciding on and developing close friendships.
- Play, hobbies, and adventures, alone or with others.

How I face challenges involving [area of life] *physical skills/risks*

2. Fill in the person or persons you will be thinking about as you answer the questions—the person most influential in this area [mother, father, both parents, grandfather, etc.] *mother*

3. Answer the questions about how this person handled your attempts in this area by putting beside each listed behavior or attitude a 1 for rarely, a 2 for sometimes, or a 3 for often.

   _2_ a. Expressed considerable fear for me if I took even a small risk—piled on the "Be carefuls."

   _1_ b. Looked for or saw a physical condition (besides overarousability) as the reason I failed or I had not taken/should not take a risk.

   _2_ c. Within some limits, told me he or she trusted me to do what I needed to do.

   _2_ d. Did not allow me to take a risk.

   _1_ e. Paid no attention to what I did.

   _1_ f. Tried to lead me into new situations in small steps, giving me plenty of time to get used to each step.

   _1_ g. Pushed me to do more than I wanted.

   _2_ h. Was very upset with me when I could not do as much as he or she wanted me to.

   _2_ i. Enrolled me in a class outside of school, or otherwise found instruction for me, with my permission.

   _1_ j. Made me take classes I did not wish to take.

   _2_ k. Ignored or denied the whole issue.

   _1_ l. If I failed, tried to comfort me with food, gifts, etc.

   _2_ m. Compared me to others in a negative way.

   _1_ n. Compared me to others in a realistically positive way—tried to build up my self-esteem.

   _1_ o. Compared me to others in a positive way that I knew was false.

[handwritten margin notes: piano, dancing, cheerleading, sewing, drawing, traveling]

       3   p. Criticized my decisions.

       2   q. Praised my good decisions when I made them.

       3   r. Said little about my decisions but seemed worried or dissatisfied with me or them.

       2   s. Consulted a professional for advice about me.

       1   t. Discussed with others my issues, with my permission.

       3   u. Discussed with others my issues, without my permission.

4. You will do steps 5 through 7 on another day. Go on now to "Second Area of Life," page 110, and do steps 1 through 4 again there.

5. For each of the behaviors listed below, put a 1 for something *you* do in the first area of life rarely, a 2 for sometimes, and a 3 for often.

Some 2   a. Feel considerable fear, even if the risk is small.

       2   b. Look for or see a physical condition (besides overarousability) as the reason I should not or do not take a risk.

Some 2 * c. Trust my decisions and how I make them—my judgment, reasoning, intuition, or "inner voice."

Some 2   d. Do not take any risks.

       2   e. Do not think about the whole issue.

Some 1 * f. Try to enter new or difficult situations in small steps, giving myself plenty of time to get used to each step.

       2   g. Push myself to do more than I really want to.

       1   h. Get very upset with myself when I cannot do what others do.

Some 2 * i. Look for a class, teacher, or book to teach myself how to handle this situation.

Some 1   j. Force myself to get instruction, even when I don't want to.

       3   k. Try hard not to think about this.

opp. 3   l. If I fail, or think I will, I comfort myself with food, drink, buying something for myself, etc.

Some 2   m. Compare myself to others in a negative way.

Some 1   n. Compare myself positively to others, pointing out to myself my real assets.

       2   o. Notice my assets, or hear another praise them, but then doubt they are real.

       2   p. Criticize or doubt my decisions after I make them.

       3   q. Take pride in my good decisions.

Some 3   r. Generally feel vaguely anxious, worried, or dissatisfied with myself or my decisions.

Some   _2_ ✗s. Consult a professional for advice.

_2_ ✗t. Discuss my issues in this area with those carefully chosen people who can support or teach me.

_2_ u. Discuss my issues in this area with anyone who will listen, even if they are not likely to be helpful.

6. Compare each question that you answered about yourself in step 5 to the question with the same letter in step 3, about how your parent (or whomever you named in step 2) reacted. Write next to those in step 5 "same" if you do the same with yourself as your parent did with you. Write "opposite" if you do the opposite.

7. Reread this second set of questions and, regardless of how you answered them, put a star by those that you think are good ways to approach a challenge. Add up the number of starred items you actually do (rated 2 or 3), underlining them as you go so that you can see them later. Hopefully, there is not a large discrepancy between what you do and what you think you should do. More on this later.

Now do steps 5 through 7 for the "Second Area of Life," on pages 111–12.

Second Area of Life

1. Write the area of life you want to explore (refer to the list on pages 107–8 or choose your own).

   How I face challenges involving [area of life] _Stranger faces / risks_

2. Fill in the person or persons you will be thinking about as you answer the questions—the person most influential in this area [mother, father, both parents, grandfather, etc.] _mother_

3. Answer the questions about how this person handled your attempts in this area by putting beside each listed behavior or attitude a 1 for rarely, a 2 for sometimes, and a 3 for often.

   _3_ a. Expressed considerable fear for me if I took even a small risk— piled on the "Be carefuls."

   _3_ b. Looked for or saw a physical condition (besides overarousability) as the reason I failed or I had not taken/should not take a risk.

   _1_ c. Within some limits, told me she or he trusted me to do what I needed to do.

   _3_ d. Did not allow me to take a risk.

   _1_ e. Paid no attention to what I did.

   _3_ f. Tried to lead me into new situations in small steps, giving me plenty of time to get used to each step.

_3_ g. Pushed me to do more than I wanted.

_3_ h. Was very upset with me when I could not do as much as she or he wanted me to.

_1_ i. Enrolled me in a class outside of school, or otherwise found instruction for me, with my permission.

_1_ j. Made me take classes I did not wish to take.

_2_ k. Ignored or denied the whole issue.

_1_ l. If I failed, tried to comfort me with food, gifts, etc.

_2_ m. Compared me to others in a negative way.

_1_ n. Compared me to others in a realistically positive way—tried to build up my self-esteem.

_2_ o. Compared me to others in a positive way that I knew was false.

_2_ p. Criticized my decisions.

_1_ q. Praised my good decisions when I made them.

_2_ r. Said little about my decisions but seemed worried or dissatisfied with me or them.

_2_ s. Consulted a professional for advice about me.

_1_ t. Discussed with others my issues, with my permission.

_3_ u. Discussed with others my issues, without my permission.

4. You will do steps 5 through 7 on another day. Go on to the "Third Area of Life," page 112, and do steps 1 through 4 again there.

5. For each of the behaviors listed below, put a 1 for something *you* do in this area of life rarely, a 2 for sometimes, and a 3 for often.

Same _3_ a. Feel considerable fear, even if the risk is small.

Opp. _1_ b. Look for or see a physical condition (besides overarousability) as the reason I should not or do not take a risk.

_2_ ✗c. Trust my decisions and how I make them—my judgment, reasoning, intuition, or "inner voice."

Same _3_ d. Do not take any risks.

Opp. _3_ e. Do not think about the whole issue.

Opp _1_ ✗f. Try to enter new or difficult situations in small steps, giving myself plenty of time to get used to each step. ✓

_2_ g. Push myself to do more than I really want to.

_2_ h. Get very upset with myself when I cannot do what others do.

Same _1_ ✗i. Look for a class, teacher, or book to teach myself how to handle this situation. ✓

Same _1_ j. Force myself to get instruction, even when I don't want to.

_3_ k. Try hard not to think about this.

o pp __3__ l. If I fail, or think I will, I comfort myself with food, drink, buying something for myself, etc.

Some __2__ m. Compare myself to others in a negative way.

__2__ *n. Compare myself positively to others, pointing out to myself my real assets.

Some __2__ o. Notice my assets, or hear another praise them, but then doubt they are real.

Some __2__ p. Criticize or doubt my decisions after I make them.

__3__ *q. Take pride in my good decisions.

__3__ r. Generally feel vaguely anxious, worried, or dissatisfied with myself or my decisions.

__1__ *s. Consult a professional for advice. ✓

__2__ *t. Discuss my issues in this area with those carefully chosen people who can support or teach me.

pp __1__ u. Discuss my issues in this area with anyone who will listen, even if they are not likely to be helpful.

6. Compare each question that you answered about yourself in step 5 to the question with the same letter in step 3, about how your parents (or whomever you named in step 2) reacted. Write next to those in step 5 "same" if you do the same with yourself as your parents did with you. Write "opposite" if you do the opposite.

7. Reread this second set of questions and, regardless of how you answered them, put a star by those that you think are good ways to approach a challenge. Add up the number of starred items you actually do (rated 2 or 3), underlining them as you go so that you can see them later. Hopefully, there is not a large discrepancy between what you do and what you think you should do. More on this later.

Now do steps 5 through 7 for the "Third Area of Life," pages 113–14.

Third Area of Life

1. Write the area of life you want to explore (refer to the list on pages 107–8 or choose your own).

   How I face challenges involving [area of life] _____

2. Fill in the person or persons you will be thinking about as you answer the questions—the person most influential in this area [mother, father, both parents, grandfather, etc.] _____ *mother* _____

3. Answer the questions about how this person handled your attempts in this

area by putting beside each listed behavior or attitude a 1 for rarely, a 2 for sometimes, and a 3 for often.

_3_ a. Expressed considerable fear for me if I took even a small risk—piled on the "Be carefuls."

_1_ b. Looked for or saw a physical condition (besides overarousability) as the reason I failed or I had not taken/should not take a risk.

_1_ c. Within some limits, told me he or she trusted me to do what I needed to do.

_2_ d. Did not allow me to take a risk.

_1_ e. Paid no attention to what I did.

_1_ f. Tried to lead me into new situations in small steps, giving me plenty of time to get used to each step.

_1_ g. Pushed me to do more than I wanted.

_1_ h. Was very upset with me when I could not do as much as he or she wanted me to.

_1_ i. Enrolled me in a class outside of school, or otherwise found instruction for me, with my permission.

_1_ j. Made me take classes I did not wish to take.

_2_ k. Ignored or denied the whole issue.

_1_ l. If I failed, tried to comfort me with food, gifts, etc.

_2_ m. Compared me to others in a negative way.

_1_ n. Compared me to others in a realistically positive way—tried to build up my self-esteem.

_1_ o. Compared me to others in a positive way that I knew was false.

_3_ p. Criticized my decisions.

_1_ q. Praised my good decisions when I made them.

_3_ r. Said little about my decisions but seemed worried or dissatisfied with me or them.

_2_ s. Consulted a professional for advice about me.

_1_ t. Discussed with others my issues, with my permission.

_3_ u. Discussed with others my issues, without my permission.

4. Now stop. On another day, turn to step 5 under "First Area of Life," page 109, and do steps 5 to 7 for it, and for the "Second Area of Life" and "Third Area of Life" as well.

5. For each of the behaviors listed below, put a 1 for something *you* do in this area of life rarely, a 2 for sometimes, and a 3 for often.

Same _3_ a. Feel considerable fear, even if the risk is small.

      _2_ b. Look for or see a physical condition (besides overarousability) as the reason I should not or do not take a risk.

  opp _3_ c. Trust my decisions and how I make them—my judgment, reasoning, intuition, or "inner voice."

      _3_ d. Do not take any risks.

  opp _3_ e. Do not think about the whole issue.

  Same _1_ f. Try to enter new or difficult situations in small steps, giving myself plenty of time to get used to each step.

      _2_ g. Push myself to do more than I really want to.

  Same _1_ h. Get very upset with myself when I cannot do what others do.

  Same _1_ i. Look for a class, teacher, or book to teach myself how to handle this situation.

  Same _1_ j. Force myself to get instruction, even when I don't want to.

      _3_ k. Try hard not to think about this.

  opp _3_ l. If I fail, or think I will, I comfort myself with food, drink, buying something for myself, etc.

      _1_ m. Compare myself to others in a negative way.

      _2_ n. Compare myself positively to others, pointing out to myself my real assets.

      _2_ o. Notice my assets, or hear another praise them, but then doubt they are real.

      _2_ p. Criticize or doubt my decisions after I make them.

  opp _3_ q. Take pride in my good decisions.

  Same _3_ r. Generally feel vaguely anxious, worried, or dissatisfied with myself or my decisions.

      _1_ s. Consult a professional for advice. ✓

      _2_ t. Discuss my issues in this area with those carefully chosen people who can support or teach me.

  opp _1_ u. Discuss my issues in this area with anyone who will listen, even if they are not likely to be helpful.

6. Compare each question that you answered about yourself in step 5 to the question with the same letter in step 3, about how your parent reacted. Write next to those in step 5 "same" if you do the same with yourself as your parents (or whomever you named in step 2) did with you. Write "opposite" if you do the opposite.

7. Reread this second set of questions and, regardless of how you answered them, put a star by those that you think are good ways to approach a chal-

lenge. Add up the number of starred items you actually do (rated 2 or 3), underlining them as you go so that you can see them later. Hopefully, there is not a large discrepancy between what you do and what you think you should do. More on this later.

The Last Steps—Do for All Three

8. Look at the items that are both starred and underlined, those good things you actually do. For those with "same" beside them, give credit to your parents for their help in your upbringing. For those with "opposite," give credit to yourself for overcoming some bad training and consider whether this has been a conscious choice or an unconscious reaction (the latter being a riskier situation, as you may revert to the "same" under pressure).

9. Look at the starred items you don't do, and the unstarred items you do—these are the places you want to change. If these have many "sames" beside them, you know you have some prior training to undo. If these have many "opposites" beside them, you need to ask yourself what this is about. There are too many questions for me to discuss each one, but basically, doing the opposite on starred items would suggest that you are rebelling against some good ideas, perhaps for the sake of rebelling, which ultimately means your parents are running your life as completely as if you were doing the same as what they had wanted.

Pairs and Groups: Bs and Cs can discuss the results, but this is primarily an individual task.

In CONCLUSION: Use this space to reflect on what you have learned and to decide on ways you might want to change how you help yourself handle new or challenging situations.

I don't seek/don't trust "professionals"

Try something in small steps!

I was taught/learned on my own not to take risks — self fulfilling prophecy? I have an inappropriate response to risk-taking

Getting to Know the Child Inside You

A lot has been said—and joked—about the inner child. Personally, I know the little girl inside me, being a very private person, hates all the undignified hoopla around the topic. But there's no getting around the validity of the underlying idea. Of course we carry with us who we were at each age. When working with childhood, it would be foolish and insulting to that child if we did not treat him or her as our most respected consultant.

Why Listen to a Child?

These inner children are remarkably wise, especially the highly sensitive ones. They warn when troubles from childhood are revisiting, they help us play, they have strong instincts about what is good and bad for us. If this doesn't convince you, think about whether you sometimes feel as if a powerful childish or needy person has taken over your life. They can do that. Suddenly we behave like angry, abandoned, abused, frightened, or ashamed children, sometimes at only the slightest provocation. Once you listen to this inner sensitive child, and perhaps negotiate with it a little, it will no longer need to take over. You and it can arrange a life that works for both of you.

How do we make contact with these inner boys and girls? They show up in thoughts, "childish" fantasies and behavior, and especially our dreams. We can also reach them through active imagination, discussed in Chapter 2, on page 61.

The Child in Your Dreams

What about this child in dreams? At first my little girl appeared as a young animal. I suspect she was too afraid to show herself—or she thought I couldn't handle it. Then she came in her most distressed form—sick, abused, suffering, dying. I know now that it wasn't to upset me. It was to get my attention and tell me that she, we, were in trouble.

Probably the most important point of any dream is the emotion being felt or not felt. The stronger the feelings being expressed by anyone in the dream, or the stronger the feelings that *ought* to be expressed (as when someone dies tragically and no one cares), the more your attention needs to be given to the dream and to this feeling which is either repressed or in some way dominating your life right now.

The age of the child in a dream indicates the age in your life that is relevant to your current situation. So if you dream of yourself at seven, ask yourself what happened to you at seven. Maybe your grandfather died or you changed schools. Whatever comes to mind first is *usually,* not always, the connection you were meant to make. The setting of the dream is also important—it gives the topic of the dream. For example, your childhood home usually indicates the dream is about your family dynamics. A classroom may mean your learning process right now, while a foreign land represents unfamiliar territory.

Women have dreams of little boys, and men have dreams of little girls. One has to think carefully in each case about why. If it is a boy or girl you know, as I said in Chapter 2, the dream may be about that child. But it can also be about a child part of you like this real child. A man might dream of his new niece being abandoned because he is not ready to see himself as having been abandoned in some way as an infant. The dreamer is protected from the full realization of himself as a child in that situation by the child being "someone else." In general, when a part of one's self appears as a figure of the other gender, it represents aspects far, far from our concept of who we are or can be, especially given our view of our gender. For example, a woman beginning to be more assertive may first dream of an active, assertive little boy—a part of herself still young and developing and also still strange to her and her ideas of the feminine. A man beginning to acknowledge his sensitivity may first dream of a delicate, sweet little girl—a part of himself that in his mind cannot yet be allowed to appear in a little boy.

A dream with toys in it or in which you are much smaller than everything around you can also be your psyche's cautious way of introducing your child part to you.

Your Task

Your task is to make contact, renewed or for the first time, with the child inside of you. If this is the first time, be prepared for anything. It's not always teddy bears and music boxes. One or both of you could be feeling ambivalent or even hostile. I found my first, uncontrollable impulse was—it's hard to believe—to beat and kick the Little Girl viciously, in my imagination of course. I realize now that I just *hated* myself as a child—as a "too sensitive" child. Even recently I had a dream of being a busy man and drowning her because she got in the way. Not good, but we all have setbacks!

On this same note, again, please seek professional help if things become too intense. And go slow.

There are two ways to make contact with your inner child:

- Through active imagination, by inviting him or her to speak. If you need to "prime the pump" a bit more, you could ask for the child who is unhappy with you right now, or who was most affected by being highly sensitive, or who lived through the event you reframed on page 99.

- By working on a dream you have had about a child and thinking about it in the ways described above—the emotions, age, setting, and situation of this child (there is more on dream work on pages 62 and 234). You can also combine active imagination with dream work by doing active imagination that flows out of a dream.

Use this space to record your active imagination or to make notes as you do your dream work.

To the [one] most affected by being highly sensitive: Will you talk to me? Maybe... I don't know if I can trust you. You don't protect me or value me enough. You listened to others and made their judgments your own. You saw me through their eyes. You thought I was WRONG — wimpy, shy, scared, silly, a baby, unable to control myself. So I hid — had to, to live. I had all these gifts to give you — a special kind of knowing & being — fragile, precious gifts. A rich & playful interiority, a sensitivity to everything fragile & precious. You hated me; you hurt me. You loved them (THEM) more than me. You let THEM hurt me. You abandoned me. I'm a wild child, at home with trees and sky & creatures, small & vulnerable. You couldn't hear me

anymore. I cried and cried for you. Then I hid.
You tried to force me to behave, but I could
only Be WHAT I AM. I was the one who shouted
silently, LEAVE ME ALONE! You couldn't stop THEM.
THEY HURT ME. YOU HURT ME, silenced me,
hid me. Now my voice is very small. You want it
back — just like that — but it isn't so easy.
You'll have to WORK for this!

Pairs and Groups: Cs only.

IN CONCLUSION: Write a message to the child you have found through your active imagination or dream work. Express your respect, love, intention to help, and intention to provide her or him with privacy—promise that you will not discuss him or her with anyone you do not trust greatly. You may also want to tell this child why things are as they are, especially if you have had to do things he or she did not like. This is important for all your future talks with this child. You *will* have to do things it doesn't like. Life will not always be fun. And do not assume it knows what you know. But listen to the child's response, and if it is miserable, try to strike a compassionate compromise. Best wishes to both of you in your growing relationship.

I'm so sorry, Dear. I didn't know any other way
to survive. I couldn't protect you because I
couldn't protect myself, couldn't value you in
a world that had nothing but contempt
for you. But that was then. I can learn to
heal you, respect you, value you, love you

Now. It won't be easy for either of us —
sometimes I will have to do things you don't
like — sometimes, to protect you, I will
still have to hide you. But I'll
try very hard to hear you into speech.
I want to, I do.

5

HSPs in the Social World

Thirty percent of HSPs are extroverted, the sort who are usually quite comfortable socially. But all HSPs can be overaroused and overwhelmed by social situations, which is probably why 70 percent of us do choose to become introverts—that is, to avoid groups and strangers, and especially big, noisy, or tensely formal social situations. We are just avoiding the overstimulation. (Extroverted HSPs usually grew up exposed often to such situations, so they are familiar and comfortable, but they still need lots of downtime alone and quiet.)

The problem is that this whole pattern of avoiding strangers and groups can sometimes turn into something more permanent and problematic—shyness or social phobia. So while I am *not* equating sensitivity with shyness, this chapter is about reframing the shy moments that can happen to all of us so that we can handle them in an HSP way. It is also about rethinking any other social "flops" and generally brushing up your social skills, all in the light of your sensitivity.

FOUR REASONS FOR SHYNESS

Shyness. It is such a big deal, isn't it? This is because our culture idealizes its opposite, being very outgoing and not very sensitive. The fact is, almost no one meets that ideal. Hence, 40 percent of all people (which means lots of non-HSPs as well as many HSPs) see themselves as shy.

One reason you sometimes feel shy is that you are aiming for a style of behavior so outgoing and idealized that very few feel they measure up to it. A second possible reason for shyness is a difficult, unsupportive childhood home life. As with depression and anxiety, I have found that HSPs who have had unhappy childhoods are more likely to be shy as adults than non-HSPs with equally unhappy childhoods. If you think about what you read about Megan Gunnar's research and the three attachment styles at the beginning of the last chapter, you can see that a fear of meeting strangers and being judged would have to be more common among those with insecure attachment styles, and that overarousal with cortisol would be more true of insecure HSPs, making their overarousal an extra problem when trying to "perform" socially. Specifically, anxious ambivalent HSPs would be so anxious to attach themselves that their arousal would have to be high when meeting people in social situations. Avoidant HSPs would withdraw, perhaps excusing themselves too much because of the overstimulation, and act like meeting people did not matter to them anyway—a sure way to be left alone. Privately, however, they may be unhappy or sense something is the matter with them. We are all social beings, after all.

A third reason HSPs might become shy is the well-researched fact that traumatic social experiences, usually in adolescence, are a frequent cause of shyness. Many people can recall the exact moment they became shy, and many of those people are probably HSPs, too. Finally, there's what I describe as the "slide into shy." A social situation makes us as HSPs overstimulated and overaroused, so we aren't as clever or socially adept on that occasion. If we don't understand overstimulation as the reason (often it is due just to a noisy, stimulating environment), we are even more nervous the next time we are in such a situation, do even worse, dread the next time even more, and so forth. We start to avoid these situations, become even less comfortable in them because any social skills we had are getting rusty, and we and others begin to judge us in a global way—that we are shy or "socially avoidant" or "social phobics."

In all four cases, your sensitivity plays an important or even the only part in your shyness. So here's my approach to shyness in HSPs.

THREE ATTITUDES TO HOLD ABOUT SHYNESS

1. *Stop labeling yourself shy, and don't let others do it either.* It has so many negative connotations and sounds so final. You were not born shy. Everyone is shy sometimes. So you and they should knock off. It only becomes self-fulfilling.

2. *Remember that overstimulation leading to overarousal is often the initial problem.* It can feel like fear and shyness, but it's not the same. Don't call your response fear or shyness when it is really overarousal. Sometimes "All we have to fear is fear itself." So in social situations, see if you can explain your fear as overarousal and then reduce your arousal.

3. *Stop buying into the impossible ideal:* Stop expecting yourself to perform like a non-HSP extrovert in social situations, and appreciate what you contribute socially with your introverted style. For example, your intimate relationships are probably thriving thanks to your sensitivity, and you are probably a good listener and far more at ease and helpful than others when conversations turn to problems, loss, death, and the like.

We'll return to shyness later in this chapter. But the next task is even for extroverted HSPs. We *all* have our social flops.

Analyzing Your Flops

In any skill area, one must look at the instant replay and see if there are any moves that could be improved. You don't need to fix what's working, so let's concentrate on what's not working—and also what may be working better than you think when you look more closely.

Think of the last few times you felt socially inept, speechless, or rejected during a conversation with another person.

Describe one or two such times here: *Holly in a crowd.*

Palmer - Trinity functions.

Now go over the following list and check anything that you think might have been going on.

☐ *The other person didn't seem to want to talk to you.* This is the big fear, isn't it? You will be judged and found wanting. This is the essence of a shy moment.

First, are you sure it had anything to do with you?

Second, attraction doesn't always happen. It happens mostly between people who are similar, and since you are part of a minority and not similar to most people, especially those at social gatherings, there may be very few people present with whom you are compatible.

Third, does it really matter if this person did not want to talk to you? Can you please everyone? Or is this the perfect chance to liberate yourself from caring so much?

Fourth, maybe it does matter, in that this seems to happen so often, with so many different people. It may seem that it has to be your fault. But be careful about coming to this conclusion. Research finds people troubled by shyness think others don't like them far more often than is the case.

Let's assume for the moment that you are doing something wrong. First, you can get feedback and instruction to improve your social skills. There are books on social skills and shyness, there are probably therapists in your area offering group therapy that can address social skills, and there are courses and even shyness clinics (see Resources, page 312).

If you have already tried learning skills without success, you may want to think about whether this is an attachment problem (see page 96). Both insecure styles can turn others off—the one with a subtle message of desperate need, the other with a subtle message of "who cares." In either case, individual therapy would be most effective in helping you develop a secure relationship with someone reliable who does not mind your spells of neediness or coolness as you learn to trust, and who can later support you as you develop relationships with others. In the meantime, work with the inner child you met in the last chapter. Ask him or her not to come out when you are first meeting people, insecure as he or she may be. The child's needs are just too much for people who don't know you well enough to realize there's more to you than that.

☐ *The other person didn't want to talk to anyone right then.* Never thought of that, did you? Not your fault, is it? Think how often you haven't been in the mood to talk to anyone. Some people are often in a nontalking mood and let it show in a conversation, which you may not do because you don't want to hurt the other person. Or they may think they aren't showing their I-don't-want-to-talk mood because, not being as sensitive as you, *they* would not notice that mood in anyone else behaving the way they are behaving. A slight variation on this is that you may have caught the person at a busy or tired moment, or at a time in the person's life when many people are approaching him or her and making demands (such as an author at a book signing!). Do not take the person's leave-me-alone attitude personally.

☐ *It's you who really didn't want to talk.* Trying to do something you really don't want to do is like rowing upstream—of course you "failed." Your task was not social, but internal—sorting out the inner conflicts and getting what you *want* in synch with what you *do.*

☐ *You just couldn't think of anything to say.* No big deal. This is easily fixed—next time come prepared. See the next task, on chitchat.

☐ *You did all the talking, went on and on, and afterward felt embarrassed, ashamed, or that you were inappropriate.* There can be several causes of this. First, someone may have been "interviewing" you because he or she did not want to talk. So you let the other person run things. That's okay, now that you see what was going on.

Or this person was very interested in you. That should be all right with you, although you may not be used to it.

Or you may have been with a non-HSP who was simply stunned and overwhelmed by your perspectives on the world. Then you realized, too late, that from the non-HSP perspective, you were way out in left field. That's okay too. You can't be exceptional without being exceptional.

It is also possible that you were speaking to another HSP. We can overwhelm each other, you know, and then realize it afterward. We get so used to non-HSPs that we forget HSPs are out there too, and they can react sensitively to things we don't expect.

Perhaps during this communication you slipped into one of your "complexes." A complex is a topic around which you have high emotional energy, very strong feelings, heated opinions. *Everyone* has them. In Chapter 8 we will talk more about complexes. They can be mostly personal, but they always have an "archetypal" (almost universal, instinctual) vein beneath, feeding them intense energy. You know you are in a complex, or the other person is, when the energy intensifies (this is heard especially in the voice), and you or the other person—or both of you if you hit a mutual complex—just can't stop talking. You feel a bit out of control, like you're going downhill too fast. Examples might be the whole topic of divorce, because you are in the midst of one, or of traumatic childhoods, if you had one, or of gender. Almost inevitably you feel later that you said far more than you wanted and worry about what the other person thought about you—sometimes, alas, with justification.

Certain complexes are not so personal, more collective, and great for conversations, but dangerous ground because of the intensity of opinions. Religion and politics are perennials. A recent one was child abuse and repressed memories. The difference between women and men. Abortion. Disasters. Anyone's recent surgery or childbirth also hits that archetypal vein. If there's agreement or common experience, these conversations can be exhilarating, but both parties will usually feel a little odd afterward. Often it is good to acknowledge that something unusual happened by saying words to this effect: "It's obvious from my energy around it that I still haven't worked through it *at all*." Sometimes that admittance can reassure the other person and deepen the relationship more than if the whole event had not occurred. A complex in a conversation can even be a friend in disguise—although some of them are best left in disguise.

It takes practice to stay out of complexes and to manage them gracefully when in them. Be most careful about getting into the story of your life if it has been traumatic. In fact, one way researchers identify an insecure attachment style is by the tone and style of discussing one's childhood. "Secures" just tell you. "Avoidants" can't remember. And "anxious ambivalents" can't stop telling you. I think you'll feel better if you keep that private history for your intimate relationships.

☐ *The other person did all the talking and you felt bored.* Women and introverts in particular may find this happening. We think that if we politely listen and ask questions, the other person will soon ask us questions and return the compliment of listening. But some people are used to different rules. For them, interrupting is okay and getting in there with your thing is pleasantly assertive. The trick with them is to be more aggressive yourself. They will usually like it, or at least not mind. You might surprise yourself and enjoy it too. Anyway, equal time is your right, so if you get in the mood to demand your right, do it.

☐ *The other person walked away after a while.* There are many reasons why someone might exit a conversation, and usually you will never know why. The trick is to assume the reason most flattering to you and don't dwell on it further.

Even better, walk away first. Seriously. At parties, we HSPs may be so glad to be in any conversation that we never stop it. Or we don't know how to slip gracefully away even when we know the chat is reaching its natural end.

Plan ahead how you will liberate both of you. "Gee, I've enjoyed this conversation, but I think it's time for me to get something to eat." This can feel very assertive.

☐ *The other person was rude, argumentative, and hurt your feelings.* This is their failure, *not* yours. And if you are unusually sensitive to such things, that's no flaw or failing. That's just who you are. People with good manners will never pursue hurtful lines of conversation, at least not intentionally. They respect differences in personality, opinion, and temperament, and are prepared to leave room for them in conversations. The only thing you might have done differently was to be certain the other person knew you were experiencing discomfort and did not like the treatment.

Pairs and Groups: As, Bs, and Cs—it is very good to discuss each other's flops and share experiences and opinions.

IN CONCLUSION: Have you learned anything useful here? If so, let it sink in by reflecting about it and then writing down your insights.

I really didn't want to be there, but just obligated.

Recognizing the Patterns of Chitchat

HSPs tend to dislike social chitchat or small talk. It can bore us, and it's something we aren't very good at it because we have such a habit of plunging so deep so fast. We're intense. Just knowing in the moment that we ought to engage in some small talk doesn't help much. We aren't used to it and don't know what to say. If we become at all aroused, we really don't know what to say. So, dumb as it sounds, for us success at small talk requires some planning.

It helps to begin by recognizing the patterns of chitchat—they are used by HSPs and non-HSPs alike—so that you can steer things into the pattern that works best for you, given the person and your mood. This also keeps you alert, with your "umbrella up," rather than just "receiving." So first you will read about these patterns, then practice using them.

A word about sincerity. You may think that steering a conversation or planning what to say before you have even met a person seems unauthentic. Well, it is in a way. If you can be authentic in the moment, go for it, of course. But if a little planning can lead to a lengthier conversation and a chance to find out if the two of you like each other, then at least the planning seems to have an authentic purpose, and certainly not a harmful one. To speak very generally, I think HSPs are hard to get to know, but really worth knowing. So give people a chance to get to know you, and if the other person is another HSP, give both of you a chance.

You Interview Them

One pattern is that you ask and listen while the other person does a monologue. This is easiest on you, and can be either boring or enlightening, depending in large part on what you ask. The trick here is to have good questions prepared—somewhat personal but not too much so. And you want to word questions so that they can't be easily answered with a simple yes or no. Questions with a little cleverness (again, think them up ahead of time) help make the other person feel that the conversation is going to be worthwhile. One I use is, "What do you do when you aren't coming to _____'s parties?" (Well, it's not that clever, but it's as good as I get at this.)

Some others might be, "You seem happy [if the other does not, of course]. Are you enjoying yourself these days?" Then you follow up with questions about the other's work, home life—whatever was brought up.

"I've been looking at that [painting, flower arrangement, tree, outfit someone is wearing] for a while now and trying to decide what's so appealing about it to me—do you have the same reaction? Can you put into words what's so special about it?"

"Being away from my work like this makes me think I need more time off, but I can never decide the kind of vacation I'd like—been on any good ones lately?"

"Well, since it's on my mind, I can't help but wonder what you think about [a recent movie, a hot topic in the headlines]."

So try your hand at it.

For those for whom small talk is difficult:

Write three questions below that you could ask strangers and that might start an interesting monologue on their part. You can also try a follow-up to an imaginary response of theirs, just so you feel a little more prepared to keep the ball rolling.

For those who are adept at small talk in most situations:

Think of a person or situation that makes you feel *very* anxious or shy, either remembering or anticipating a conversation with this person or in this situation. Write three questions below specifically for use in that situation, and then for each try a follow-up to an imaginary response of the other person.

Question 1: _____

_____

Your follow-up: _____

_____

Question 2: _____

_____

Your follow-up: _____

_____

Question 3: _____

_____

Your follow-up: _____

_____

During an "interview" pattern you are learning a great deal about the other person. That means you can also make compliments. A sincere compliment is always welcome. And research shows that in general it has to be really over the top to be seen as insincere. What to say? Try "That's clearly the most interesting opinion about [the topic—say, a movie] I've heard in a week. Are you a film critic—does that explain your insights? Or is it something else?"

Try writing three inventive compliments. If it would help, imagine a new person you met recently or expect to meet and what would apply to that situation and person.

1. _____

_____

2. _____

_____

3. _____

_____

They Interview You

Stirring someone's interest so that you are the one interviewed is another skill you can develop. It has the advantage of keeping you from getting bored. And you may need the other person to know about you, as when you are trying to network. The trick here is to plan ahead the kind of titillating comments you can make that people *have* to ask more about. You can turn anything to your most interesting specialty, even the party's food, if you use your sensitive, creative, intuitive mind and stay active, not passive. For example, "Great food—perfect for getting me ready for my race." Or "Great food—my snakes would like this." Or "Great food—I'd love to photograph that table for my book."

Think of three topics you could easily talk about and that are unusual enough to interest someone—that is, a topic you know something about that others don't. Often this comes from your work or hobbies. After each topic, write your titillating comment, to use as a lead to drop into any conversation at an appropriate pause—something that anyone wanting to talk at all would certainly pounce on and run with.

Topic 1: _____

Leading comment:_____

_____

Topic 2: _____

Leading comment:_____

_____

Topic 3: _____

Leading comment:_____

_____

Volleyball

The most difficult and rewarding conversations are those in which there is a back and forth repartee that *goes beyond* being brief versions of the above two conversations (in which I interview you and you interview me, about work, living arrangements, recent vacations, movies seen, and so forth, with neither listening deeply). The volleyball sort of conversation is what romantic comedies are full of—because the writers are sitting with their feet up in a Malibu condo thinking of these things while not under the pressure of another person's last witty comment. They don't do it impromptu at a party. Certainly not many HSPs do.

Still, when there's a special connection, you may find yourself wanting to *converse,* back and forth, not just manage a series of monologues. You may be falling in love, or in friendship, or just enjoying an interesting person. Obviously such conversations can't be rehearsed. But the opening can be thought about, just as you can learn to serve in volleyball.

Try writing two or three opening lines that might initiate a deeper conversation: Examples:

> *"Funniest thing—when you walked in the door, I had this strong feeling we were supposed to talk today."*
>
> *"I've been waiting all evening for a chance to talk with you a little bit alone. I often find what you say to be, well, provocative."*
>
> *"For some reason I always feel good when I'm with you."*
>
> *"To be honest, I often find you in my thoughts, and I try to trust things like that when they happen to me."*

Opening line 1: _____

Opening line 2: _____

_____

Opening line 3: _____

_____

Try extending one of these into an imaginary dialogue. If it helps, imagine it as a scene in the kind of really good romantic or dramatic movie you most like—maybe the scene in which the two leads first realize they find each other interesting.

Imaginary dialogue _____

_____

_____

_____

_____

_____

_____

_____

_____

_____

Groups

Small talk in groups can be difficult for HSPs in that we like to process things deeply and the conversation can move too fast for us, or we can be so stimulated by just watching and listening that we forget to speak. Those HSPs with low self-esteem, shyness, or a history of being criticized in their family, school, or workplace may have a particular problem speaking up. Others may not want to bother saying much because it is too overarousing to have the group's attention.

The first thing to remember in groups is that being silent never makes you invisible. On the contrary, eventually it draws attention to you. So always say just a little bit of something innocuous if you want people to think you are fine and ignore you. "Air space" or group attention is limited and most people want it—they'll be glad if you don't.

On the other hand, if you want to have influence, stay quiet a while and see what's going on. Then they'll be curious about what you'll have to say, and your comments will be saturated with the reflectivity of a well-functioning HSP priestly advisor. You will probably be asked to say more, and then you are involved *and* moving the group past the superficial small talk.

Chapter 11 is all about groups. But here's a task to help you put more in and get more out of the small talk in every gathering. Think of a group you have been in recently and reflect deeply on what may have been going on. Then make some notes on these points.

- What you thought was really going on or being said, beneath the chitchat. For example, if the topic was divorce, maybe you noticed someone in the group whom you knew was newly divorced was either falling silent or expressing intense opinions.
- What you might have said or done in this situation that would have been helpful to you or the group.
- If you did not do this, why?

_____

_____

_____

_____

_____

Pairs and Groups: As, Bs, and Cs. The three small-talk patterns are *best* practiced in pairs or groups. In groups you can break into pairs. Set a time limit—five to ten minutes—and allow time to discuss your experiences in the larger group.

IN CONCLUSION: Think a bit about yourself as a social being, given what you have learned from these tasks, and write your conclusions here.

_____

_____

_____

_____

_____

Reframing Your Shy Moments

Below are the familiar steps you learned in "Reframing Your Past" (page 24). Think about a time when you felt *very* shy, socially uncomfortable, or awkward (*everyone* has in some situation, although they can be hard for us to remember—we try to forget them as soon as they happen). If there's one that seems to stand out as decisive in developing whatever low spots you have in your social self-esteem, pick that one. This is more than a social "flop." This might be a single moment that has deeply shaped who you are, such as when you were speechless the time you were supposed to give a speech. Or it might be a whole category of events, such as every time you have to do something formal, like give a toast or make introductions.

The experience needs to be one that you can eventually see in a new light, knowing about your trait. But don't consider that at first—just think about the most decisively upsetting event or class of events, even if it doesn't seem related to your sensitivity. Chances are it was, because you were probably overaroused.

Write here the shy moment you wish to reframe.

_____

_____

_____

_____

Now let's reframe it. I have not given an example this time, as by now you know what to do.

1. Recall how you responded to the event—as many emotions, behaviors, images as you can bring up.

_____

_____

_____

_____

_____

2. Recall how you have always tended to feel about that response.

_____

_____

_____

_____

_____

3. Consider your response in light of what you now know about your trait.

_____

_____

_____

_____

_____

_____

4. Think about whether the negative parts of the event might have been avoided or would have gone differently if you or others had known you were an HSP and had made adjustments for that.

_____

_____

_____

_____

5. If this knowledge would have prevented your suffering or wasting a portion of your life, take time to feel whatever you feel about that.

_____

_____

_____

_____

_____

_____

6. Write down your new understanding of the event and read it over often until you have absorbed the full meaning of it.

_____

_____

_____

_____

_____

_____

_____

_____

Pairs and Groups: As, Bs, and Cs.

In Conclusion: Reflect on what you have learned from this reframing and about yourself as a social being. Summarize your thoughts on page 30.

6

Vocation, Work, and Sensitivity

HSPs face a real challenge in choosing a vocation and finding a comfortable work environment. Some reasons why we have a harder time sorting all of this out are that others tell us what we should be good at or do, or we try to imitate others, or we try to tolerate something that for an HSP is really intolerable and so we are often slower to settle into what is right for us. That means we may change jobs or careers more often than others.

It's okay to make a mistake or two. It's your life and only you can be the judge of when you are working in the right spot for you on this planet. I hope this chapter helps you deal with this difficult topic.

THE PROBLEM OF VOCATION FOR HSPs

Your vocation is generally what works for you, what "calls" you (the literal meaning of the *voc* in vocation). If you want to be a bit romantic about it, it is what you were "born to do." For HSPs, usually it is something with the priestly advisor aspect to it.

It is a great blessing to be able to earn your living doing your calling, or even be well paid working at the job where "your own greatest bliss intersects with the world's greatest need." But many HSPs have trouble finding that intersection. Many artists and musicians, for example, find that the world won't pay them well unless they do something that seems to them to be too commercial or simply against their nature. Sometimes you know you were meant to have a particular vocation, but the way it is practiced these days is too stressful (many nurses and teachers complain of this), or you could not obtain the education, perhaps because you had to support others and could not take the time for further training. These are all real tragedies to be grieved, or obstacles to overcome later in life.

THE PROBLEM OF THE WORKPLACE

Some of us have to earn our living in ways that we don't enjoy that much, and perhaps have to pursue our true vocation on the side. But if the workplace is congenial, any job can be enjoyable. Research finds that enjoying one's fellow workers is often the highest reason for job satisfaction. For HSPs, being able to work at home, out of doors, or in a region where they want to live can also be reason enough to be satisfied with a job.

But many, many HSPs labor in situations that make them unhappy. The fact is, HSPs are *different*—we have special abilities to contribute and some special needs, but these can usually be easily met. Of course we don't look different. And in today's temperament-ignorant social climate, if we claim we are different, we are thought to be weird, whiny, or arrogant. If we just try to do our work differently without explaining ourselves, people tell us we are going about our work "wrong" or "ineffectively." So this is not entirely your personal problem—it is a social problem, in that you are not understood or appreciated.

Our trait is basically a "human diversity in the workplace" issue—a hot topic in human resource management these days—and this one is often more relevant and inescapable than gender or ethnic diversity. Biologically, we HSPs are different. We are welcome for our conscientiousness, vision, creativity, cooperativeness, vigilance for errors, perfectionism, and sensitivity to every sort of issue and need of the organization, the customer, those we supervise, our product. But if we show the other side of our difference—that we are more easily overwhelmed, we need more downtime, and we are prone to illnesses if we ignore our trait—we sense we will be discriminated against. Again, we'll do what we can about this in this chapter, but it may take time to see real progress in the world.

THERE *WILL* BE PROGRESS

Someday we will be so valued, I believe, that organizations will compete for their share of HSPs. Our needs will be met because it will be economically wise to do so. Of course we will have to be unusually well educated and competent. That is always the responsibility of the priestly advisors. Meanwhile, those of us who have been fortunate enough to develop unusual competence can use our influence to begin the job of reeducating the work world by asking for different treatment (telecommuting, quiet office space, reasonable hours, recovery time after travel, etc.) commensurate with our special contributions.

Still, until the work world changes, the problem of the kind of work you as an HSP do and the workplace where you do it is your problem to solve, fair or not. The first task is to fully appreciate yourself as an HSP. Then you must teach others to appreciate your sensitivity.

The Inventory of an HSP's Assets

If there is any task you must complete in this workbook, it is this one. Whenever possible, I have every class of mine do it. There is always resistance before, but gratitude after: "Finally I have the words for describing my sensitivity in a positive way." Do it.

In the space below, list every possible asset, virtue, blessing, or talent an HSP might have. These can be traits of HSPs in general or of yourself in particular. List not just those that are obviously work related, but any type. You can also write down all your other assets, virtues, and talents. But do not miss any of your HSP qualities. That's what you need to highlight right now.

This is a "brainstorming" activity in which you open your mind to every possible idea, without criticizing anything. It doesn't matter if you list two words that are similar or if not all HSPs have the quality you think of. Just write each down and go on, pouring out as many as you can. If you get stuck, think systematically about each chapter you have worked through or about areas of life (mental, emotional, social, spiritual, natural, physical, etc.).

You *must* try to fill *all* the blanks provided. More traits, written in the margin, are welcome. I have primed the pump with the first five.

compassionate   _sensitive_   _listener_   _perceptive_   _articulate_

careful   _writer_   _conscientious_ _intelligent_ _knowing_ good listener

creative

think deeply

Pairs and Groups: As, Bs, and Cs. Definitely do this task. In a group, work together to make a list of the traits of HSPs in general.

IN CONCLUSION: Take a moment to absorb this list. I know you are probably afraid of becoming conceited or developing an "inflated" ego. But you won't. Doing this is just an antidote to too much devaluing of who you are, so that in time an objective valuing can replace it. Now, write how you feel about yourself and this list.

Writing a Letter or Script About Your Trait

This is also an essential task for you to do in this workbook, even if at the moment you are thoroughly appreciated where you work. It is good practice for all your relationships. The task is to write a portion of a letter, or a script for a little speech to be inserted into an interview or conversation, in which you more or less sell yourself, or make your virtues known, including your high sensitivity. Use the language developed in the previous task. Also, hint about what conditions bring those virtues out. In other words, in a carefully worded way, express some of your needs as an HSP.

Here is an example of a letter:

> *As for the assets I believe I would bring to this position, in my years of experience as a quality control manager, many have noted that I seem to have an innate sensitivity to subtleties (a talent I've had since childhood) that I bring to any production team, as well as a keen intuition for what is likely to become a problem and what will not. For example, past supervisors have commented that I seem to possess a "sixth sense" about what is required to maintain a harmonious team without sacrificing efficiency.*

> *My sensitivity and intuition also seem to force me to be conscientious, making me vividly aware of the answers to the question, "what happens if this gets by us?" I simply cannot allow mistakes or misunderstandings to linger for long.*

> *I have found that maximizing this sensitivity and intuition requires a certain amount of quiet and privacy during the day—which more than pays off by improving my productivity. One approach is telecommuting, working from my home one day a week. But I am flexible about how we accommodate this requirement of a certain amount of "protection."*

Write your own letter or script on the lines below. If there is an employment change or work review coming up for you, or one from the past you wish you had handled differently, you can think of that specifically as you write. If it would be more relevant to work on an entirely different setting—such as school, friendship, or dating—feel free to adapt the task to that need. Prepare a letter or script for a prospective teacher, friend, date, or life partner.

_____

_____

_____

_____

_____

_____

_____

_____

_____

_____

_____

_____

_____

_____

_____

Pairs and Groups: As, Bs, and Cs. Definitely do this task. Each can read his or her script or letter out loud and others can comment, sensitively of course.

IN CONCLUSION: How did it feel doing this task? It will be good to observe your reaction to valuing yourself and make note of it.

_____

_____

_____

_____

_____

_____

Freeing Up Your Vocational Choice

There are dozens of excellent books on finding a vocation that will be right for you and bring you joy (see Resources, page 312, for a few). There are also vocational counselors listed in phone books and made available by many schools and organizations. So I don't want to reinvent the wheel here. But for those of you struggling with "what to do," the following task does seem worth having you complete in the context of this workbook, where you are thinking about your trait so deeply. If you are entirely happy with your work right now, you can skip this task, although you might enjoy doing it as a fantasy or an exercise in creativity.

1. On the lines provided below, list *all* the things you love to do *or* the areas where you would like to have extensive competency. Pay no attention to whether these are potential careers. If you like to bicycle, list it. If you like to be around dogs, list that. If you love to read about disasters or diseases or heroic escapes or alternative health treatments, list that.

Write - think - research - play the piano - travel -

art museums - concerts - buy books - read - teach -

be alone - listen to music - establish order - walk -

talk w/ friends - go out to eat - be on or near

water - nature - plan courses - learn - write

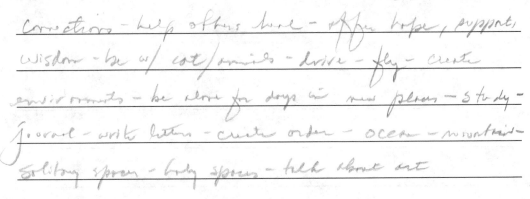

2. Now, think creatively about whether there might be a way to support your-self doing one of these. If it is something many people do or know about, then there may be room for more of it, or for a new service or product. If it is something few do, but enjoy, more people might get involved if they had the help of a specialist like you. (Or maybe you aren't a specialist yet, but would love to become one.) Knowledge is a resource you can sell, as a con-sultant, author, teacher, and so forth—natural roles for HSPs as priestly advi-sors. *Think: Is there a need or desire here that you could meet?* If there is, peo-ple will probably pay you to meet it.

I recall very well one night paddling around a pool in San Juan Bautista, California, excited by a "brainstorm" I was having: "People keep saying they want me to teach a course for highly sensitive people, or even write a book for them. People have been asking for it. I'll bet they would pay me." This was after I had done my research and become an expert, out of pure love for the topic, not for income. But it did turn out to meet a need for which I have been compensated, paying the cost of my time while I do what I love.

Of course you don't know for certain something would support you. You may overestimate the needs of others or how competent you are. After you have an idea, you have to "test market" it. The HSP way is to take few risks: Do something small scale while you still have your steady job and see how it goes.

For three of the things you listed above, brainstorm how you might support your-self doing them. Don't be too critical yet—rather, emphasize creativity and playing with possibilities.

1. _____

_____

_____

_____

_____

2. _____

_____

_____

_____

_____

3. _____

_____

_____

_____

_____

Pairs and Groups: As, Bs, and Cs. Discuss this task, encourage each other, and share ideas and experiences.

IN CONCLUSION: Reflect a moment about how it felt to play around with your future during this task, perhaps noting if you tend to limit yourself, and why, or whether you are uncomfortable thinking too much about material goals. Write your discoveries here.

_____

_____

_____

_____

_____

Assessing Your Work History

For each statement below, note whether the statement is *Very* true of you by marking it with a **V,** *Somewhat* true with an **S,** or *Almost never or not at all* true with an **N.** Then read the discussion of each question in the section that follows.

Questions

1. _S_ I have held positions with many different organizations.
2. _S_ I leave positions on my own, even if most people want me to stay.
3. _N_ Employers have asked me to leave.
4. _V_ Anyone knowing my work would say I am underpaid.
5. _S_ Few people where I work understand what a good job I do.
6. _N_ I have had job offers I have declined because I was afraid of what the change might entail.
7. _S_ My work is the most important thing in my life.
8. _S_ I get along well with my coworkers—these relationships add greatly to my pleasure at work.
9. _S_ My unhappiness with my work is the major source of pain in my life.
10. _V_ I fear that the physical conditions under which I work are harming my health.
11. _S_ I am hassled or mistreated by my supervisors.
12. _V_ I am proud of the work that I do.

Evaluating Your Answers to These Questions

1. If changing jobs often is *very* or *somewhat* true of you, the standard thinking is that you must be unstable or unable to commit, and that's always a possibility. But changing jobs often can be quite typical and reasonable for an HSP. It takes time for you as an HSP to figure out what you need as opposed to what others need or think you need.

If your response was *almost never*—you have always stayed in the same place—has this been due to it being a very good job for you? Or has it been out of a fear of change?

2. If you often leave, even when others want you to stay, the same issues apply as above, but more strongly. Are the moves advancing you or improving your life? Or do you have trouble committing yourself? Are you being unfair to those who value you? Do you fear being too attached or dependent? Do you move when you are given more responsibility or asked to manage or supervise others? (Managing

others is not always a good idea for an HSP, however, especially managing non-HSPs. To be taken seriously, we must speak as they would, firmly, even harshly by our standards. And take it when it's given back. We *can* and will manage others, but it's hard on us.)

On the other hand, if you have *never* left a job for your own sake, ignoring your being needed where you are, you may be undervaluing yourself and it might be time to take a chance on a change.

3. If you responded *very true*—you have been frequently asked to leave—the reasons are obviously very important. You may have had some bad luck in a bad economy or job specialty. Or if employers have often truly fired you, you may be having real problems learning from others what they expect and what you are willing or able to do. Try to look back to see if there has been a common pattern or problem. Then work on it, on your own or with an appropriate professional. On the other hand, losing a job for whatever reason at least once is probably inevitable, given the wide range of employers' personalities and reasons they have for "letting people go." As with falling off a horse, perhaps it is even necessary to have survived the experience once just so that one does not live in perpetual fear of it.

4. If it is *very* true that people often tell you that you are underpaid, they are probably right. Research on shy people (which may not quite describe you but it does some HSPs) shows that they are underpaid. I find that HSPs often hope they will be rewarded if they are quietly good enough for long enough. Or they are loyal and claim not to care that they make less than they should—they are even glad to save the company the money. But it isn't fair and isn't good for you. Nor is it good for the world. It fuels the stereotype of HSPs as easy to take advantage of. Stand up for all of us.

On the other hand, HSPs often gravitate to fields chronically underpaid, like teaching or the arts, or they work in nonprofit or government agencies. So you have to compare yourself to others of your caliber in this field and others. Ask yourself, is this really a case of accepting low pay for the sake of doing what I want, or am I underpaid by any standard and allowing myself to be treated unfairly? An important motto taught to me by someone I respect: *Don't give yourself away*.

5. If few people where you work understand what a good job you do—if this is *very* or even *somewhat* true of you—that is probably typical given that you are an HSP, but it needs to change. Again, it is unfair to you and to the organization, because those above you will make personnel mistakes if they do not have all the relevant information—that is, if they do not understand how valuable you are.

6. If you have declined *some* job offers because of the fear of change, that is probably both reasonable and a good sign. But if it is *very* true of you, and the jobs are within your vocation, then perhaps people are seeing considerable potential in you that you refuse to acknowledge and develop. Responsibility is good for us if we can grow into it without undue strain. The world needs us.

7. I think that if it is *somewhat* true that work is the most important thing in your life, that's fine. If it is *very* true, consider whether more balance in your life might even improve your work. There are few callings that are not enhanced by reading a book having nothing to do with your work or having relationships with people not involved in your profession.

If your work is not important to you, it may be time to change. What do you most enjoy doing? What is your play? Somewhere in that is your vocation, even if you never make money at it. Or you may be misdefining work. My son loved to draw pictures of everything. But one day he came home with an assignment to draw a picture of Columbus's *Nina, Pinta*, and *Santa Maria,* and he groaned about doing his homework. That word "work" had taken all the joy from his creativity. Does it still do that for you?

8. A *very true* is fine here—enjoying coworkers is an often overlooked factor in job satisfaction. It can be one of the best parts. Listening and helping each other, laughing together—it can make up for a lot of other stuff. Your true vocation may even live unnamed somewhere in your role in this team.

An *almost never* is not good. You may need to enter into conversations a little more. If you haven't because of one or two people who are unpleasant, do consider changing jobs. Just as there are good families and terrible ones, there are good workplace social environments and bad ones. You need a good one to be healthy and work well. See the comments to question 11.

9. If it is *very* true that unhappiness with your work is the major source of pain in your life, obviously something needs to be done! Admitting this is important. The reasons could be numerous. If absolutely nothing can be done about the external situation, you may need to think about ways to use the situation to develop your own character.

10. If it is *very* or *somewhat* true that the physical conditions under which you work seem to be harming your health, that also needs to be addressed. There's some physical wear and tear with every job (even sitting still and writing). But if the dangers are unusual, just the strain of staying in an environment that a part of you wants to flee is very stressful. Fortunately, employers

cannot dismiss major risks for long before they get into legal trouble. But if only one person complains, managers naturally want to blame the bothered employee's unusual sensitivity. And since you are indeed more sensitive, you may have to accept that this job is not for you rather than fight it. One's health is the foundation of everything else, as anyone in poor health will tell you.

On the other hand, you might be able to suggest minor changes that will improve the productivity of you and the other 20 percent or so of the employees who might be HSPs. You may even be able to use your knowledge of your trait to demonstrate that it is more cost-effective to accommodate HSPs like yourself than lose the special assets they bring.

11. If it is almost *never* true that you feel mistreated by those you work for, celebrate your good fortune. (And you just might also ask yourself if you are being treated so well because someone knows you are worth more than you are being paid, and this is a way to keep you around.) But if being mistreated is *very* true for you, consider if this has been a regular pattern. If it has not been, and especially if many others are having the same trouble with the type of management and supervision they work under, this should help you appreciate that you may need to act to escape a bad situation. If it is a regular pattern, or if others are not as bothered as you are, your sensitivity may well be part of the reason for this repeating pattern. Not only do HSPs take harsh words more to heart, but we can be easy targets for bullies—we react more. We may even get used to being bullied and fall into the victim role without realizing it. This nasty, subtle situation is exacerbated by our not understanding the value of our trait and by having it devalued by our culture. Of course we tend to feel inferior, weak, and powerless. That makes domination seem natural and deserved.

Other reasons we may repeatedly get into and stay in a bad work situation is that we may fear the other's anger (or our own, when it is finally felt), so we don't set the necessary boundaries at the outset. ("I'm sorry, but I don't take that kind of treatment.") We may fear change—perhaps we fear losing a job or benefits. Then there is being nice, loyal, and conscientious, or justifying the other's behavior because the work he or she is doing is so important or others respect the person so much.

Everyone has his or her "shadow," the not-so-pretty side. It just seems to be part of the human condition. I believe a relationship—work, friend, romantic—has not really begun until we know the other's shadow and decide if we can live with it. But especially when HSPs feel flawed or weak, not understanding our trait, we can tend to idealize others. Then we want to be close to the people stronger than us, lean on them, and be part of their lives. But it is also as if we want to stay innocent of our own strength and of the shadow in everyone else. The idealized other's shadow then becomes a disillusioning shock when we finally acknowledge it. Sometimes we can overreact by hating or dreading the person. But too often we remain stuck in some bad reciprocal role—we are the admiring audience for the narcissist, we are the slave for the great master, we nurture big babies who should be taking care of themselves (and if they are our supervisors, of us).

It takes experience to sense after a little time with a person the kind of shadow problems you will be dealing with eventually. But the first step is to expect, rather cheerfully, *some* kind of problem. Expecting a shadow in everyone is especially helpful when you have to decide whether you would really be happier in a different job or would just be going from frying pan to fire. A known entity you have learned how to deal with has its advantages, as long as it is not totally abusive—there is a fine line. On the other hand, some people's difficult qualities would be too distressing for anyone. You have to decide how bad is too bad.

You need to pay particular attention to those types of bad relationships that you enter into over and over, or stay in for much too long. For these, you'll need to do inner work with whatever part of you, internalized from some past relationship, that lets you or makes you do this.

12. If you are *very* proud of the work you do, congratulations. That is *so* important. If you do not feel pride, you do need to look at why. "Life is not a rehearsal"— this is it. Do not go to your grave regretting how you spent your energies.

Pairs and Groups: Cs only. This is all probably very good to discuss, but there are serious issues here. You will need some safety in order to receive the feedback and suggestions you need, from people who have come to know you well.

IN CONCLUSION: Reflect on this interaction between us—my questions, your answers, and my thoughts about your answers. Please take my thoughts as just that— some ideas to stir your thinking. Since I don't know you, but you know yourself very well, what you write below is probably far more important. So given this start, see what more insight you can gain about your work history, and write that here.

_____

_____

_____

Reframing a Critical Moment in Your Vocational and Work History

By now you should be in a good position to reframe one of the crucial events in your career—for example, how you decided on your career, or failed to decide; why you had to leave a certain job or did not take a certain job or stayed in one too long; difficulties you have had at work. If you are unhappy with your career or job, pay particular attention to who or what influenced you to enter it.

Below are the familiar steps you learned in "Reframing Your Past" (page 24). As usual, choose something that stands out as decisive in damaging your self-esteem. This might be a single moment or decision that has deeply shaped who you are, such as the remark of an instructor or an employer, or a whole category of events, such as every time you are tested, observed, or evaluated. The experience needs to be one that you can eventually see in a new light, knowing about your trait. But don't consider that at first—just think about the most decisively upsetting event or category of events, even if it doesn't seem related to your sensitivity. Chances are it is.

Write here the vocational or work moment you wish to reframe.

_____

_____

_____

_____

Now let's reframe it.
1. Recall how you responded to the event—as many emotions, behaviors, and images as you can bring up.

_____

_____

_____

_____

_____

2. Recall how you have always tended to feel about that response.

_____

_____

_____

3. Consider your response in light of what you now know about your trait.

_____

_____

_____

_____

_____

4. Think about whether the negative parts of the event might have been avoided or would have gone differently if you or others had known you were an HSP and had made adjustments for that.

_____

_____

_____

_____

_____

5. If this knowledge would have prevented your suffering or wasting a portion of your life, take time to feel whatever you feel about that.

_____

_____

_____

_____

6. Write down your new understanding of the event and read it over often until you have absorbed the full meaning of it.

_____

_____

_____

_____

_____

_____

_____

_____

Pairs and Groups: As, Bs, and Cs.

IN CONCLUSION: Step back from all of this a moment and reflect on what you have learned about your vocation and work life. Then summarize your thoughts on page 30.

7

Developing Your
Close Relationships

HSPs specialize in close, long-standing relationships with people, perhaps with a romantic partner, but always with a few friends or selected family members. We HSPs tend to have different, more intense experiences in these relationships than non-HSPs and we can be unusually skillful in developing and maintaining closeness. But there are always insights to gain, especially about how our sensitivity affects our closest relationships, and there are always skills to hone. That is the purpose of this chapter.

HOW IMPORTANT IS "BIRDS OF A FEATHER"?

Before getting to work, there are two issues to think about as you proceed. One of the big ones, arising again and again as I talk with HSPs, is whether we are better off "flocking together" or better off with non-HSPs, who can complement our trait. The question is important, of course, since we often can choose whom to be close to.

My experience suggests that there may be a very slightly higher percentage of satisfying relationships among those in which both are HSPs. It makes sense. There are fewer conflicts over what's fun and for how long. The other doesn't feel rejected when you need time alone. You rarely or never have to say, "Could you do that more quietly?" or "That 'little joke' hurt my feelings." You don't have to hear "You're too sensitive" or "Tired already?" The nervous systems are kind of humming at the same frequency. It feels so good to be with someone like yourself, given how many there are out there who are not.

All this compatibility does *not* mean that relationships between HSPs and non-HSPs can't be exceptionally successful. My thirty-year, slightly stormy but wonderful marriage is testimony to that. You bring each other talents, perspectives, and sheer gifts that each probably could never fully access without the other. For example, the non-HSP will take you on adventures, handle the tasks and situations that overwhelm you, and hopefully truly honor and protect you as a sensitive person, because you bring to his or her life depth, intensity, insight, loyalty, spirituality, creativity, an awareness of the briefness of life, and a dozen other sweetnesses and bitter sweetnesses that are hard to find in this world. It requires extra effort to respect and tolerate each other, but it is perhaps effort that builds character.

I should add that about 20 percent of the population is at the other extreme from HSPs. The positive term for this group is "uninhibited," a relatively neutral term is "sensation seekers," and they have also been called "impulsives." Appreciate them—they make great ambulance drivers and firefighters—but do *not* imitate their lifestyles. As for a relationship with one, an HSP would have a rocky ride with a non-HSP sensation seeker.

As you work on particular relationships throughout this chapter, you will need to do some mental gymnastics and think, along with everything else you are asked to think about, how the other's temperament and its match with yours is affecting each task.

TROUBLES: ARE THEY DUE TO SENSITIVITY OR PERSONAL HISTORY?

The other big issue to keep in mind while working through this chapter is one I wrestle with as a psychotherapist. How much of the trouble in a given relationship is due to the innate temperament of each person, and how much is due to their past relationship experiences, starting with infancy and all the way up to how you each are treated these days on the job. The question is important because, of course, you try to *adapt* to each other's temperament, but you want to have insight about and *change* learned patterns that don't work.

The temperament versus personal history question is never easy to sort out. Temperament always interacts with personal history. But how, exactly, does it interact in your history? There is a way to come closer to the answer: Review your relationship history, looking for repeating patterns.

One way to see patterns is to think in terms of attachment style (see page 96). I emphasize it because there's a tendency to underestimate the impact of infancy—we don't remember it or it seems a bit absurd to think our baby self is that important. But infants are highly programmed to relate—their lives depend on it—and they adopt the style that will work for their caretaker and then stick to it with all subsequent people who claim to care unless there's substantial reason to change this style.

An example of how temperament and attachment can interact is the successful, confident, outgoing person who claims to be an HSP, but who seems to feel safe in many environments where other HSPs would not. You inquire, and discover that this person has a history of secure, happy relationships and may even be an extrovert. In such cases, a few more questions unfolds the happy tale of this person's great parents, understanding teachers, and good childhood friends.

Then there's the "obvious HSP" who complains of needing more time alone and of a partner who is "all over me" and "too needy." A conflict of temperament? The partner complains that the more he or she wants to be with this HSP or express love, the more the HSP seems unhappy or even hostile. In this case, I'll place my bets that I'll hear a history of a mother too busy, ill, neglectful, or whatever to give much attention to her HSP infant, creating an avoidant attachment style. The HSP suppressed fear and pain about this abandonment and learned to "get along without" and is uncomfortable with closeness or with someone else's often normal need for closeness, which seems too needy to an avoidant.

So here's your second twist to perform in these mental gymnastics—while you go through this chapter, thinking about your and the other person's temperament, also think about your attachment styles and general relationship histories.

Your Love Story

Before doing anything else, use this page to write out an experience of your own of falling in love or beginning a friendship. It will be interesting to contemplate as you work through this chapter, so you should do this now. Include the state of your life at the time you fell in love, your overall mood before you fell in love, the situation in which it happened, what each of you said and did, and how the relationship worked out.

_____

_____

_____

_____

_____

_____

_____

_____

_____

_____

_____

_____

Now, look back at this story and write answers to the following questions. My comments follow each question.

    1. Were you feeling good or not so good about yourself at the time? How did this affect the relationship's later development?

_____

_____

      In general, *on average,* when you are in a period of low self-esteem, you are more likely to be responsive to someone who expresses interest in you. Also, low self-esteem is associated with less happy relationships. But that's a chicken and egg problem—it's hard to say which causes which.

    2. Had you already learned to live alone? Were you feeling lonely?

_____

_____

      If you need to enter a relationship, any relationship, to avoid living alone or feeling lonely, you obviously will be less choosy and may end up with a less happy relationship. On the other hand, a dash of loneliness can be a great motivation for an introverted HSP to consider entering a relationship.

    3. Were you in an unfamiliar situation or otherwise aroused? Do you think this increased your initial sense of attraction?

_____

_____

      When people meet while in an unfamiliar, arousing situation—perhaps while traveling or weathering a crisis together—they are more likely to be attracted. Since HSPs are more easily overaroused, we ought to be falling in love more often! (But the effect meeting this way has on the happiness of the long-term relationship is probably negligible.)

    4. Who confessed loving feelings first (this and the next three questions assume it got that far), and to what degree did that cause the other to realize his or her own affection?

Again, on average, this is the way many people fall in love: They learn the other person likes them, then "discover" they feel the same. That's important for HSPs to realize—it may seem very risky to confess your feelings, but it is an excellent way to usher love into your life.

5. Did the two of you disclose many personal things about each other quickly? If you did, were you delighted or a bit afraid to have gotten so close so fast?

Rapid self-disclosure—if not too rapid—feels good. But for HSPs it can be almost too arousing. It can especially be overarousing if you also have an avoidant attachment style.

6. Were you similar or different in degree of sensitivity? How did that affect your meeting and early communications?

Two HSPs might fall in love practically from the sheer joy of being with another HSP. On the other hand, an HSP and non-HSP may be stunned by the almost magical abilities of the other. These are not bad reasons to be attracted to another in either case, except that if you have had very little experience meeting different types of people, you may not realize that this amazing person you have just met is not all *that* unique, and other qualities need to be considered too.

7. Looking back over all of this, use this space to reflect on the outcome of this falling-in-love experience. If a relationship started, what has happened to it? How have you felt about this experience? Do you feel differently about it now, having written about it and answered these questions? If so, write a bit

about that and share it with someone so that your new understanding stays with you.

_____

_____

_____

_____

_____

Pairs and Groups: As, Bs, and Cs. But consider how much personal material you want to reveal in the story.

Reframing Important Moments in Your Relationship History

All humans are deeply shaped by their relationship histories. Again, one reason may be that the human brain is specifically designed, due to our long dependency in infancy, to maintain and gradually revise an attachment *style* that optimizes our chances for survival, given the people around us. Revising it in the direction of more security is what we hope to do as adults. One way to do that might be to see that the experiences we've had that maintain an insecure attachment style carried extra force because of our sensitivity, or our sensitivity may even be the cause of these insecurity-creating experiences, as when we've been repeatedly hurt by non-HSPs. In that case, reframing your relationship history may well also help you revise your attachment style.

Below are the familiar steps you learned in "Reframing Your Past" (page 24). Choose a relationship event that stands out as decisive in developing any sense of insecurity you have in relationships. Pick something that you can now see definitely involved your sensitivity. (In this area more than most, other factors besides sensitivity, such as the histories of both of you, may well have been central, and reframing too much in terms of sensitivity might be a distortion of what actually happened.) The event might be a single moment that has deeply shaped who you are, such as when you failed to take the town's most popular girl to the prom after she practically asked you herself, and she was the one you secretly always adored and still think you should have married. Or you might focus on a whole category of events, such as partners always wanting you to spend all your spare time with them, and your not being able to do that without getting irritable, so that several relationships have ended over this.

Write here the event you wish to reframe.

_____

_____

_____

_____

Now let's reframe it.

   1. Recall how you responded to the event or relationship—as many emotions, behaviors, and images as you can bring up.

_____

_____

_____

_____

_____

   2. Recall how you have always tended to feel about that response.

_____

_____

_____

3. Consider your response in light of what you now know about your trait.

_____

_____

_____

_____

_____

_____

4. Think about whether the negative parts of the event or relationship might have been avoided or would have gone differently if you or the other had known you were an HSP and had made adjustments for that.

_____

_____

_____

_____

_____

5. If this knowledge would have prevented your suffering or wasting a portion of your life, take time to feel whatever you feel about that.

_____

_____

_____

_____

6. Write down your new understanding of the event or relationship and read it over often until you have absorbed the full meaning of it.

_____

_____

_____

_____

_____

_____

_____

Pairs and Groups: Bs and Cs only.

IN CONCLUSION: Reflect on what you have learned from this reframing about yourself in close relationships and summarize your thoughts on page 30.

About Reflective Listening

Reflective listening is the simple-sounding skill of repeating back to the other person the feeling component of whatever he or she is telling you, so that the person knows you have heard right, and so that through this mirroring the person can fully experience what he or she is feeling. It is especially useful when someone you are close to is having strong, confusing, even overwhelming emotions—about anything, but particularly about you.

There is usually some resistance to practicing this skill, since out of context it can seem stilted. But this is an invaluable tool for HSPs. For example, with it we can help non-HSPs recognize what's going on with them, and we tend to feel better when those around us are as aware of their feelings as we are. Further, we are exceptionally good at reflective listening, once we get the idea.

The list of "dos" for reflective listening are short.

1. *Appear attentive physically*—look at the person, never look at your watch, do not sit with your arms crossed.

2. *Use words that reexpress the emotional content* of what you have heard, largely ignoring the factual content, focusing on getting right the feelings being expressed.

The "don'ts" are remarkably difficult to avoid.

1. *Don't ask any questions.* You'll hear the answers that matter soon enough.

2. *Don't advise.* You haven't heard enough to give good advice, and besides, if you play your role well, the other person may come up with a solution on his or her own. This is better for the person, and it is probably a better solution too.

3. *Don't talk about your own similar experience.* That's fine when mutual sharing is the goal, but while a person is having strong feelings, talking about yourself just shifts the attention off of what's going on inside that person.

4. *Don't explain "what's really going on"* or "what you are really feeling" or generally play the psychologist. This might be helpful later, but right now your task is to listen and not distract the other person from his or her highly personal experience.

Even a single sentence indicating this kind of attuned listening, this kind of gift, is powerful. We've all had the other experience so often we consider it normal. We say to someone, "I'm so happy—my dog Patsy just had puppies." The person says back, "How nice! I spayed my Ginny, but she did have one litter. Want to see the pictures?"

So much for *your* experience.

How about this response: "How nice! I can see how happy it has made you. You are glowing, just like a proud grandparent." It's even better than the interested question, "How many did she have?" That can come next, of course.

You can use reflective listening like this, right in the midst of conversation. But its real importance is in helping others be grounded in their own experience and in maintaining (and sometimes saving) a relationship. Before you try it, let's look at an example.

An Example of Listening to Another Person's Experience

I'll begin with an example of using reflective listening to help a close friend or relative explore an issue that does not relate to the relationship the two of you have. This is really a brief course in the most important fundamental of psychotherapy. If a therapist only uses reflective listening and nothing else, that in itself *works*. So this is a potent skill.

You and someone you are close to have set aside time to talk at the end of a day which the other has dreaded—the first day of a new job. He says, "Today was a thousand times worse than my worst fears. It was really awful. I was so nervous sometimes that I just wanted to hide, or die. I'm not sure I can ever go back."

All your alarms go off inside. You fear he will lose the job, or lose confidence. You may be angry he did not handle the day better. You are certainly confused about how this happened. You want to ask questions. However, you are going to control all of this. So you just say, "Sounds like today was one long nightmare." Maybe you add, "You never want to see that place again."

You ask no questions—it will all spill out in good time, without your asking. You don't start giving advice, like "Sounds to me like you need to talk to your boss to clarify what's expected of you." Because you don't even know what happened. And you do not sneak in covert messages that you don't want to hear these feelings, like, "It must be terribly hard, but I'm sure it will get better once you are used to it, don't you?" You definitely try not to say, "But you promised me this would be an easy switch" or "Sounds like if there's going to be any money earned around here, it will have to be earned by me."

By giving the feelings room, you trust the other person to find a way through this problem—if not consciously, then with the psyche's help. You cannot, however, listen with any kind of expectation or subtle demand that things come out a certain way. The more you simply trust the other person's psyche, the more you will find that you like the result.

Based on my experience, here's how I can imagine this conversation working through.

> *You: You never want to see that place again.*
> *Other (starting to cry): I hated it.*
> *You (sounding deeply sympathetic): Oh, how hard.*
> *Other: I can't go back.*
> *You: Yeah, it's really clear to you—that place is not for you.*

Other: It was a big mistake. I feel so ashamed of not seeing that before.

You: Yeah, I hear you. You're feeling ashamed too—you think there's something wrong with you for not seeing this coming.

Other: Most people could do it, but that cash register . . .

You: The cash register really fouled you up.

Other: Customers were backed up, getting impatient. I just froze. So the supervisor came and did it for me. He whispered, "Imbecile." Everybody heard. Afterward he said he'd never seen anyone so slow at learning.

You: Boy, the pressure of everyone waiting, then those rude, ridiculous comments . . .

Other: I'm no imbecile. I learn fast. But I can't handle that kind of pressure.

You: We both know you're smart. But some situations . . .

Other: I couldn't believe any supervisor saying that to someone on their first day.

You: Pretty amazing. No one with a brain would dream of training someone that way.

Other: No. I would have seen the nervousness. Remembered the references, the good grades, and figured this person needs less pressure. Not more.

You: Sounds like it's pretty clear to you that with different supervision, today would have turned out differently for you.

Other: Maybe I'm just making excuses.

You: Yeah, it's hard for you to trust your version of what happened today, even though you were right there.

Other: No, not really. This supervisor was out to get everybody. I heard him call somebody else a bastard when he thought no one else was around.

You: A real bully.

Other: I can't go back there.

You—silence.

Other: Although the person who hired me really wanted me, and he's the boss of this other guy. I should at least tell him what I saw going on.

And so the person problem-solves what to do—report to management, try another job, or whatever. You sigh with relief.

Of course, if you think the other person's solution is really wrong, you can take two approaches. If possible, let him or her go ahead and learn from a mistake. If you can't, then try to begin with an action/feeling statement (page 174) like this: "When I imagine you doing that, I get afraid for you." Or "When I think of you doing that, I am afraid you will lose your job, and then I'm afraid we'll not be able to pay the rent." If that doesn't generate some deeper reflection on the other's part, add what you might do in that situation, but try to avoid directly telling the other person what you think he or she should do. Straight-on advice to a distressed person often is met with resistance or creates more shame that she or he did not think of your solution. Besides, you probably do not know the whole situation. Further, it becomes your responsibility if your advice doesn't work!

Listening When the Other Person Is a Threat

The most important use of reflective listening—and the most difficult to do successfully—is when a conflict has arisen in a relationship and both of you are getting defensive or out of control. In this case, some complex has been stirred and each person is being seen as a threat to something central to the other. Reflective listening does not solve the conflict, but airing feelings without allowing any defensive responses seems to force us to hear the other's point of view, and that view gets into the unconscious and creates change at a deeper level.

Here's another example. This time you can practice filling in responses. The example is followed by how I would respond to what the other person says. But there's always more than one good response.

Let's assume you and your partner need to work on an argument you had last night that began like this:

> *Other: Where have you been? You said you were just going to have coffee with this Joe guy, and you've been gone three hours. I don't really want you to see Joe any more. I don't think it's just a friendship and if you love me and are committed to this relationship, you will give him up.*

So tonight you have agreed to listen reflectively, and do only that for a half hour. After a break, your partner will do the same and listen to your feelings about the situation. (Sounds stilted, but again, it can really work *if* you can stick to reflective listening and not boil over.) So you get started.

Other: I want you to give up this "friendship." (Said sarcastically.)

You (taking a very deep breath): _____

_____

Other: If you love me, you will give him up. (Angrily.)

You: _____

_____

Other: I can't trust you. After all, you left Neil to be with me. Why shouldn't you leave me to be with Joe?

You: _____

_____

Other (sounding more upset than angry): Why should I trust you?

You: _____

_____

Other: God, I hate to hear myself talk like this. I sound like a jealous nut. But I am jealous.

You: _____

_____

Other (near tears.): I love you. Desperately.

You: _____

_____

Other: I have seen you with Joe. You really like him. Maybe more than me. How the two of you smile *at each other. It just kills me.*

You: _____

_____

Other (crying): I don't want to lose you.

You: _____

_____

Other: I feel so *ashamed.*

You: _____

_____

How I might respond

Other (sarcastically): I want you to give up this "friendship."

You (taking a deep breath): You feel strongly about me and Joe. You don't believe for a minute that this is just a friendship.

Other (angrily): If you love me, you will give him up.

You: You're mad.

Other: I can't trust you. After all, you left Neil to be with me. Why shouldn't you leave me to be with Joe?

You: You think you can't trust me.

Other (sounding more upset than angry): Why should I trust you?

You: I hear you—right now you can't think of any reason to trust me.

Other: God, I hate to hear myself talk like this. I sound like a jealous nut. But I am jealous.

You: You feel ashamed of wanting so much not to lose me to someone else.

Other (near tears): I love you. Desperately.

You (silent awhile): I hear you. Your love feels truly desperate tonight.

Other: I have seen you with Joe. You really like him. Maybe more than me. How the two of you smile *at each other. It just kills me.*

> *You (with deep empathy):* *You feel I like him a lot and it really hurts you.*
>   *It's like it's going to kill you. Like I'm killing you,*
>   *being with Joe.*
> *Other (crying):* I don't want to lose you.
> *You: I hear you, how much you want me in your life, how much you don't*
>   *want to lose me.*
> *Other: I feel so ashamed.*
> *You: Yeah. I can see it's hard to admit so much need, so much love, with*
>   *me seeming happier with Joe, not needing you at all.*

You and I have no idea how this will work out. It could be you later express total rage at all this unreasonable jealousy. Or you face the fact that an attraction has happened that threatens this relationship and violates your intention to keep this relationship central to your life, whatever the sacrifices involved. Or you may feel both the rage and a determination to end it with Joe—one during one listening session, the other in another session. But one thing is certain: You know the feelings you have created in your partner and probably cannot avoid dealing with them any longer.

Ending the Session

In the example on pages 168–69 about the first day on the job, the ending came rather naturally. In an ongoing, heated conflict or crisis, it is better to agree ahead of time how long one will listen to the other. Then the clock ends the session, whatever is going on. The listener can only take so much, after all.

Should you switch roles right afterward? That should be agreed upon ahead of time, too. But usually it is better not to. Even if powerful feelings have been stirred up in you as listener, the other person needs time to digest whatever feelings and insights have come up.

The listener can make *some* feeling response at the end—maybe "That was intense for *me*. I will really need to talk about my feelings later." And the listener can make some notes for when he or she will be the one listened to.

In the after-the-first-awful-day example, you might say, "Boy, I knew something was up the moment you walked in. Thank you for opening up like that to me. I'm glad you can trust me, and that I didn't have to wonder and worry about you all evening." If this is someone you do this with regularly, at another time you could talk about the feelings that came up when you first heard those words, "Today was a thousand times worse than my worst fears."

By the way, when doing reflective listening around a conflict, be careful not to let the conflict subtly spill over by berating the other for not doing the reflective listening just right.

Now for a Live Performance

Obviously the best way to practice reflective listening is with another person. Perhaps show this task to your partner or a close friend and ask if you can practice together, to have this tool available when you have conflicts or one of you needs help working through a difficulty. For the first practice, one of you starts by choosing a real issue in your life, but one that is not so distressing that it would be hard to stop and switch roles. And for now, don't pick anything to do with your relationship to each other. You talk about your issue, the other listens. Then you reverse it. Decide at the start how long you will each listen—ten to twenty minutes might be enough— and stick to it. Then you can discuss how it went, coaching each other on how to improve. Again, don't pick an issue *too* big or intense for these first tries.

Pairs and Groups: As, Bs, and Cs. Groups should break into pairs, with someone timing the listening sessions, which could be ten to fifteen minutes. Large groups can break into threesomes, with people taking turns in three roles: listening, being listened to, and coaching the listener.

IN CONCLUSION: Make a few notes here on what you have learned about yourself from practicing reflective listening.

_____

_____

_____

_____

Making Action/Feeling Statements

This activity is based on Claude Steiner's book, *Achieving Emotional Literacy,* which I recommend to everyone, whether they are in a relationship or not. He distilled years of experience into a powerful, clear handbook for communicating about feelings.

After reflective listening, the next most basic building block of good communicating in close relationships is to be able, when things get complicated, to make a simple, factual statement about what you feel when the other person does something. Alternately, it is the ability to help the other person make a simple statement about what he or she feels when you do something. This is called making an action/feeling statement. It sounds easy, but can be quite tricky.

As with reflective listening, one reason HSPs need this skill is to help them clear up their communications with non-HSPs, who are often less in tune with their feelings, or with HSPs who may be overaroused, and thus out of tune with everything.

An action/feeling statement involves first an action, *not* an interpretation of an action: "When you left early, I was sad," *not* "when you decided you wanted to go, I was sad." Unless the other person said he or she wanted to go, all you *know* is that he or she left early.

Here's another statement that interprets rather than sticking to the action: "When you treat me like your mother, I get angry." This is not a specific action, and whatever made you angry may or may not be something your partner does to his or her mother. A better action/feeling statement is, "When you don't call me to say you'll be late, I get angry."

Here's an example of how we might work with a non-HSP on an issue dear to us. The other person says, "It makes me furious when you are so overly sensitive." So you can say, "Excuse me, but can you tell me specifically what I have done that is making you angry?"

Try rewriting these statements. How I would rewrite them follows them.

When you are rude, I am embarrassed.
Better: *When you* _____, *I am embarrassed.*
Here's a tricky one. *When you drive unsafely, I get afraid.*
Better: *When you* _____, *I get afraid.*
Here's an interesting one. *When you don't respect my sensitivity, I get angry.*
Better: *When you* _____, *I get angry.*
Here is how I would rewrite these statements:
When you are rude, I am embarrassed.
Better: *When you don't remember the name of someone you were just introduced to, I am embarrassed.*
When you drive unsafely, I get afraid.
Better: *When you leave less than three car lengths between us and the next car, I get afraid.*
When you don't respect my sensitivity, I get angry.
Better: *When you say that you can't understand "how anyone can be so silly" get-*

ting upset about our staying a few hours more when I had already said I was ex-hausted and wanted to go, I get very angry.

The second half of the statement is also hard to get right. There are only a few real emotions: anger, fear, sadness, hate, shame or embarrassment, happiness, love, pride, and joy. Maybe you could add loneliness, curiosity, worry, anxiety, jealousy, guilt, envy, hopelessness, and hope. But these last are more often derivative. Other "feelings," like feeling ignored or ridiculed, imply a motive and action (ignoring, ridicule) by the other that may not have been present. Another part of the difficulty is that in English it is common to say "I feel" when you mean "I have a hunch" or intuition, so it can be especially hard to notice that you are not stating a feeling in the sense of an emotion when you say "I feel." For example, "When you don't speak to my friends, I feel you are rejecting me" is really an intuition that the other is rejecting you. You don't know—maybe this person is feeling reclusive.

Here's another example of confusing feeling with thinking or intuiting: "When you smile, I feel I've made you happy." This is your thought about what caused the smile. Better reaction/feeling statement is: "When you smile, I feel happy."

Here's one for HSPs: "When you shout, I feel how insensitive you are." But you don't know for certain that the other person is insensitive. Has no HSP ever shouted? Why not just say, "When you shout, I feel angry."

Here's an example of why we need this skill to straighten out other people's statements: "Every time you refuse to go to a party with me, I feel put down." To understand better and perhaps alleviate the feeling without having to go to more parties, you could try asking, "Could you tell me exactly what you feel? When I refuse, are you angry with me? Afraid of something? Sad?"

Try rewriting these. How I would write them follows these examples.

When you broke the glass, I felt you were breaking a part of me.
Better: *When you broke the glass, I felt* _____.
When you turn away, I feel you are looking for someone more interesting to talk to.
Better: *When you turn away, I feel* _____.
When you say you "just forgot," I feel like you really wanted to forget.
Better: *When you say you "just forgot," I feel* _____
_____.

When you sighed, I felt you were letting me know that you don't like my being so sensitive.
Better: *When you sighed, I felt* _____.

Here's how I would rewrite these statements:

When you broke the glass, I felt you were breaking a part of me.

Better: *When you broke the glass, I felt deep sadness.*

When you turn away, I feel you are looking for someone more interesting to talk to.

Better: *When you turn away, I feel afraid.*

When you say you "just forgot," I feel like you really wanted to forget.

Better: *When you say you "just forgot," I feel angry.*

When you sighed, I felt you were letting me know that you don't like my being so sensitive.

Better: *When you sighed, I was worried.*

It's not that you *always* have to talk this way, and certainly you will want to explain why you feel sad, angry, or worried. But as with reflective listening, when there is a conflict, a muddle, or a lot of strong emotions flying around, you want to get down to the facts of the feelings themselves and eliminate the interpretations, advice, defensiveness, and accusations. Feelings aren't right or wrong, they just are. The person receiving the action/feeling statement may not have intended to create this feeling in the other, but in a good action/feeling statement, accusations about intentions are not present, so the receiver need not feel accused. The other's feeling response may seem stupid, irrational, or sick. But again, it is a fact that cannot be eliminated by attacking or denying it. Especially because you are an HSP, you will be wise to learn to welcome an action/feeling statement from someone, whatever its contents. It is invaluable information about where you both stand. From there, you can take whatever action you want—use some reflective listening, change your behavior, apologize, express some anger, suggest reasons for your behavior or the other's reaction, and so forth.

If you haven't yet, show this activity to your partner or friend and ask if he or she would be willing to do it with you. One of you should pick a minor conflict or bit of unfinished business (hopefully not a big issue still masquerading as a small one) that you have around an event or exchange of feelings.

1. You begin by making a clear action/feeling statement.

2. The other person should sit with the statement a while, letting it sink in, then just repeat back the idea, using the same words.

3. You then make a second action/feeling statement about what you feel *now.*

An example of what I'm asking you to do for each other:

1. You begin with this action/feeling statement: *"When you don't take out the trash, I feel angry."*

2. Your partner lets this sink in, then simply repeats the idea: *"When I don't take out the trash, you feel angry."*

3. You then see how that feels, and make a new action/feeling statement: *"When you repeated my words, I felt angrier still about it."* Or *"I felt happy."* Or *whatever.* This is very basic stuff—attending to what you are feeling.

That beginning should launch a good discussion about the trash, perhaps followed by who is feeling taken advantage of these days, who is feeling life is too short to do everything, and so on, in which reflective listening, intuitions, apologies, and lots of other stuff can happen. But return to action/feeling statements if things get fuzzy.

Pairs and Groups: As, Bs, and Cs can practice hypothetical statements, or statements you would use in relationships, not in a pair or group. But statements made by pairs or group members about each other's behavior toward each other should only be attempted by Bs and Cs—and can be extremely useful in advancing the pair's or group's closeness.

IN CONCLUSION: What have you learned from trying to make action/feeling statements? Make a few notes about that here.

_____

_____

_____

_____

Letting Your Psyche Tell You Why You Are in This Relationship

This activity is very roughly based on the work of Harville Hendrix, and I do recommend his book, *Getting the Love You Want: A Guide for Couples.* Like Steiner, Harville Hendrix has depth and complexity to his thinking, along with years of experience. This task is complicated, but for a reason. I'm trying to help you access your unconscious psyche. So I think it's worth it.

The Terms You Use for Describing People

1. Think of three traits you liked best and least about your mother, father, and any other very influential person in your childhood: a brother, sister, best friend, daytime caretaker, grandparent, or whomever. Below is an example *only,* that I will refer back to often.

	Best Liked Traits			*Least Liked Traits*		
Mother	kind	serious	devoted	tired	overreacts	dull
Father	funny	strong	successful	angry	unavailable	rigid
Sister	smart	wealthy	light-hearted	controlling	not sensitive	mean

Do your own below

	Best Liked Traits			*Least Liked Traits*		
Mother	*sympathetic*	*listener*	*friendly*	*critical*	*cruel*	*blistering*
Father	*funny*	*wry*	*kind*	*logical*	*critical*	*impatient*

2. Now write down the three best and worst traits of yourself. Here are examples:

	Best Liked Traits			*Least Liked Traits*		
Myself	hard working	compassionate	sensitive	poor	slow to understand	lack energy

Do your own below

	Best Liked Traits			*Least Liked Traits*		
Myself	*smart*	*creative*	*mystical*	*compulsive*	*angry*	*lost energy*

3. *On another day*, so that the traits of you and your family won't be fresh in your memory, write out the best and worst traits of your partner—what do you love this person for, what do you most criticize? Examples:

	Best Liked Traits			*Least Liked Traits*		
Partner	funny	energetic	committed	works too much	uses clichés	not careful with money

Do your own below

	Best Liked Traits			Least Liked Traits		
Partner	funny	love 4 kids	honesty	critical	mean	cruel

Identifying Your Complexes

Now we can talk about the purpose of this task, which is to help you see how any troubles you may be having in your relationship with your partner—your complaints about her or him that make you sometimes or often consider ending the relationship—are related to your own issues, your complexes (complexes were introduced on page 125 and are discussed further later in this task). The step on page 183 is the reorganizing of the traits you used above into the major categories you use for thinking about people—that is, your complexes. The example will help.

1. Using all the terms you used to describe people, you put them into categories, under either the positive or negative pole of that category. As you enter each term, put in parentheses the person you used it to describe. One way to do this is to start with the first trait you wrote down, the first about your mother, and think of it as a category, then look for any other terms like it, checking off each term for that trait as you put it into a category. If the next trait does not fit in your first category, make it part of a new one, and so on. (You can use the same trait more than once if it fits into more than one category—but put every trait into at least one category.)

In the example filled in on the next page, your first trait and major category section would be "kind" (with "mother" in parentheses). Since to you it is a positive trait, it goes under the positive pole. Continuing through the most and least liked traits for mother, there are no other very similar traits or opposites to kind. However, when you get to father, you come to "angry," which to you is a fairly close opposite to kind. So you put "angry" (with "father" in parentheses) under the negative pole, as shown in the example. Continuing further, you come to "mean" (sister) and put that on the negative side. Coming to "compassionate" (self), you put that on the positive side.

2. Continue categorizing all the terms you used to describe people. It does not have to be done perfectly. In the example, you would go back to the second term used for mother, "serious." This one is harder, because while you like her seriousness, you realize already that its opposite is humorousness, and you enjoy your partner's humor far more than mother's seriousness. So you put "serious" on the negative side and your partner's "funny" on the positive side. Then your father's "funny" and your sister's "light hearted" go here too. Important: None of this has to be done perfectly.

3. If some traits seem only vaguely similar or opposite to a category you have already created, put these on the next lines, as "Could-Be-Related Terms." In the example, on the lines for "Could-Be-Related Terms," we'll imagine that in your mind "devoted" (mother) and "committed" (partner) seem related to kind, while "controlling" (sister) and "works too much" (partner) have a mean quality to you, so you put them on the negative side.

What about a term that seems to fit nowhere, so it is a category by itself? Make it one if it is important to you. Otherwise, try to put it into one of the categories under "Could-Be-Related Terms." Again, none of this has to be perfect.

4. Make up a title for the whole category—the positive and negative poles—and write it in on the line by "Major Category." In the example, you might decide to title the first "Major Category" "kindness/meanness."

5. Go on with this process, creating additional categories, until you have used up (checked off) your most liked and least liked traits for all the people you rated.

The imaginary example:

*Major Category*_____kindness/meanness_____

	Positive Pole	*Negative Pole*
All Similar Terms	kind (mother)	angry (father)
	compassionate (self)	mean (sister)
Could-Be-		
Related Terms	devoted (mother)	controlling (sister)
	committed (partner)	works too much (partner)

*Major Category*_____humorous/serious_____

	Positive Pole	*Negative Pole*
All Similar Terms	funny (partner)	serious (mother)
	light-hearted (sister)	
	funny (father)	
Could-Be-		
Related Terms		hard working (self)

Major Category _____ energetic/tired _____

	Positive Pole	*Negative Pole*
All Similar Terms	energetic (partner)	tired (mother)
		lack energy (self)
Could-Be-Related Terms	strong (father)	
	successful (father)	
	hard working (self)	

Major Category _____ available/unavailable _____

	Positive Pole	*Negative Pole*
All Similar Terms	devoted (mother)	unavailable (father)
	committed (partner)	works too much (partner)
Could-Be-Related Terms	successful (father)	hard working (self)
	hard working (self)	

Major Category _____ smart/stupid _____

	Positive Pole	*Negative Pole*
All Similar Terms	smart (sister)	slow to understand (self)
		using clichés (partner)
		dull (mother)
Could-Be-Related Terms	successful (father)	not careful with money (partner)

Major Category _____ wealthy/poor _____

	Positive Pole	*Negative Pole*
All Similar Terms	wealthy (sister)	poor (self)

Could-Be-
Related Terms _____ successful (father) _____   _____ not careful with money (partner) _____

_____   _____

_____   _____

Major Category _____ sensitive/not sensitive _____

                   Positive Pole   *Negative Pole*

All Similar Terms _____ sensitive (self) _____   _____ not sensitive (sister) _____

_____   _____

_____   _____

Could-Be-
Related Terms _____ overreacts (mother) _____   _____ strong (father) _____

_____   _____ rigid (father) _____

_____   _____

Do your own below

Major Category _____

                   Positive Pole   *Negative Pole*

All Similar Terms _____   _____

_____   _____

_____   _____

Could-Be-
Related Terms _____   _____

_____   _____

_____   _____

Major Category _____

                   Positive Pole   *Negative Pole*

All Similar Terms _____   _____

_____   _____

_____   _____

Could-Be-
Related Terms _____   _____

_____   _____

_____   _____

Major Category _____

	Positive Pole	Negative Pole

All Similar Terms _____

_____   _____

_____   _____

*Could-Be-
Related Terms*   _____   _____

_____   _____

_____   _____

Major Category _____

	Positive Pole	Negative Pole

All Similar Terms _____

_____   _____

_____   _____

*Could-Be-
Related Terms*   _____   _____

_____   _____

_____   _____

Major Category _____

	Positive Pole	Negative Pole

All Similar Terms _____

_____   _____

_____   _____

*Could-Be-
Related Terms*   _____   _____

_____   _____

_____   _____

Major Category _____

	Positive Pole	Negative Pole

All Similar Terms _____

_____   _____

_____   _____

Could-Be-
Related Terms   _____   _____

_____   _____

_____   _____

Major Category _____
                 Positive Pole   *Negative Pole*

All Similar Terms _____   _____

_____   _____

_____   _____

Could-Be-
Related Terms   _____   _____

_____   _____

_____   _____

More on Complexes

Look back at the description of complexes on page 125 and then look at what you have just filled out. For the purpose of going along with me on this task, assume the "Major Categories" are a rough sketch of your complexes, at least in regard to relationships. They are where your energy goes, they are the topics which are likely to make you touchy and opinionated. Another way to define a complex is to say it is like a black hole into which any experience vaguely related will be sucked. If you have a victim/dominator or controlled/controlling complex, for example, everyone will be assessed by you, consciously or unconsciously, for their place in a hierarchy of those above you, who want to dominate, abuse, or control you, or those beneath you, whom you could easily dominate or control if you wanted to.

Complexes always have two sides to them, two poles. One pole of the complex is the side we identify with, "own," or are conscious of. The other is what we reject, dislike, or are not conscious of existing at all in ourselves. It's always one pole or the other when we are in a complex. Another sign of a complex is that in this area you engage in rather "black and white" thinking—there are fewer nuances. You tend to label people as this (good) or that (bad). Again, it's one pole or the other—nothing in between.

Some other common categories/complexes not in the example:
- self-sufficient/needy
- masculine/feminine

- trustworthy/likely to betray
- rational/irrational
- refined/gross
- close/distant
- submissive/dominant
- achieved greatness/achieved nothing
- shy/outgoing
- responsible/irresponsible
- virtuous/sinful

The list could go on and on, but it is not infinite. If there are some topics here that are "hot" for you but that you forgot about, go ahead and make them "Major Categories" too for the next step of this task.

Now we get ready to consider the connections between your complexes and your relationships. To do this, you will make a fresh list—of your complexes (as represented by the "Major Categories" in the previous list) and whom you have identified with the positive and negative poles. When you are one of the people, list yourself last.

Here is how you might create a list for our example:

Positive Pole	People	Negative Pole	People
kind	mother, partner, self	mean	sister, father, partner
energetic	partner, father, self	tired	mother, self
humorous	partner, sister, father	serious	mother, self
available	mother, partner	unavailable	father, partner, self
smart	sister, father	stupid	partner, mother, self
wealthy	sister, father	poor	partner, self
sensitive	mother, self	not sensitive	sister, father

Do your own below

Positive Pole	People	Negative Pole	People
_____	_____	_____	_____
_____	_____	_____	_____
_____	_____	_____	_____
_____	_____	_____	_____
_____	_____	_____	_____
_____	_____	_____	_____
_____	_____	_____	_____
_____	_____	_____	_____

Making the Connections

Next we'll look for connections. But leave out your partner for now.

1. The first connection is found by asking, who are you identifying yourself with? Who does *self* appear with? In the example, it is most often mother. Then think about the "package deal" by looking back at the start of this task, at what you most liked and disliked about this person with whom you identify. How do you feel about yourself concerning the traits this person has that you did not mention for yourself? Would you like to have these other traits as well as those you share with the person? Or do you see them in yourself but hate them and try to pretend they aren't there, or emphasize their opposites? Or, liking them or not, have you been utterly unaware of their presence?

In the example, if this were you, there's quite a bit that you listed about yourself that does overlap in some way with your mother. So you'd be looking at what else you said about her. "Overreact." Do you feel you overreact, as your mother does? Is that okay? Or is this something you have struggled against?

Describe here how you feel about the traits of the persons you are most like (not counting your partner) but which you did not list for yourself.

_____

_____

_____

2. Who is most your opposite (again, leaving out your partner)? In the example, there seem to be two strong candidates, your father and sister. The person most your opposite "carries your shadow." This is especially true with someone of the same gender as yourself, and of a sibling. Very often two sisters or two brothers will become "complete opposites" in personality. Sometimes they are almost forced to by their families, who are always comparing them. "Joe is so smart—if only Josh had half his brains, and Joe had some of Josh's sense of humor." The worst one may be, "Sally is so good and Jane is so naughty."

The traits "assigned" to your sibling by your family are in a sense lost to you. You probably could never be those things or you would "disappoint" (disprove) your parents, and even if you acted in ways you weren't supposed to according to your assigned traits, those acts would just be ignored. But these lost opposite traits and behaviors are still at least potentially strong in you, if for no other reason than that you had someone so close to you who was such an expert in them! Your knowledge of how to be the opposite (bad instead of good, funny instead of serious, controlling instead of controlled) is still there, lingering in the unconscious.

When you become the opposite of a parent, it is usually because you did not admire that parent, and that is usually because he or she did not treat you well. But whatever the reason, you often reject and therefore lose the benefits of that person's knowledge and perspectives. You may have learned a great deal from this parent, of course, but be resisting manifesting that latent self.

In the example, if this were you, what about your repressed but potentially wealthy self? You must have observed something about making money from your successful sister and father, although you may not admire them. What about your funny self? Do you have to be serious, just to avoid being like them?

Now, write here about aspects of your own repressed self that are similar to the person or persons (not counting your partner) whom you dislike or are supposedly most unlike.

_____

_____

You and Your Partner

Now here's the biggy. Look at the original list of things you don't like about your partner. In the example this would be works too much, uses clichés, and is not careful with money. Hmm. Pretend this example is a list of your own traits; we are looking for how your issues might be affecting how you see your partner's personality. This is not to say that your partner doesn't have real faults. But this task is designed to see whether you are making any mountains out of molehills, or why you picked these particular faults to be upset about. For example, could you be projecting (assigning to the other person) something of yourself that you know about and dislike, or even deny altogether? To see this, it helps to look for where you put yourself on the positive side of the ledger and your partner on the other side.

In the example, still pretending this is your list, you are seeing your partner as both kind and mean. Your partner landed on the mean side because back at the start you listed "works too much" (although he or she can't be too bad in this area, as you've admitted to his or her kindness through describing your partner as "committed"). You see yourself as kind ("compassionate"), and it is a big issue for you to be kind and compassionate like your mother, not cruel like your sister and father. To be cruel is probably one of the last things you ever want to be, or see your partner as being. Yet it is hard not to make your own issue an issue in your relationships. So when your partner works a lot, you tend to see it through your kind/mean glasses.

Yet you admit to being "hard working." Do your work behaviors really differ that much from your partner's? You may see your own working hard as a kind thing, part of making your contribution, or just as how you like to be. Have you ever asked your partner the reason for all of his or her working "too much," and really listened?

Let's look at "uses clichés." Still pretending the example is yours, here it seems that you and your partner are getting the same bad treatment—you seem to be projecting your disliked "stupid" self ("slow to understand") onto your partner, seeing both of you as inferior to your sister and father. Do either of you really deserve this labeling?

Finally, consider the trait "not careful with money." Perhaps you originally liked your partner being unlike your father and more like you—not good with money. But it was bound to become a problem too, because being rich or poor is so much an issue for you. Do you ever find yourself blaming your partner for your being poor?

This kind of thinking is hard, hard work, but very good for a relationship. So try doing this for your own relationship. That is, in light of the examples above, think about how what you have listed as your partner's faults might relate to your complexes. Write down here what you learn.

_____

_____

_____

_____

_____

_____

_____

Continuing this kind of thinking, look at where your partner shows up on a line with others and try to see *who* you are projecting onto your partner, by seeing whose traits you equate your partner's with. Do you sometimes treat your partner like someone else, even though your partner is only slightly like this person?

Pretending again that the example is your list, you should ask yourself if you sometimes react to a few similarities by projecting your entire Terrible Sister, or your entire Unloving Father, onto your partner. I capitalized these because they are the sort of bigger-than-life beings that develop in childhood. Everyone knows about them, probably because they are in our collective unconscious as archetypes. They are certainly taught and fed by fairy tales and stories—stories that teach us how to recognize and handle these nearly universal, archetypal, dangerous sorts of people and situations. But the stories exaggerate them for their own purposes: Wicked Stepmother, Murderous Brother, Abandoning Mother.

By adulthood, our emotional brains can be steeped in automatic reactions to certain small cues warning that we are with one of these dangerous beings. A certain phrase, a certain look, even a sound or smell, and we are treating our partner like, well, a major archetype.

The classic situation is this: Your partner is only asking a question or expressing a need, and suddenly you feel attacked. Or wounded. And it is so *hard* not to believe that the reasons for your reaction all reside in the other person! But if there's incredible energy around this issue for you, and the other person is mystified by your response, suspect a complex at work.

Write here your thoughts about who (which person, and which archetype behind that person) you might be sometimes projecting on to your partner.

_____

_____

_____

_____

_____

You may now want to make a list of more of the faults and issues you have with your partner, and look for more connections with your past. Go for it.

1. Fault/Issue: _____

    Connections: _____

_____

2. Fault/Issue: _____

    Connections: _____

_____

3. Fault/Issue: _____

    Connections: _____

_____

4. Fault/Issue: _____

Connections: _____

_____

5. Fault/Issue: _____

Connections: _____

_____

Your Sensitivity Complex

Last but never least, what about your sensitivity? Who has it? What goes with who has it? Where is your partner on sensitivity?

In the example, again pretending this is you, you knew right away that your pain-in-the-neck sister was not sensitive. Interestingly, you did not rate anyone else on the trait, although your seemingly worn-down mother "overreacts," which may be your negative feelings about sensitivity showing up, embedded in the context of your mother's "tiredness" and "dullness." These are other ways you may unconsciously view a sensitive person—that is, yourself. Sensitivity-insensitivity was not a category you applied to your partner. Could this be out of fear of noticing a difference between you two?

Write your thoughts here:

_____

_____

_____

_____

_____

Pairs and Groups: Cs could discuss this task.

IN CONCLUSION: This was a long, difficult task. Sit back and close your eyes a while and just drift. Or wait a day or two to write your thoughts below. With some time, you may find your entire relationship changing from this type of work.

To me, respect is the most difficult, most precious element in a relationship, and you cannot force it. You definitely cannot feel respect if, when you are around your partner, flaws and faults are always in your face. Everyone has them, of course. But to love someone in spite of these—that is the trickiest, most precious thing of all. And to see what part of your partner's flaws are your own issues seems to be an important step, not only for your relationship, but for your own self-understanding. I titled this task, "Letting Your Psyche Tell You Why You Are in This Relationship." Does the title make some sense to you now?

You can write on any of these points here.

_____

_____

_____

_____

_____

_____

_____

_____

8

Working with the Deeper Wounds

HSPs are not born wounded, neurotic, anxious, or depressed. When we are in good-enough environments—not special, protected environments but just normally kind, respectful ones—we are fine. Indeed, the evidence from medical research is that when growing up in adequate home and school environments, HSPs are actually physically healthier than non-HSPs, which probably means we are mentally healthier too.

On the other hand, not-good-enough environments do exist all too often. For example, about half of children in most industrialized cultures are not growing up in secure relationships with their primary caretakers (usually their mothers, and usually because the mothers also experienced insecure attachments). That means about half of HSPs also did not have secure attachments in childhood.

Similarly, the whole family environment can be wonderful or hellish or somewhere in between, as can be the neighborhood and school. Then there are the various traumas that can happen to anyone in adulthood—being the victim of a crime, witnessing or surviving an accident or disaster, losing a loved one, developing a catastrophic illness. HSPs are often good in emergencies, but we can be more vulnerable than others to the aftereffects, particularly if our mind/body state is not in excellent condition because of previous stressors.

HSPs who have had tragic childhood and/or adult histories do seem to be more prone than others to anxiety and depression. Psychologically, we have a much harder time trusting the world and its people. That's no surprise. Being "deep processors," of course HSPs are going to see the world differently after such experiences. In biological terms, we are built for handling subtleties, not gross overloads, so our brains are probably a bit more damaged by these overload experiences. Our brain's flexibility for handling future stressful events then becomes a little lessened, so that when we hit a stressful period again, even a mild one, we can have more difficulty than non-HSPs.

One *could* then argue that HSPs are born more vulnerable to anxiety and depression, but that would be about as odd as saying of a blonde, "look at that nice blue-eyed, skin-cancer-prone person." A potential for some should not be a label for all, so you as an HSP should not accept any label for your trait that pathologizes it.

At the same time, you can and should accept that, according to research, you may need to put more time into healing past hurts than non-HSPs do. A typical accusation you may hear is "Why do you spend so much time in therapy?" Or "reading self-help books?" Or "going to *those* courses?" The answer is, yes, HSPs are affected more by painful life events. (I also like the other answer, that we thrive on inner work the way athletes thrive on physical workouts.)

This chapter will begin with steps for finding a good psychotherapist, because I am so often asked how to go about it, and you will then do some tasks that may stir up enough feelings to cause you to want to see a therapist.

In the Appendix on page 316 you will find the diagnostic criteria for some of the types of depression and anxiety anyone, HSPs included, can develop. It is good to be able to sort out ordinary "blues" from more serious conditions. The longer you let a heavy case of depression or anxiety continue, the more difficult it is to stop and the more likely you are to relapse. However, since just reading these lists of symptoms in the appendix can give an HSP "medical student's disease" (convince you that you have them), I would not bother to read them if you feel no interest or need to do so.

How to Choose a Psychotherapist

I receive many requests for information about how to choose a therapist, and I have recommended therapy repeatedly in this workbook. The truth is, however, I am extremely particular about whom I refer people to and even then prefer to give several names and ask the person to check them all out before deciding. How do you decide? It's a process, and here are the steps I advise. Check them off to be sure you did not skip any.

☐ *Appreciate the fact that this decision will have profound impact on your life.* You will incorporate this person into your life. Be aware that therapists vary far more than dentists or doctors in their training, methods, personalities, and the all-important issue of ethics (most of which amounts to "maintaining good boundaries"). You need to meet with several therapists before deciding on one. *Don't* call the first name you see in the phone book.

☐ *Anyone you see should be licensed.* A license guarantees little, and there are probably therapists out there without licenses (in spite of licensing laws, people always find loopholes) who are quite okay. One still has to wonder and ask, why aren't they licensed? If you are in doubt whether someone is licensed, ask to see the person's license and check out their name with the licensing board that issued it.

☐ *Investigate what your insurance will cover and read the fine print.* Usually you will have some mental health coverage, but things have gotten pretty weird with HMOs. You will probably have to go through a screening person, to whom you will have to tell all your problems. You will have to think about whether you want that information floating around, because you really have little control over what happens to it. Your number of sessions will almost always be limited, meaning you will be given a treatment that will fit into that time limit, even if longer treatment would be more effective. Find out what the therapist would charge you if your treatment takes longer than your coverage allows.

☐ *Ask friends and professionals for referrals to therapists whom they know very well personally,* and pay particular attention to those who can tell you what it is like to be in therapy with the person. However, don't see someone a close friend is already seeing, unless you can't avoid it because you live in a small town (and obviously don't see a friend or relative who is a therapist). If your partner sees a therapist, don't see the same one (and beware of the therapist who suggests it). And watch out for any subtle sense of obligation to see a certain psychotherapist because of who made the recommendation.

☐ *Call a professional organization or school that you respect and ask for names of members, graduates, or interns.* If you prefer some particular method, such as Freudian psychoanalysis, gestalt work, or transactional analysis, contact those teaching that method. (For example, try your local C. G. Jung Institute or Society of Jungian analysts—see Resources, page 312.)

☐ *After you have assembled a list, call at least two or three psychotherapists* and find out if they have openings at the times you are free, if you can reach their office easily (think carefully about driving a long distance— which you will be doing week after week), and if you can afford their fees. They may want to discuss fees in person, to see what your needs are. However, the busiest—usually the best—may not reduce their fees for anyone (more on fees below). It's probably better not to try to find out much more on the phone unless they encourage you. Most therapists feel that the two of you need to meet to decide on each other, so set up an appointment.

☐ *Don't see someone unlicensed or poorly trained, just to save money.* It could cost you dearly in other ways. Go for the best. These therapists are often moved by someone's keen desire to do inner work, as long as you don't act entitled to their help and respect their need to make a living (and that they really earn their sometimes high fees—this is *hard* work). State what you can pay and ask whether they have a sliding fee scale or low fee places in their practice (some do this as a public service), or if they know anyone who does. Most know of interns, low-fee clinics, or schools training interns. Ask schools and professional organizations (see above) if they know of interns or other low-fee opportunities. Interns may lack experience, but are enthusiastic and up on the latest developments in psychotherapy. Those seeking the highest level of licenses usually need thousands of hours of experience (depending on the state), and are often well supervised, giving you the input of a true expert, albeit secondhand. Try to find one planning to start a private practice that you could become part of (usually they'll keep your fee low).

☐ *For the first session, plan to pay* (although a few do not charge for the first session) and know ahead of time how much that will be. HSPs should not go to see two potential therapists on the same day—these sessions require your full energy, and the second may seem dull because you were.

☐ *In the first session, bring up enough of your deepest issues for you to have an idea of whether this person will have some useful insights.* If you want to do dream work, you can even present a recent, recurring, or disturbing dream.

Whatever you want help with, ask how this person would work with your situation. The therapist may want to ask you questions too, but use at least half of the session to ask your questions and assess the therapist.

☐ *Discuss your sensitivity* and the book *The Highly Sensitive Person*. Since this is important to you, you want to be sure they appreciate the concept. Indeed, you probably want to work with someone highly sensitive (I would), although other factors are important too. I used to think most therapists were HSPs, but they are not.

☐ *Afterward, expect to feel that the person was kind and empathetic*—psychotherapists are trained to be that way. If this one was not, don't go back. Assuming the empathy as a given, did you feel you gained something from the session, or were you at least engaged enough to want to try another session?

☐ *Do not go back to therapists who push you to work with them,* discourage your interviewing several potential therapists, or who make you feel for any reason that their needs are going to get in the way of yours—for example, if they use you as an audience for personal stories or try to impress you with their talents.

☐ *After seeing several therapists, pause at least for a few days to sort out your feelings* (otherwise the last person may leave the strongest impression). What was your response to each therapist? Don't ignore your reaction to "little details" like their offices—these reflect much about who they are.

☐ *Pay attention to your dreams for clues about your psyche's response to each therapist.*

☐ *If you are planning to do long-term work, arrange to see the person you like most for four to six sessions,* with the understanding that you will both think about how it is working out after that time. For your next session with "the front runner," decide what else you need to know about the person, including office policies, such as what happens if you have to cancel suddenly or how often fees are raised. These tell you a great deal about how you two will work together.

☐ *Once you decide, you have decided.* Trust your choice through the ups and downs, unless something very unusual occurs, such as requests for sexual intimacies or friendship (absolutely unethical and wrong) or other failures to keep good boundaries (like meeting outside of the office). Do not try to see two psychotherapists, except when one has referred you to another, as for marital counseling, which by the way is probably best not done by the same therapist you see individually. If things don't seem to work out as you expected, discuss why with your therapist, in some detail, before ending.

Pairs and groups: Bs and Cs. You may be able to offer each other names of therapists and help each other work through the choosing process, but choosing a therapist should be honored as a very personal decision.

The Healing Power of Telling Your Story

Research is finding, not surprisingly, that people are significantly physically and mentally healthier, sometimes for years, after simply writing down a distressing event, even if they never show what they have written to anyone. The next two tasks are based on that method of healing.

The first story you will write, if you decide to, will be about your childhood in general. The second will be about a specific traumatic event in adulthood. You can write both stories or just one, or neither. I say neither because both of these can be very intense tasks. If you have never before given much thought to the events I am suggesting you chronicle here, you could have a strong emotional reaction. In that case, I urge you to go to a therapist to talk about these events.

You can, of course, show what you write to your therapist if you have one. If you don't, you could perhaps show it to someone else. But it is crucial that the person you choose provide a healing response—not become upset, tell you to try to forget it, blame you for being too sensitive, and so forth. I want to underscore this warning, as you can be badly hurt by trying to share your stories with people not prepared to listen well.

Telling the Story of What Hurt You, Who Hurt You, How It Happened

The first of the two writing tasks is especially for those whose childhoods involved repeated, chronic trauma or neglect, who had very insecure attachment styles, or who lived in very dysfunctional families. Some of you have worked through this story of yours with therapists or others to the point that you can skip this if you want. But even after therapy, sometimes you have not put it all together in one place where you are forced to see just how much you had to struggle with.

This is *not* about blaming anyone. It is about telling the story, very privately, so that you can stop feeling so much anger, shame, and so forth.

Write, or simply list, all the events, factors, and disturbed relationships that shaped you while you were young and vulnerable. I have provided a list of possibilities to help you work around the tendency to forget certain unusual circumstances because they may have seemed so *normal* to you as a child.

- Moving often
- Loss of a parent or sibling
- A major illness in your family
- Your having a major or chronic illness
- Mental illness in the family
- Suicide by a family member
- Alcoholism or other addiction in the family
- Poverty
- Discrimination
- Neglect
- Physical abuse
- Verbal abuse
- Sexual abuse
- Divorce
- Absence of a parent
- Cruel or dominating siblings
- Teasing by peers
- Multiple caretakers or baby-sitters to whom you became attached, then lost
- Mistreatment by teachers
- Being overweight
- Being underweight
- Parents being under stress due to illness, unemployment, etc.
- Parents fighting constantly
- Parents fighting over you (for custody, for example)
- Violence in your family
- Violence in your neighborhood
- Parents not wanting you to be born
- Parents disliking your sensitivity
- Being overly rewarded for achievements, not rewarded enough for just being yourself
- Having, as a child, to take care of your parents
- A parent who was a narcissist, a sociopath, or in other ways had a deeply disturbed character
- Being abandoned by a parent
- Feeling guilty about something you could discuss with no one

- Often feeling hopeless or wanting to die
- Often feeling afraid
- Being sent to school or camp against your will; being homesick
- Being criticized for your appearance
- As a teenager, being especially troubled, abusing drugs or alcohol, feeling suicidal
- As a teenager, being in trouble with the authorities

Begin your writing or listing on the lines below but stop if this task becomes highly distressing. Come back to it in small pieces, or take the task to a therapist, to do it in the company of someone who can help you express yet contain the feelings. The idea is to *record the facts* as a whole, the whole story, and feel whatever you feel about it. Then review this history as often as you can, thinking about it any way you can, reading, learning about, and discussing the issues if you'd like, until your reaction feels contained and you sense some resolution, some calm. Do not mistake continued dissociation, denial, or numbness for a true lessening of the feelings, which only occurs after assimilating your story. (One way to know the difference is that unexplainable bad dreams, stress-related symptoms, addictions, and poor self-care should also be declining.) Fresh feelings of distress may return throughout your life, but hopefully with decreasing strength. At these times, return to this task, or if the distress becomes greater than ever, seek professional help.

_____

_____

_____

_____

_____

_____

_____

_____

_____

_____

_____

_____

_____

_____

Telling the Story of a Specific Trauma

Specific traumas—such as being in an accident, having someone close to you die, witnessing a crime, being raped—can undermine anyone's trust in the world. But an HSP will think about it even more—if not consciously, then subconsciously. The research on treatment of the aftereffects of trauma is rather clear: For most people, if effects are still lingering, the only way through these aftereffects is to face what happened, reexperience it until it is assimilated, find the meaning in it if you can, and develop a way through to a new, modified trust in the world.

Some of us think there's something heroic about being stoical and something disgusting about thinking or talking "constantly" about one's troubles. But the fact is, those who express themselves are more likely to heal. There's nothing heroic about refusing to heal. If you don't allow yourself to think or talk *to anyone* about your painful inner experiences, most likely this prohibition came from childhood, or from some aspect of the trauma that gives you shame or guilt. This reluctance is in itself a trauma that needs to be discussed and worked through, but will almost certainly require a therapist's help.

Reliving a trauma is terribly painful work, and you definitely should not do this task without professional help if the event is recent and major, and you have received no prior professional help with it, or if you are experiencing the symptoms of full-blown depression or posttraumatic stress (see the Appendix, pages 315–16).

If it seems right that you try some processing of the event on your own, let's proceed. The idea of retelling the event is that it helps end the avoidance of the bad feelings and of the whole subject. This avoidance *seems* so necessary, and maybe it was at first, but the cost is high. The feelings remain repressed and surface as physical or psychological symptoms—those mild states of anxiety, bouts of fatigue, frequent illnesses, and that lack of enthusiasm for life.

Just retelling and thereby reliving the experiences is not quite enough, however. As time passes, calmer parts of your mind will start to work on the event and try to put it in perspective. You may begin to see that the event is really not likely to happen again and not something to let ruin your entire life, or that this has happened to others and you can learn how they healed, or that you can put this experience to use by helping others, or you have been made a deeper person by the experience, and so forth. If this kind of more positive thinking does not begin to happen spontaneously, even if only bit by bit, then you need professional help.

So please consider using this space to write a detailed account of any trauma that is still troubling you. Then read it over as often as you can, until there is a noticeable decrease in your distress about it and fewer related bad dreams or flashbacks. As an alternative, make a tape recording of yourself telling the trauma, and listen to it over and over. (If you wish or need to work with a professional, have the therapist read psychologist Edna Foa's *Treating the Trauma of Rape*—see Resources, page 312; her method is not limited to the treatment of rape.)

_____

_____

_____

_____

_____

_____

_____

Pairs and Groups: Cs only. Share these stories with each other with great caution, sensitivity, and, I hope, healing.

IN CONCLUSION: Reflect on your emotional state after having written these stories. Are you emerging out of the intense feelings? Is there a sense of perspective and meaning to your life, or are you feeling numb or distressed? Write about your feelings here, and if you feel distressed, write about how you will get help for yourself.

_____

_____

_____

_____

_____

Learning More About Your Complexes

Everyone, absolutely everyone, has complexes. We have already discussed them some in chapters 5 and 7. Complexes are yet another way of thinking about your past hurts and traumas. Psychological wounds leave complexes, places where energy gathers as the psyche tries to heal or at least draw your attention to the issue, sometimes relentlessly. Getting to know your complexes is another way to work on healing.

Carl Jung, who most popularized the term "complex," also developed the word-association test for mapping complexes. The tester says a word and times how long it takes the testee to say the first word that comes to mind, the word most associated with it. The longer the time, the more likely it is that a complex has been activated, with all of its complicated feelings and resistances to having the rejected pole brought into awareness. After presenting all the words, the tester considers the time it took for the testee to make each association and reviews the unusual associations, the patterns among them, and the testee's reasons for making those particular associations. I don't see why you can't approximate that for yourself. To time an association is tricky, but you can certainly observe how much hesitation and "mental noise" you experience when free-associating to a word. You can think later about the unusual associations you made. Ready?

1. Before turning to the next page, slip in a piece of thick paper that you can't see through.
2. Turn the page, be ready with a pen, and slip down the paper so you can only see the top word on the list. Write beside it the first word that comes to mind.
3. Circle the 1 if the association only took a moment. Circle the 2 if it took more than a moment. Circle the 3 if the word really stopped you for several moments, as if a war about what to write was going on.
4. Do the same for the next word, and all the others.

dog	*love*	① 2 3
day	*long*	① 2 ③
stop	*go*	① 2 3
mother	*mother*	1 ② 3
moon	*soft*	1 ② 3
skin	*gentle*	1 ② 3
holiday	*confused*	1 2 ③
dark	*closet*	1 ② 3
pain	*vague*	1 2 ③
love	*larger*	1 2 ③
father	*gone*	1 ② ③
work	*great*	1 ② 3
grave	*red clay*	1 ② 3
friend	*loss*	1 2 ③
hurt	*deep*	1 2 ③
money	*shrine*	1 2 ③
clown	*funny*	① 2 3
sister	*none*	1 2 ③
victim	*sorry*	1 2 ③
friend	*none*	1 2 ③
brother	*empty*	1 2 ③
happy	*sad*	① 2 3
joke	*pain*	1 ② ③
sex	*problem*	1 2 ③
success	*none*	1 ② 3
teacher	*distrust*	1 2 ③
abuse	*bad*	1 ② 3
gift	*joy*	1 ② 3
pretty	*not!*	1 ② ③
slow	*bad*	1 ② ③
baby	*wonder*	1 2 ③
cat	*silk*	① 2 3
police	*scared*	1 ② ③
sad	*me*	1 2 ③
handsome	*him*	1 ② 3
control	*important*	1 ② ③
stupid	*me*	① 2 ③

victim	_rape_	1	2	③
pet	_cat_	①	2	3
funny	_laugh_	①	2	3
death	_loss_	1	②	3
winner	_loser_	①	2	3
child	_adult_	①	2	3
hate	_love_	1	②	3
grade	_fork_	1	②	3
lie	_bad_	1	2	③
good	_bad_	1	②	3
baby-sitter	_mean_	1	2	③

5. Go back over the list and look for unusual responses. "Cat" for "dog" and "night" for "day" are not unusual. "Scared" for "dog" and "snake" for "day" would be. Circle the three after any word to which you made an unusual response, even if you already circled the one or two for time taken to make an association to that word.

6. Look back at all your 3s—the slow or unusual responses. These probably point to complexes, especially when several hint at the same issue. Suppose that "mother" gave you a long pause, before you answered "abandoned." Then "pain" brought up "John," the name of a neighborhood boy whom your parents hired to baby-sit and who was in fact cruel and beat you up. "Victim" brought up "me." "Abuse" brought up "guilt." That's one to think about. Your guilt? Why? And of course "baby-sitter" brought up "bad." There may have been many other associations pointing to this distressing victim/dominator complex as well.

7. Reflect on and try to answer the following questions:
   - What do you know about the origin and nature of the complexes pointed to by your 3s and other associations to these words? (If the above example were yours, why did "mother" equal "abandoned" and who exactly is John?)

• How do these complexes affect your life and relationships?

_____

_____

_____

_____

• What are you trying to do to learn more about your complexes—through therapy, dream work, self-analysis, and relationships with close others? (We never get rid of a complex, but we can better harness its energy, as when we decide to work for the good of other victims, or have it control our life less. And we can lessen its influence. Maybe we feel like a victim for a couple hours now and then instead of for two weeks out of a month!) Write about the progress you have already made, too.

_____

_____

_____

_____

Pairs and Groups: Cs only, and only those with the deepest mutual trust should discuss their complexes with each other.

IN CONCLUSION: Reflect on yourself as a "complex" person (like all of us), someone living with conscious but also unconscious thoughts, desires, and fears. How does this change how you see yourself?

_____

_____

_____

_____

_____

_____

_____

9

Becoming Mindful Around Medical Care and Medications

According to the estimate of one physician (see volume II, issue 2 of *Comfort Zone,* referenced on page 313), less than 10 percent of medical doctors are HSPs—and at least 45 percent of office visits are made by HSPs. We are *not* sicker than others. We make more visits because our illnesses (usually stress-related) are often chronic, even if mild, and require more visits, plus we need extra visits in order to discuss treatment options in greater depth. But given the many HSP visits to the many non-HSP doctors, it would not be surprising if there were communication problems—if they saw us as hard to treat, even weird (that is, not like them), and we found them brusque and unfeeling. We come away loaded down with prescriptions we aren't sure we need and with most of our questions unanswered because we were too flustered to ask them. We often have a strong sense of being hypochondriacs because we tried to describe all those subtle details that a professional found irrelevant. So we have to prepare ourselves better for our meetings with the non-HSPs in the medical world, particularly around the issues most commonly brought up by HSPs.

What are these issues? Many of us are more sensitive to pain and to medications and experience more side effects than other patients. We prefer to think longer about undergoing procedures and so need to ask more questions, take time, change our minds, consider alternatives. We are more easily overaroused by all things medical, because they tend to be unfamiliar, painful, or anxiety provoking.

All of this would make us "difficult" patients, and we may be told that or feel it. But we also have pluses as patients. We are more likely to be conscientious about following advice, sensitive to warning signs, quick to take responsibility for our health care, and considerate of staff. So we're a package deal—for our health-care providers to get the benefit of our pluses, they have to accept our more "difficult" side as well.

So let's begin to work on helping you stop taking the blame for having a sensitive body.

Reframing a Significant Illness or Medical Care Experience

The task is to reframe past physical or emotional reactions to a medical care experience that you have always felt ashamed of or bad about. For example, I remember a dentist who had given me a shot to numb my mouth, and I was still in pain when he drilled. He told me over and over "That *can't* hurt!" He muttered much more under his breath, while I cried and tried to endure it. Later another dentist told me that my nerves came into my jaw at a different place than other people's. For years I had carried that familiar flawed feeling of, once again, being impossibly sensitive.

Choose a time when you had a reaction to an illness, injury, medication, medical procedure, or treatment that you have always, perhaps only secretly, felt was abnormal or your fault. The event might be a single moment that has deeply shaped who you are, such as when you broke your leg and cried and the doctor lectured you on how big boys don't cry, or a whole category of events, such as how you always react to certain kinds of medical exams or procedures, like having blood drawn. If right now the event does not seem to be related to being highly sensitive, don't worry too much about that—your being overaroused certainly affected it in some way.

Write here the event you wish to reframe.

_____

_____

_____

_____

Now let's reframe it.
1. Recall how you responded—as many emotions, behaviors, and images as you can bring up.

---

2. Recall how you have always tended to feel about that response.

---

3. Consider your response in light of what you now know about your trait.

---

4. Think about whether the negative parts of the experience might have been avoided or would have gone differently if you or the person treating you had known you were an HSP and had made adjustments for that.

_____

_____

_____

_____

_____

5. If this knowledge would have prevented your suffering or wasting a portion of your life, take time to feel whatever you feel about that.

_____

_____

_____

_____

6. Write down your new understanding of the experience and read it over often until you have absorbed the full meaning of it.

_____

_____

_____

_____

_____

_____

_____

Pairs and Groups: As, Bs, and Cs.

In Conclusion: Reflect on how your feelings about yourself and your body have shifted due to this reframing, and summarize your thoughts on page 30.

A Different Kind of Team Approach to Health Care

This task is meant to help you stay healthy and avoid stress-related illness in particular (HSPs' most common problem) by using your sensitivity to keep you in touch with your body's needs.

Go back to the "Adventure Party" on page 49 of Chapter 2. In the spaces provided here, list the names of the ten or so "major players" you identified there. In the lines under each, list what that major player needs from you on a daily, weekly, monthly, and/or yearly basis: diet, exercise, stretching, examinations, and so forth. Give adequate attention to the heroes as well as to the ones needing extra help to make it through the big trip of life. If you don't know what a part needs, begin by asking it in active imagination. Then do any needed research (ask a specialist, read a book, or check the Internet).

Example (not necessarily what *your* heart needs): *Strong Heart. Daily: Regular aerobic exercise, meditation, not going too long between meals, no caffeine, enough sleep. Monthly: some time off, blood pressure check. Yearly: cholesterol and lipid check. As needed: Expression of emotions.*

1. Major Player: _____

_____

_____

2. Major Player: _____

_____

_____

3. Major Player: _____

_____

_____

4. Major Player: _____

_____

_____

5. Major Player: _____

_____

_____

6. Major Player: _____

_____

_____

7. Major Player: _____

_____

_____

8. Major Player: _____

9. Major Player: _____

10. Major Player: _____

It is very important to work out a schedule for getting each character/body part to the right professionals as needed. Enter dates for making appointments into your datebook. You probably already do much of this. If you have already seen a professional, ask this character/body part if the care was good enough or if something more needs to be done. Make note of your progress on this task here.

If you sense that after all of this you are *still* going to neglect a particular part, the question is, why? Consider how you have imagined it in the "Adventure Party." You should also think about your parents' attitudes about this part of themselves and how they took care of it for themselves and how they took care of this part of you.

You can also try active imagination with this part, seeing your attitudes toward it, and its toward you! Write the results of this self-exploration here.

_____

_____

_____

_____

_____

Pairs and Groups: As, Bs, and Cs.

IN CONCLUSION: Consider what you have learned about your attitudes toward the various parts of your body and to your body as a whole. Given that everything else in life depends upon good health, are you thinking of making any changes?

_____

_____

_____

_____

Learning About Gentler Treatments

I am not a fanatic about alternative or holistic medicine. Yet I find these health-care providers often do solve problems practitioners of mainstream medicine cannot. Further, they have often come forth first with treatments adopted later by the skeptical mainstream; they often understand HSPs better, probably because so many of them are HSPs themselves; and their treatments are gentler. Many, many HSPs tell me their illnesses have been solved by nontraditional methods when "regular doctors failed." Perhaps the best solution is to see one of those few medical doctors willing to use both approaches, or at least read a book by one (see Resources, pages 312–13).

This task is not difficult—it just asks you to take any health problem you have and explore alternative treatments for it. (Skip this task if you have already done this on your own.) Browse on the Internet, at a health food store that has a book section, or in the health section of a large bookstore. Use the book indexes to look up information on the problem you want help with.

The trick, to me, is reading with the right amount of open-mindedness and skepticism. The good news *and* the bad news here is that the Food and Drug Administration (FDA) and the American Medical Association (AMA) are not supervising these treatments. It's good that there's another faction exploring remedies that may be cheaper, more natural, or too new to be researched. For example, there are herbs that can help with many problems, but doctors hesitate to prescribe them (partly because they are not used to them, partly because they are more liable to lawsuits if they prescribe something "not the standard of care"). The bad news about the lesser involvement of the AMA and FDA in alternative medicine is that it's up to you to be sure an alternative really works, that it isn't just an expensive or time-consuming hoax, and is safe. For example, herbs can be just as potent as any prescribed medication, but the purity and dosage of the effective ingredient of an herbal preparation is not as certain. You really have to do your homework, which is what I am recommending here.

So again, your task is to go to wherever there would be a collection of the latest holistic health books and browse for one or more alternative treatments for your health problems (or a preventative approach to the problem you are most likely to develop, given your family history). Take with you the following list of questions as guidelines for you in your research.

1. What is the treatment's purpose—that is, what is the symptom or illness it treats?
2. How does it work in the body?
3. What is the basis for believing it is effective and safe? (This is very important. You should try to read any research on effectiveness and safety, and research subjects should not just be patients saying it worked. There should have been a control group of people *not* getting the treatment who did not improve during the same period of time.)
4. What are its known side effects and possible long-term effects?
5. Are there problematic interactions with other drugs, alcohol, etc., to watch out for?

6. What happens when you stop using it—will there be a withdrawal problem?
7. Has it been used on people like you (people of your age and gender, with your other health issues)?
8. What is the likely cost and time expenditure for achieving the results you want?
9. Are there potential issues about the purity of the preparation or skill and training of those giving the treatment?

Write here what you learned about the treatment from your research.

_____

_____

_____

_____

_____

_____

_____

_____

_____

_____

Pairs and Groups: As, Bs, and Cs. You can report on what you learned from your research and also share your experiences with herbs, holistic medicine, and alternative medical treatments in your area, as long as no one pushes anyone else to try something. In particular, do not push any product or service you offer onto others.

Learning About Medications Often Prescribed for HSPs

If there's nothing wrong with us, you ask, why learn about medications? First, many of you are already taking medications for depression and anxiety, which is not surprising given that, if you have had a stressful life, you are indeed more likely to develop some anxiety or depression at times of stress or simply as you age. Second, as you become more forthcoming with medical professionals about your sensitivity, you may find someone suggesting one of these medications only "because you are so sensitive." If you are doing fine, then you have the perfect chance to correct this person. Say that you *enjoy* sensitivity, and you would prefer to guard it with the right lifestyle rather than try to medicate it away. But it helps in these high-medication times to be knowledgeable about what you are rejecting. One could also argue that depression and anxiety medications should be in the domain of the priestly advisor (you). People around you, including HSPs, are talking about taking these medications. They will probably be interested in your opinion. If you say anything at all, it ought to be an informed opinion. Finally, if you end up in a crisis and are perhaps changing your mind or being pressured about using these medications, you will feel more confident about your decision if you are already well informed, or know how to be.

The decision to take depression and anxiety medications is entirely yours. Let no one bully you about it. But whether you take them or refuse them, or refuse them until you need to take them, it seems reasonable for you as an HSP to know about them.

This task is another research venture, in which you go in search of information. This time you will learn about a couple of the medications listed below. You can choose. Maybe you are taking one, one has been suggested to you, or someone you know is taking one. Probably you'll want to choose one from each category. But having learned about a couple, you will know how to get the information you need in the future.

Since new medications are always coming out, and research is changing what's known about existing medications, be sure to use the latest reference books. The classic is the *Physicians' Desk Reference.* However, many books on particular problems describe the medications for those problems too. For depression, I like Michael Norden's *Beyond Prozac* because it includes a discussion of alternatives to antidepressants and Edmund Bourne's *The Anxiety and Phobia Workbook,* which also discusses anxiety medication. (See Resources, page 313.)

I. Antianxiety medications (note that all these are potentially addictive)
  A. Benzodiazepines
     1. Xanax (alprazolam)
     2. Klonopin (clonazepam)
     3. Ativan (lorazepam)
     4. Valium (diazepam)
     5. Restoril (temazepam)
     6. Dalmane (flurazepam)
     7. Librium (chlordiazepoxide)
     8. Halcion (triazolam)
     9. Tranxene (clorazepate)
    10. Serax (oxazepam)
    11. Centrax (prazepam)
  B. BuSpar (buspirone)
  C. Herbal or "natural" alternatives—chamomile, valerian
II. Antidepressants
  A. Cyclics or Tricyclics (developed before SSRIs—see below) such as:
     1. Tofranil (imipramine)
     2. Pamelor (nortriptyline)
     3. Elavil (amitriptyline)
     4. Surmontil (trimipramine)
     5. Desyrel (trazodone)
     6. Sinequan (doxepin)
     7. Norpramin (desipramine)
     8. Vivactil (protriptyline)
     9. Anafranil (clomipramine)
  B. MAO (Monamine Oxidase) inhibitors
     1. Nardil (phenelzine)
     2. Parnate (tranylcypromine)
     3. Marplan (isocarboxazid)
  C. Selective Serotonin Reuptake Inhibitors (SSRIs)
     1. Prozac (fluoxetine)
     2. Zoloft (sertraline)
     3. Paxil (Paroxetine)
     4. Luvox (fluvoxamine)
  D. Others
     1. Wellbutrin (bupropion)
     2. Effexor (venlafaxine)

    E. Herbal or "natural" alternatives—for example, St. John's Wort, 5-HTP

III. Betablockers

    A. Inderal (propranolol)

    B. Tenormin (atenolol)

Now to the activity. First, select two medications you want to learn about. If other types of medications have been suggested to you to help with anxiety or depression, you can research these at the same time. For example, estrogen replacement hormones (be sure to explore natural progesterone and the alternatives to Premarin). Or thyroid (be sure to learn about T3 and T4). However, for purposes of this research activity, also select two medications from the list above.

Medication 1. _____

Medication 2. _____

The following questions are only suggestions as to what you'll want to learn.

1. What is the drug's purpose—what is the illness or symptoms it treats?
2. What is considered the lowest "clinical" dose (or the least dose that is thought to work, keeping in mind that HSPs may need much less).
3. How does it work in the body?
4. What are its known side effects?
5. Does it interact with other medications, alcohol, etc?
6. What happens when you stop the medication? Is there difficulty withdrawing?
7. Has research been done on its use with people like you (your age, gender, and problem)? What have been the results?
8. Are there long-term effects? If so, what are they?
9. Under what circumstances would you take it? (This question is perhaps most important. Of course, in a crisis, you may be more willing to take medications, but any previous reluctance would surely cause you extra worry, and it will be a bad time to have to do this research and decide.)

Write here what you learn about Medication 1:

_____

_____

_____

_____

_____

_____

_____

_____

_____

Write here what you learn about Medication 2.

_____

_____

_____

_____

_____

_____

_____

_____

Pairs and Groups: As, Bs, and Cs. You could systematically select different medications to learn about and share what you learn, including photocopying the best information. You should consider, however, how much you want to discuss your own medical history with others.

A New Script for Talking to Health-Care Professionals

Now that you have reframed a medical experience, assessed what your "team" needs to stay healthy, and learned a little about alternative treatments and how to research medications in general, you are well prepared for this next task. This activity will help you practice how to assert your HSP self when you are faced with a nonsensitive medical professional. Always remember, of course, that *you* are the consumer—if you aren't heard, you can go elsewhere.

Think of an incident that has happened, happens repeatedly, or is likely to happen eventually, in which your sensitivity is not being respected by a medical professional. Perhaps you are being told you are overreacting, or that you couldn't possibly be experiencing a side effect at such a low dosage, or that there's no reason for anxiety about a procedure. Write what you want to say back to that doctor or nurse. If you can imagine the other's retort, then write an entire dialogue. I wish I could be with you to coach you, but I'm hoping that what you've learned so far by using this workbook, plus the following example, will leave you prepared to enter the fray with a wealth of good responses.

> *Me: I was hoping there was a woman gynecologist [male urologist] available to do that procedure.*
>
> *Nurse: Everyone likes Dr. Blank. You'll do fine.*
>
> *Me: Well, I think I stated that wrong. I need to have a female [male] doctor for this purpose.*
>
> *Nurse: (Sighs.) Some patients do feel that way, but it's really not rational. We doctors and nurses are all very professional . . .*
>
> *Me: I'm not questioning Dr. Blank's competence. I simply know that I relax better with a woman [man]. It's a physical reaction of mine due to emotional conditioning.*
>
> *Nurse: That's just what I mean—this feeling of yours is emotional, not rational.*
>
> *Me: But the physical reaction is real and part of my nature, like my blood type. I'm highly sensitive, which makes me highly aroused in unfamiliar situations anyway. There's no reason for me to add extra physical arousal to my body resulting in extra cortisol in my bloodstream, by having Dr. Blank do this procedure.*
>
> *Nurse: Extra cortisol?*
>
> *Me: Yes. It's the physical reaction to stress and it's not conducive to health, as you well know. But fortunately, I know what I require for the proce-*

dure to be minimally stressful—and also for it to be successful and easy for the doctor, all of which is better for my health. I'm not trying to be difficult. I'm trying to be helpful by stating my needs for a successful outcome of this procedure.

Nurse: I'm sorry, but it is not our policy to comply with such requests.

Me: I appreciate your position. But if I told you I was allergic to a certain medicine, would you still give it? This is exactly the same issue—I will have an adverse physical reaction that I am trying to warn you about. But since you are unable to correct this situation, I will have to go elsewhere for the procedure. I will also have to write a letter to the director of this clinic, detailing this conversation and my dissatisfaction with its outcome and with the clinic's policy.

Feeling empowered? Go for it! Write your dialogue here.

_____

_____

_____

_____

_____

_____

_____

_____

_____

_____

Pairs and Groups: As, Bs, and Cs—you could even role play the situation.

IN CONCLUSION: Reflect on what assumptions you have held about yourself that may have caused you to passively accept from health-care professionals treatment that was not good for you, and what new assumptions you need in order to speak to them in the way you must for your health's sake.

Envisioning Your Death (Or, "I Warned You This Is No Lightweight Workbook")

I once helped to teach a health psychology class at a time when I was also studying postmodernism. Postmodernism was teaching me to "deconstruct texts" and see what was missing. As I read the health psychology text, I realized that death was missing. The tone seemed to imply that if we do all these good health practices, death will be optional.

HSPs, however, know better. We tend to think a great deal about death, but guiltily, because in this culture, that's morbid, pessimistic, anxiety provoking, and depressing. Goodness knows we must not go off in *that* direction.

In other cultures, death is a part of life. When spiritual practices are taught, they are often centered around practicing for death, that last great initiation. One must prepare for an initiation. At the very least, one must have some idea of what one wants to have happen, how one wants to behave. We may not have control over our death. But then again, all traditions teaching about death believe that the more we prepare, the more control we will have, even in choosing the time, setting, and cause.

Above all, living life with an awareness of death helps us eliminate petty thinking, cherish the moment, and get out of bad situations that waste our energy. It helps us recall that life is not a rehearsal. It is the performance itself.

So use this space to plan your own death: How do you want to direct your mind in your final days or hours? Who or what could help you with that? Whom do you want present? (Consider who probably won't be there, having died ahead of you, and imagine some of the fine new friends or new young relatives you might have.) What do you want to say to them, leave with them? Where do you want to be? What do you want the environment to be—light, sounds, music, smells? How might you want to deal with pain?

_____

_____

_____

_____

_____

_____

_____

_____

_____

_____

_____

_____

Pairs and Groups: This is a task to do alone, but Cs might wish to share what they wrote.

In Conclusion: Use this space to write about how you are feeling after doing this planning.

10

Working the Spirit

You finally made it to the chapter that I know some of you wish there had been twelve of—the one on spiritual matters. But soul and spirit require a foundation, and hopefully you have been building that up to here. That is, maybe it has all been spiritual work.

From my research, I've concluded that HSPs have a spiritual talent. When I first interviewed HSPs for *The Highly Sensitive Person,* they always wanted to tell me about their spiritual lives. Since then, their greater spiritual interest always shows up on questionnaires. And on a less objective note, in large groups of HSPs I often notice a quietness that is more than lack of noise—to me it's more like a sacred space.

Recent research suggests that spirituality (interest in God or spirit, liking to pray or meditate, thinking about the meaning of life, etc.) is to some extent inherited. If the researchers had tested for sensitivity, I'm sure they would have found an overlap with spirituality, or even that it was the same inherited trait, or the cause of the spirituality.

I see it this way: When humans first tried to understand death, the people who processed things more deeply, the HSPs, were going to think longer about death, too. They were going to wonder more where the life goes after death, where the spirit goes. They would wonder if the wind or the rain or the stars have anything to do with that spirit, or if the spirit is what causes dreams of the dead person. These deeper processors, the HSPs, would be more likely to think of prayers and ceremonies to help the dead on their journeys, and create methods like meditation and yoga to help the living prepare for death. Later, religions would deal with these issues, of course, and HSPs have certainly been at the fore-front of religion, too.

As most modern cultures have adopted a scientific or materialistic atti-tude about such matters, however, those without much spiritual talent have felt better about themselves and tended to think spiritual interests are not very important, or even a sign of weakness or superstition. Some-times we HSPs actually accept those ideas. Of course the nonspiritually talented can often change their minds and develop an interest when they are near death. That's one more reason the warrior kings, mostly non-HSPs, have always kept around the priestly advisors, mostly HSPs. So take pride in your spiritual or philosophical bent if you have one. (And if you have thought hard about it and concluded that you are an atheist, that is a very HSP thing to do, too.)

When I think of the depth of spirit of the HSPs I know, I feel very out of place trying to tell any of you what to do in this area. What I offer here are only some starting places. And of course, now that we have entered this realm, I am no longer writing from the basis of scientific research, because the spirit level of life is difficult to research usefully from the empirical level. But I am certainly writing from the experiences of many HSPs, myself included.

We'll begin with dreams, because in many traditional cultures they are believed to be sent to us from the spirit world to help, and from my own experience, that's a hard idea to refute.

An Embarrassingly Quick Course in Dreams

To try to teach you to work with your dreams in a few pages is pitifully silly on my part. But dreams are essential resources for HSPs. There are good books on the sub-ject that I urge you to read (see Resources, page 313). However, these are not writ-ten with HSPs in mind. And to get to the HSP-relevant aspects of dreams, I have to cover a few basics first.

I'm going to leave out the "maybes" and "oftens" and write in succinct, flat state-ments, but dreams do not follow any rules, so nothing I say here is unequivocal.

First, dreams are certainly *not* meaningless. Nor are they meant to be obscure. They are attempts by the psyche to communicate.

What does the psyche want to communicate? "The rest of the story," what you aren't aware of, and your "real" attitudes and situations, which then can suggest quite new solutions. Sometimes a dream is showing you what you don't realize about how you actually react to a situation, sometimes it shows a whole new way to react.

Usually dreams are about the present as it stands. Yes, sometimes they seem to predict what will happen. More often if there is a prediction, it is a warning of what will happen if you behave as you have been, or as you do in the dream.

If a dream's meaning seems obvious, or it seems to be telling you something you already know, look again at the details and all the little places where what happens is not quite what you would expect in the situation, or where your reaction is not typical of you. No detail in a dream is irrelevant. Odd details are especially important. Watch for puns. A dog collar kept showing up in my dreams, until I got the message to "call her."

The language the psyche uses to reach you is all symbolic and metaphoric. The particular symbols and metaphors are the ones most likely to reach you personally. There's no meaning of any dream symbol that is universally true—if you dream about a bird or a taxi, you need to think about what a bird or a taxi means to you personally.

Settings of dreams and your age in them usually tell you the general topic—work, school (the lessons you are learning), home. A dream set in the house where you grew up is probably about just that, your childhood. If you are an adult in that house, it is probably about your childhood and you now.

The amount of emotion in a dream is roughly equivalent to the amount of emotion you need to express or be aware of around that issue. Nightmares and recurring dreams are very important—they are attempts to get your attention, to get you unstuck; they show you that you have vast amounts of emotion bottled up around this issue.

People and Animals in Dreams

Go back to page 61 of this workbook and reread, under the discussion of active imagination, about people and animals in dreams—people are usually (*not* always) parts of yourself, and animals and ancestors have lessons to impart. For example, you may need to ask yourself, why did Lizard appear in my dream, or why did Grandmother come to me at this point in my life? By the way, you may have to learn more about lizards or your grandmother before you see an answer to that question.

Acting on Dreams

It is important to honor a dream with some kind of action, as I urged you to do with the results of any active imagination you do. But even though dreams can add vast amounts of insight, they should not be acted on without careful thought. The psyche tends to be like nature—factual, neither cruel nor kind. The conscious mind has to think about what needs to be done and the consequences for you personally and for those around you.

In the Judeo-Christian Bible, there's the account of Joseph interpreting Pharaoh's dreams of the thin cows eating the fat ones. It's a simple statement from nature about nature: famine, hunger, survival. The dreams did not advise saving up food for seven years, then distributing it. A lesser man than Joseph might have advised Pharaoh to have the rich build high walls around their homes to keep out the poor when the famine comes so that the thin could not eat the fat. What was moral and feeling-oriented was Joseph's reaction to the dream—not the dream itself.

Remembering Dreams

Most HSPs remember dreams often. If you are one of the exceptions, one reason may be that you are not getting enough sleep or are having trouble with insomnia. Do what you can to sleep more. (Sleeping medications, however, will also interfere with dreaming.) Try not to use alarms to wake up—the dreams most easily remembered are usually the last ones.

When you do wake up, stay in bed until you have searched your memory a bit for any dreams. At first you won't remember any, but if you stay with it, you often will. You can even try stirring your memory by running through categories—was there a dream set out of doors, at work, with animals, with people, at the beach? Write down any dreams you recall, and think about them during the day and before falling asleep that night. All of this tells your psyche that you are interested in communicating. You don't need lots of dreams—a few a week will keep you busy.

If you usually dream but have stopped for no apparent reason, go back to the last dream or the last big dream and work with it more. In my experience, it is as though your psyche is saying that you don't get another if you aren't going to use what you've already been given. If you don't understand a dream, have the desire for clarification. Then, no matter how unrelated the next dream, think very hard about whether it is the clarification you asked for. In this way you will develop a dialogue with the source of your dreams.

The Dreams of HSPs

Your dreams probably already have a way of symbolizing your sensitivity. As an example only, for me it's everything to do with my feet—going barefoot on rough ground, the kind or condition of shoes or socks I'm wearing or given or need (socks are especially interesting—the cushioning between inner and outer), anything anyone else does in a dream affecting my feet. Animals in my dreams that I know are related to my sensitivity are fish, birds, and horses. Horses are my personal animal teachers. They are strong yet sensitive, quick to run but willing to fight. The animals who teach you may well be different.

As for the struggle between the sensitive and tough parts of the self, I find that dreams involving cruelty, violent crimes, and the like are usually about myself dominating or hurting my sensitive self. So then I look at my life and see where there's a cruel, dominating energy making life hard. It may be coming from within or it may be a force from outside that I'm tolerating too much.

HSPs also can have frequent dreams of being up high or down low. This may refer to your mood, or to your feelings at times of being very special, at other times of being flawed or less than others in some way. Maybe you are down in a pit of mud, in a cave, or buried. Or you could be up on mountains—beautiful or scary mountains, mountains you can't get down from or find your way into. Or you dream of towers—towers you are climbing, looking up at, on top of, towers that are flimsy or firm. Then there are the airplanes, landing or crashing, and elevators that are falling or stuck or crowded. (I always think of "elevate her.")

Alas, it is hard to know whether a dream is compensating for something or showing how it really is. If you are up on a flimsy tower, it may be that you are thinking too well of yourself, with too little basis for that opinion. Or you may instead be thinking too poorly of yourself, afraid of any little thought that would isolate you at the top of a seemingly dangerous, unwarranted sense of superiority. But then, these two fears are so similar, given the two poles to every complex. (See pages 125, 185, and 206 for discussions of complexes.)

Finally, you are ready to work with a dream.

Working with a Dream

1. Write down a dream. Pick one that seems important because it has recurring parts or creates intense emotions in the dream or afterward. Put in all the details. Write it in present tense—"I am running and then . . . "

_____

_____

_____

_____

_____

2. Look at the dream in terms of the big picture. Right away, is there something about it that makes you think of a particular issue in your life? Write this down and keep it in mind as you proceed in a more systematic way. It's good to learn to be systematic, but after you are good with these steps, you can skip some as they begin to give you the big picture.

_____

_____

3. What is the main emotion? Is there a point in the dream where you have an inappropriate emotional reaction—too much, too little, a feeling that is un-characteristic for you? Is this happening with this emotion in your life?

_____

_____

4. What is the setting, and what topic or issue does that imply the dream is about?

_____

_____

5. Go back to your description (Step 1) and underline *every* word that is a de-tail—objects, colors, shapes, people, animals, names, places, verbs like "run," and descriptive phrases that seem to be the only way to say what happened.

6. Below, write your associations, each on a separate line (write up to twenty of them). For the major ones, like a named person or an animal, describe them in twenty-five words or less as if to someone who has never met the person or seen that species of animal. Also, consider its main characteristic or relationship to you.

Example (a very short dream): *I am <u>running</u> from <u>Mr. T</u> through a <u>forest</u>. A <u>tiger</u> <u>stops</u> me, <u>asking</u>, "<u>Why the rush?</u>"*

Running—fear, not good at running, ought to do it more.

Mr. T—black man, strong, member of The A-Team, *a popular TV show in 1980s. Was afraid of flying. I watched* The A-Team *in my teens.*

Forest—dark. Lost in the forest. A forest is a dense growth of trees. Rain forests are being destroyed.

Tiger—large striped cat. Belongs in India. "Tiger, Tiger burning bright . . ." Eats people.

Stops—stop and go. I was running, now am stopped.

Asking—regular tigers don't ask questions!

"Why the rush"—I'm rushing a lot right now. Rushes grow in rivers.

_____

_____

_____

_____

_____

_____

_____

_____

_____

_____

_____

_____

_____

_____

_____

_____

_____

_____

_____

_____

_____

7. Look at the major events. Make associations to your life right now. Then look at the jumps in action and try thinking of the dream as almost a statement of logic: When I do this, then this happens in my life, then this happens. Try it—write down the dream as a series of steps in logic.

Example: *When I am chased by Mr. T (running from something big and strong from my teen years?), then I am stopped by a magical tiger (some fierce, exotic, human/animal instinctual energy has to be confronted) and then I am asked "why the rush" (could be good to stop rushing, but should I trust Tiger? How is rushing now caused by something in my teenage years?)*

_____

_____

_____

_____

_____

8. If you still are not sure of the meaning of your dream, try active imagination (see page 61) to continue it or to talk with its main character or object. You are trying to find out why this character has done what it has and what it wants to say to you. Use this space to record your active imagination. (In the example, I would probably imagine climbing a tree, so I'd feel somewhat safe, then yelling to Mr. T—"Why are you chasing me?" And waiting for the answer. Or you could answer Tiger's question, "Why the rush?" and see how Tiger responds.)

_____

_____

_____

_____

---

9. If it feels like an important dream, do something because of it—perhaps perform a ritual, perhaps make a phone call you have been avoiding, perhaps paint an image from the dream, perhaps change your lifestyle. Write here what you plan to do.

Pairs and Groups: Cs, and only pairs. A pair can do wonderful dream work together, getting to know each other's symbols and lives. Each can see things for the other that the dreamer working alone would miss. But every dream, worked on, can reveal much more about yourself than you ever imagined, so only Cs should try it.

Dream work in groups is not a good idea without a therapist skilled in such work. There's just too much being revealed and too much opportunity for others to push their own agendas, unconsciously of course.

IN CONCLUSION: Reflect on how you are feeling now about dream work and the role of dreams in your life. Write your thoughts here.

"How Many Ways Do I Love Thee?"— How Many Ways Art Thou Spiritual?

Spirituality can be defined many ways. For this task, let's call it anything to do with what is beyond the material, visible, given world—although from one spiritual perspective this is a distinction only made in ignorance. And we must remember that the material world is how we reach the nonmaterial. The world is the doorway, if only in the sense that we must pass through it. But still, we'll equate "spiritual" for now with beyond-the-material.

Some people think they aren't very spiritual because they don't go to church, pray, meditate, or any of those "spiritual things." But when they define spirituality in this bigger way, they are surprised by how spiritual their lives are.

Try listing here all the ways you sense or make contact with what is beyond the "given." A few you might overlook include music, dance, yoga, art, holiday celebrations, studying physics or astronomy, reading novels, being in nature, working with your dreams, lovemaking, certain conversations, and moments of fear.

Pairs and Groups: As, Bs, and Cs.

IN CONCLUSION: Reflect on how you reacted to this task and how you feel about being "spiritual."

_____

_____

_____

_____

The Precepts of Your Religion

Religion. "Organized religion." Does it make you rejoice or cringe? But even those of you who recoil probably have some religion organized in your mind, whether it is organized by a larger organization or quite "disorganized" and in flux. You have thoughts on the topic, even some precepts. This is an opportunity to write down what these are—what you accept, believe in, or know from experience.

As a priestly advisor, it is good to be able to put your thoughts into words. It will bring more focus to this part of your life. And someday someone may benefit from hearing your precepts from you.

Maybe you don't want to commit yourself or seem dogmatic, but you don't have to impose your beliefs on others. That might even be your first precept. Or your first might be that you are uncertain. I sometimes say, "On Monday, Wednesday, and Friday I am sure of this. On Tuesday, Thursday, and Saturday it seems almost the opposite. On Sunday I rest." On the other hand, you may stand by certain givens that you would die to uphold, and that you wish others would adhere to as well. That is another good reason to become fluent in expressing your beliefs.

List the precepts of your religion here:

_____

_____

_____

_____

Pairs and Groups: Bs and Cs. These could be read out loud. In a group, allow only about five minutes per person to keep things moving. Do not critique anyone's precepts!

IN CONCLUSION: Reflect on your precepts—where they came from, where they may be headed, how much they determine your daily behavior. Write your thoughts here.

Becoming a Ritual Leader

As far as we know, a human is the only animal that will commit suicide when it cannot find any meaning in life. Rituals are one way that meaning is provided. When we are taking part in a ritual, we feel we belong in our culture, that we are participating in something larger, older than ourselves, and when we come back from that ritual space we feel changed. If we create a ritual in private, we feel in direct communication with the Unseen. This is no small accomplishment.

Radical rituals, those meant to change a person forever from the inside, are rare today in Western culture. We still have a taste of what can be called maintenance rituals, which celebrate the identity of the community through regular festivals or observances of events, including largely secular but traditional celebrations of weddings, graduations, and holidays. Some of us are involved in important religious rituals as well. But usually these are quite voluntary and participated in somewhat mechanically, rather than being radical events in our lives. For the most part, industrialized, scientific, Westernized cultures tend to be eliminating rituals, in part because these cultures do not value community as much as, say, moving to where you can get a better job. And communities are the basis of meaningful ritual.

As people all over the world are moving away from their ritual life, I believe the resulting emptiness is a problem. I don't know which causes which, but I think this emptiness goes along with the increasing difficulty HSPs have in playing their priestly advisor roles in modern societies.

The solution is not likely to be one of going back to "olden times." We couldn't, even if we wanted to. What we can do is still unclear—a huge experiment we can all participate in. There is a definite trend for HSPs and others to try to create more ritual. Women's groups and men's groups have started this. Those concerned with family life have also discussed the revival of rituals and traditions as a way of helping family members stay connected. And individuals have created or become aware of rituals in their personal lives.

To begin, list the rituals you have participated in. Next to each, note its impact on you—for example, was it negative, a minor but positive event, life changing? And why? Was it performed repeatedly, creating a cumulative effect? To warm you up, I have created these examples.

1. *Lighting Sabbath candles with Jewish spouse. Cumulative, very positive.*
2. *Prayers before dinner. Same.*
3. *Laying out a medicine wheel. Done this several times, subtle but very positive.*

4. *Studying certain spiritual materials before bed. Not sure—getting hard to do, too tired.*

5. *Weddings, funerals, etc. Varies. Many leave no lasting impression.*

6. *Communion at church. Struggle with gaining the full meaning—sometimes mechanical, sometimes moving.*

Make your own list here.

_____

_____

_____

_____

_____

_____

_____

_____

_____

_____

The second half of this task is trickier. The creation of ritual is difficult, because almost by definition rituals ought to be old and not need to be created. Nor do I think creating rituals comes naturally to every HSP, just as we aren't all good at math, storytelling, or music making. But this task lets your try out the role. If you like it, you can read books on creating rituals. (See Resources, page 313.) But in this task, plan what you would like personally. Or imagine yourself as a shaman or an elder in a religious community. Later you can see what is proper traditionally or what others have done.

1. The most important step is the first—setting the intention of the ritual. This is a matter of inner work and the reason HSPs are *priestly* advisors and excellent ritual leaders. Setting the intention means divining what is most needed right now by the community, or if you are unable to work within a community, the individual, or yourself. You can think of all rituals as healing—healing body, soul, and relationships; healing the loss of connection with spirit, nature, community, ancestors, and parents.

   To heal, it helps to envision the end result, the wholeness. "Whole" is a word very related to healing and health because for any species to become a species that heals, the individuals need a mental representation of a whole, healthy body (or community). Only then can individuals note any variations from whole and try to fix them. Even if your ritual is one of celebration rather than explicit healing, a celebration is an experience of wholeness that can be remembered as how things ought to be.

   So what is your intention with this ritual? What do you wish to heal, restore to wholeness, or celebrate in a whole way? (There are many, many things to heal. To celebrate, there might be a birth, a passage from youth to adulthood, from being single to being married, from middle age to old age, the onset of menopause, the start or end of a career, or a new home.)

   _____

   _____

2. Where would you like this ritual to take place? How will you mark off the "ritual space"?

   _____

   _____

   _____

   _____

3. Who should come? How will they be summoned? How should they dress? What should they bring?

_____

_____

_____

4. As participants enter into ritual space, there is often a purification of some kind—sprinkling water on them, lighting incense or sage around them. How would you do this?

_____

_____

_____

5. Write an invocation—a request to the Unseen to be with you, to guide the group and you in these ritual efforts. In most Western religions, God is called upon. In many other traditions (and sometimes in our Western religions), certain ancestors, saints, or spiritual beings are called on for assistance or to intervene with a higher power. Or the elements, the four directions, or certain spiritual qualities are called on. Also write down what actions would be taken while making this invocation—for example, facing each of the four directions or having people kneel.

_____

_____

_____

_____

6. Music is an almost universal ingredient in ritual. What kind would you choose, and would there be dancing, drumming, chanting, or choral singing? If you'd like hymns or songs, which ones? How will people participate? It all affects the ritual.

_____

_____

_____

7. Besides having music, how would you use stimulation of the five senses to impact participants? What would you want them to see, hear, touch, smell, taste? Shamans and priests know that the more senses involved in a ritual, the more one reaches the soul and turns the mind toward spirit.

_____

_____

_____

_____

_____

_____

8. At some point the drama unfolds—a drama symbolic of the transformation this ritual is about. This is the heart of the ritual. It may involve a journey or a death or descent and then a return or resurrection, resulting in something or someone being brought back, made conscious, or transformed. Each participant hearing or witnessing the story makes this journey personally or receives its gifts. You may wish to tell this story, enact it, have all the partici-

pants enact some or all of it, or simply display the symbols of a story already familiar to everyone. Write here what you would do.

_____

_____

_____

_____

_____

_____

_____

9. There needs to be recognition and celebration of the transformation after it has taken place—perhaps more music. Write how you would do this.

_____

_____

_____

_____

_____

10. Write how you would close the ritual space, thanking those who were invoked for their aid, giving a blessing or talisman to those departing. The de-

marcation between ritual space and nonritual space should be clear: Participants should be led away, file out in a procession, or be signaled that the ritual space has been returned to nonritual space.

_____

_____

_____

_____

_____

11. Now the community must recognize the change in the participants. (The extroverts will want to talk or celebrate immediately. The introverts may want to be alone first.) All should remain within the vicinity of the ritual space and ritual leaders while they make their transition and receive this recognition (especially in the case of an initiation, a healing, or a celebration of a life event).

_____

_____

_____

_____

_____

_____

Pairs and Groups: Bs and Cs. You can share what you have written (allow perhaps five minutes for each person) without much comment or any critique. You could also possibly perform one of the rituals created. But be aware that some could feel uncomfortable or that the ritual might violate their religious precepts.

In Conclusion: Reflect on yourself as a ritual leader—for example, would you enjoy this role? Have you played it already?

After Your Death

Most of us do not think we know for certain what happens after death, but most of us have some ideas, and they have to affect how we live life. At least unconsciously, you make quite different choices if you think death is the end of everything, or that you will have to answer for your behaviors in heaven; that you will be reunited with your loved ones; that you will be in a celestial body or merged with the One; that you will be reborn with all your karma as baggage to be sorted through again. This task is about glimpsing your own inner wisdom about what follows death.

For this task, proceed when you are feeling very calm, centered, and have at least an hour of uninterrupted time in a safe place. Lie or sit down, close your eyes, and enter the kind of deep state described for active imagination (page 65). Then imagine your death—where you left off perhaps in the task on page 230—and what comes next. Treat this like active imagination, in which you receive contributions from your psyche as well as offering your own reactions.

As with active imagination or a dream, I think it is better not to think that what you envisioned is necessarily the truth, to be accepted without reflection. But it is your psyche's current response to your interest.

You can do this task several times, but do not treat it lightly. Give yourself time to return emotionally to the living. If you find the experience too unsettling, you might want to seek out some professional help, perhaps in this case from a spiritual director within your tradition.

Write here as much as you like of your experiences with this task.

_____

_____

_____

_____

_____

_____

_____

_____

_____

_____

Pairs and Groups: Cs only. This is actually best done together, with a sharing of experiences afterward.

Returning to What You Most Dislike About Yourself

It is time to complete the circle, to return to Chapter 1 and the difficult work you did there about the things you dislike about yourself. Why is this task in this chapter, and not in its own closing chapter? To me, spirituality comes very close to being the same as wholeness, and wholeness comes very close to being the same as healing. That is why, traditionally, the priests and shamans have also been the healers. Let me see if I can put this connection into words.

I defined spirituality as being open to what is beyond the material, or bigger than the material boundaries of things. When we see the rest of the world, beyond the material, we see the whole. To do that, we need to be whole ourselves—not too caught up in restricting complexes, for example.

Yes, but who is perfectly whole? Perhaps it is our very sense of not being whole, that ache and pain of being injured, that pushes and pulls us toward the goal.

The process of healing also develops wholeness directly. Healing psychologically means seeing the rest of ourselves—the unconscious parts, the deeper psyche. As we gain understanding of our complexes, we can behave more lovingly and morally, more spiritually. We act more in accord with how the world is, rather than projecting our issues onto others. As we receive help in this work, we may even begin to think there must be something or someone unseen that is helping us.

So now let's return to the task in Chapter 1, to see if we can heal some of those painful spots.

Turn back to page 33 and look at those aspects of yourself that you disliked so much. As you go through the following questions, you can treat each aspect separately, going through the questions three times for the three aspects you listed, or if they seem to fall together now, treat them as a whole.

   1. Looking at this issue of yours, how do you feel about it, *right now?*

I. _____

II. _____

III. _____

   2. Write down how your view of it has changed in light of your better appreciation, through this workbook, of your sensitivity, your psyche, and your

strength as an individual who has persevered. Have the behaviors you disliked diminished at all? Or do you better understand and accept them? Or has nothing changed? If nothing has changed, or these aspects seem worse in any sense, go on to the next step. If you see great change, in either your behaviors or your acceptance of them, you can stop here. It's time to congratulate yourself and celebrate.

I. _____

_____

II. _____

_____

III. _____

_____

3. Make note of how important this issue is for you now, or in the language of complexes, how much energy you have around it. You can use a scale of 0 to 10, or any words you would like.

I. _____

II. _____

III. _____

4. If the issue is less important for you now, write down why that might be. Or, if it is more important than ever, can you see a positive side to it now? In terms of a complex, remember, they all have two poles—one we accept and perceive as positive and one we reject and perceive as negative. The rejected half is often an asset in disguise, rejected with too much vehemence. So if the issue is still unchanged and still important, are there ways in which you can now see these "faults" also as strengths or potential strengths? Write any changes in your attitude toward the issue here. If there are satisfying

changes, you can stop here and celebrate, or go on. If there are no satisfying changes, definitely go on.

I. _____

_____

II. _____

_____

III. _____

_____

5. If the issue is still very important to you and you cannot see any positive aspects to it, can you see any value in this problem of yours being in your life? Is it teaching you anything, helping you grow, forcing you onto new ground?

I. _____

_____

II. _____

_____

III. _____

_____

6. However you answered the last question, now would be a good time to remind yourself of the voice or voices that helped you choose these three things you don't like about yourself. You should know something about them from your previous work on this issue (pages 18, 34, 38, and 42). What is this voice like? Is it afraid you'll fail? Cruel and wanting you to fail? Afraid it will lose control over you, that you won't listen to it anymore? Afraid for

your health and well being because you are behaving foolishly or self-destructively? You can consider each aspect as having a separate voice associated with it, or think of this judge or critic as the same voice, whatever the issue—whichever feels more true for you.

_____

_____

_____

_____

_____

7. Write something to the voice or voices. I say "something" because it probably can't be and shouldn't be your final communication with each other. What you write might be a letter, an acknowledgment, or part of an ongoing dialogue.

_____

_____

_____

_____

_____

_____

_____

8. Have you come any closer to an understanding with this voice? Have you been able to get it to respect your position more? Or should you (and can you) appreciate its perspective more? If you still can see little that is positive about the presence of these issues in your life, and still have no way to work things out with this voice—can you step back enough to see if it is objectively reasonable to feel so much about these issues? Is this a sign that you must now use this distress to make yourself change? Are you willing to get professional help with these issues? Write below whether (a) there is something objective to change and (b) you are ready to change it, with help if necessary.

I. _____

_____

_____

II. _____

_____

_____

III. _____

_____

_____

Pairs and Groups: Cs only. This is a powerful task to discuss.

IN CONCLUSION: Reflect on your pain, or the lessening of your pain, around these issues. If your suffering is still great, you really need to seek some help. I wish I could be that help, but I fear that you and I have done all that we can with the issue in this book.

Write here some of your feelings around your progress with each issue, or if there has been none, your plans to heal in a different way.

I. _____

_____

II. _____

_____

III. _____

_____

An Ending

I suspect that even the most conscientious HSPs do not usually work through a workbook from beginning to end, exactly as instructed. You do some and stop, skip around and fiddle around. But at some point you may want to end your work, or take a long pause, and I believe it is essential to acknowledge an ending. We HSPs do not like endings. Most are sad. But an experience is not whole when we leave it dangling, and we have been making wholeness very important in this chapter and in this workbook. It would be a shame to drop the ball now.

From my side, as I write these words, I am hoping so much that something here has been helpful. From your side . . .

　　1. Why are you closing this book for a while or forever? Can you feel good about this decision?

_____

_____

_____

2. Go back through this book and read all the "In Conclusions" that you have written. Take your time with this, and reflect a bit on what you read, to integrate it into your life. If you would like to write a grand conclusion, use this space to do that.

_____

_____

_____

_____

_____

3. What would you like to say to the book, or to me the author?
   Feel free to send a copy of what you write, or any other writing that was born through this workbook, to *Comfort Zone,* P. O. Box 460564, San Francisco, CA 94146–0564. I can't promise you an answer, but I try to read everything.

_____

_____

_____

_____

_____

_____

_____

_____

_____

_____

_____

_____

_____

4. Close your eyes and imagine yourself before you opened this book. Have you changed? Write down how you have changed, and above all, how you will welcome and celebrate these changes.

_____

_____

_____

_____

_____

_____

_____

_____

_____

_____

And now, please do celebrate. This moment will not come again.

Pairs and Groups: As, Bs, and Cs. If there's an ending of the pair or group relationship, it is important to do this task together and share your writing. Groups can also use the ending provided on page 307.

11

Guidelines for HSP
Discussion Groups

Many of you have asked if there are support or discussion groups for
HSPs in your area, or if I could help organize groups for HSPs in your
area, or if I am giving a course in your area soon, because you would
like to meet other HSPs. These guidelines are to help you have what you
want.

WHY GROUPS?

You are right to want to meet one another. You need to feel how it is to
be with those with temperaments like yours. You need to hear others'
stories. You need to be convinced you are not alone and not abnormal. I
have been impressed by how much every gathering of HSPs has meant
to those present, whether at a book signing, a lecture at a library, or one
of the courses I have taught.

You are also right to seek reinforcement from classes or other activities
with HSPs that are focused on what this trait means to you—your past,
your future, your whole self-concept. It is well known from social psychological research that identifying with a group of others who share
similar positive attitudes about themselves is the best way to strengthen
your own self-concept.

While many HSPs may not enjoy most social groups or even working
in groups, we often shine in groups of other HSPs, or any groups intended to help people learn, grow, heal, deal with difficulties, or explore
the meaning of life and the depths of the psyche. Further, in any kind of

group we can usually sense what's going on—who is upset, who is trying to take control, who would do a good job if encouraged. So groups are another place to appreciate and further hone your great asset, your sensitivity. We can use our sensitivity particularly well in a group that decides to encourage discussing what's going on interpersonally. We can help the group through its inevitable rough spots, rather than keep our insights to ourselves. In short, we are actually *good* in groups and for groups.

WHAT *DOESN'T* WORK

I have thousands of hours of experience facilitating groups, so I know their usefulness, even for a very introverted HSP like myself. I can also tell you a hundred stories of groups that disappointed or hurt their members. So I approach groups with a strong vision of their potential and an equal sense of conscientiousness about what happens in any group that I have anything to do with organizing.

When I began working with HSPs, I did encourage support groups. Some were started by others, and I started some myself. But those without facilitators, at least to get them started, tended to be short-lived, disappointing, and sometimes aggravating for those involved. I could not run many groups myself, or be certain of the qualifications of very many other facilitators, so I finally decided I could not with good conscience help people organize support groups unless I could supply the required leadership. So I was left with a dilemma—I wanted HSPs to have groups, but when they suggested starting groups on their own, I could not be very encouraging.

The failed groups had two problems:

1. *There was no screening* of members by a trained professional when the group started or of new members joining later. Some people, HSPs included, are not ready for a non-therapy group. They may be in an unusually stressful time in their lives, or they may need to develop more social skills, or they may need some individual therapy. They may have very, very pressing inner needs to talk, to be loved, to control others, to have attention, or simply to be helped, so they quite naturally join a group of peo-

ple who ought to understand them better than others do. Perhaps they even organize the group. But then unduly shape the group by using it too much for their own needs. It's difficult for the other members to stop it, as no one wants to be unkind.

I know what you are thinking now. "What if that's me? What if I'm too needy or 'whatever' to be in a group?" Well, it's a good question to ask. If you are very depressed, distressed, or have absolutely nowhere else to turn at this time, it's best *not* to join a non-therapy group. Instead you should seek professional help. But it's all right to join a group because you think it would be useful for your own purposes—otherwise, why bother? It's just that once in the group, you have to balance your needs equally with others', as in a family. Frankly, the problems for groups usually arise with those who are not self-aware enough even to wonder if they should join. Once in the group, their needs blind them to the effect of their own behaviors on others.

2. *Groups became boring or divisive because of a lack of common interests.* Most support groups are focused around an issue or experience, like an illness, addiction, domestic violence, or having been abused as a child. Everyone has experiences in common, and everyone else's experience is highly relevant to every member. HSPs have nervous systems in common and the problem of being easily overaroused to deal with. But at a less basic level, their personalities, backgrounds, strengths, and problems are extremely diverse. When people begin bringing in their "outside world" problems, the issues can be so dissimilar that the suggestions and even attempts at empathy are not very successful. The person with the problem gets little help and the rest of the group is bored by issues not very relevant to them.

Given these two problems, I started considering solutions.

A SOLUTION—A STRUCTURED, TIME-LIMITED, LEADERLESS DISCUSSION GROUP

Group psychotherapy and other kinds of professionally led groups can handle these two problems because the professional can screen members, and can keep people focused on the most meaningful topics. Actually, the best therapy groups tend to focus more on what's going on in the group, among the members. The "here and now" is always more interesting, scary, and full of lessons to learn. In contrast, when someone spends a half hour telling the group about a problem at work or at home, it is always hard for the group to know what's really going on. If the issue occurs within the group, there's a whole room full of witnesses to react and advise.

A variant of this kind of group that's not therapy but contributes to personal development is the "process-oriented group." These are usually only available in some corporate training settings, or in colleges as courses in group process with an experiential or laboratory component. When well guided, they are perfect for HSPs, as the whole point is to attend to the subtle events in the group and the feelings in yourself and to learn from these. These groups also train you to air the disappointments, conflicts, and irritations that most groups politely ignore; and thus you learn to help groups avoid the situation in which everyone quits in disgust without ever having said a word about what was really going on for them.

Most HSPs, however, don't want or need the expense of being in group psychotherapy or a process-oriented group. You just want to get to know well some other HSPs. So how do I provide you with the professional help you need? Fortunately, while I was involved in process-oriented groups in the 1960s, I was part of an experiment to see if such groups could work without a leader. And they did—as long as there was a carefully planned structure. The structure solves the first problem, screening, because it sees that everyone gets equal time, even if there are one or two members unaware that they put their needs ahead of others. It solves the second problem because the group moves quickly, and if one topic is not of interest, the next one will be. Plus the structure can include some focus on the "here and now," often the intensely interesting part.

The group experience I have provided here is very structured. That has disadvantages—you may feel you would rather just talk about what interests you. But that may not be what interests the others. And rather than figure out what interests who, the structure allows you to cover a little of everything, with time for everyone, and minimal time discussing and deciding what the group should do. As for the screening problem, no member can be that much of a problem as long as every member keeps to the structure. If someone doesn't, there's an objective reason to ask that person to leave—it isn't about personalities, but about keeping to what everyone agreed to at the outset.

The group is limited to six two-hour sessions, so that everyone can commit themselves without investing too much time, but anyone can gracefully depart after six meetings if it is not quite right for him or her—for example, if there should happen to be a "problem" member.

The group can continue after the six sessions if all goes well—if trust builds and people enjoy each other's company. The group can create its own structure for itself from the workbook activities, or become more free form, or a little of both. At the end of every task in every chapter you have seen the note about which tasks are appropriate for groups (and pairs), including what is appropriate for the level of trust (As, Bs, or Cs) the group has attained.

The group is leaderless, but for each session you will appoint a facilitator and a timekeeper. They will go over the structure for that session ahead of time, be certain they understand it, and gently keep the group within that structure. The group can also always decide at any time to hire a professional to facilitate.

This is a discussion group rather than a support group for three reasons. First, since many of you have enjoyed taking courses from me, which are focused on topics, it seemed you might also enjoy a discussion group focused on topics suggested by me rather than a group left to steer itself. Second, everyone has different ideas of what support groups are, and might bring those differing ideas into the group and have conflicts right at the start. Third, my own idea of a support group is that it helps people deal with a big problem they all have, and I have never liked the idea that being an HSP is a problem.

If you want to try organizing a group without using the structure I have provided, do go ahead. This might work especially well if you know the other members ahead of time, have common interests (for example, you are all HSPs who are nurses or all raising sensitive children), and some of you have group-leadership training. You can still use the tasks in the workbook, perhaps to start each session or when a topic arises for which there is a task that would be helpful.

THE GUIDELINES

The instructions you are about to read, and reread out loud in your first meeting as a group, have been tested by leaderless groups who volunteered for that purpose, and they have been adjusted according to members' feedback. Each group, however, is as different as each person in the group. There will be things here that do not work for your group. But I strongly recommend that you stick to the structure, because once you open yourselves up to changing it, you will have to agree on how to change it, and some will like the changes while some will not. Democracies take time and involve considerable debate and conflict. Benevolent dictatorships like this one, in which the "guidelines rule," are more efficient if not quite as satisfying.

The First and Most Important Guideline: If you feel unusually (for you) distressed, depressed, or anxious at any time while planning to be in the group, while in the group, or afterward, please, please go discuss this with a *good,* well-recommended, sensitive psychotherapist. See page 196 for suggestions on how to choose a therapist.

Organizing the Group

Who Organizes It. Someone has to get the ball rolling, and since you are reading this, it may be you. Or perhaps you can share the responsibility with another HSP, or interest someone else in taking on the project. From now on I will speak of an organizer. That doesn't have to be you, but it has to be someone, and so I will assume it is you for the sake of instruction.

Who Is Invited. I once asked the professional group facilitator whom I most respect what the one thing was that he knew for sure about groups. He said without hesitation, "One difficult member can ruin any group. You must screen out people who will be a problem, and if you miss one, you must remove that person—but that of course affects a group deeply. The most important thing is screening."

In organizing a group, your first impulse will be to invite anyone who wants to come. We want to think that all people are fine and certainly all HSPs are wonderful, and deep down both are absolutely true. But as I have already said, some people, HSPs or not, are not ready for a group experience, and sometimes it is these people who are the most eager to be in a group.

One solution for the organizer is to form the group rather quietly, asking only those you know well and asking them to invite others whom they know well. The disadvantage of this is that you will not meet as many new people, and you may not know enough HSPs to start a group this way.

You can also invite people openly—for example, through an announcement in the HSP newsletter *Comfort Zone* or in your local paper, and let anyone join. Then you let the tight structure take care of limiting the influence of any one person, with the very clear understanding that anyone who does not want to follow the structure must leave. The risk is that if there does turn out to be a "problem member," a group that would have otherwise continued after six weeks may choose not to continue rather than hurt that person's feelings by continuing without him or her.

When inviting people, be sure to tell them ahead of time that it will be highly structured and you want the group you organize to stick to that structure for the first six weeks. Also tell them what to bring (this workbook and two No. 2 pencils) and to read this chapter before the first session.

How Many Members. I recommend six, but start with seven in case, in spite of your best efforts, someone misses a meeting or drops out. Everyone you add lengthens the amount of time it will take to do the structured activities involving, say, five minutes for each person. You don't want people to tire, so fewer people can mean less fatigue and certainly more time for each of you.

If the group shrinks to three or four, don't worry about it. Even if you shrink to two, you can meet, using the suggestions in this workbook for pairs. But there will be upset feelings about the loss of members, so a commitment is still important.

Tell everyone that it is *essential* they commit themselves to coming to all six meetings—no trying one to see how it is or starting later in the time-limited period. Groups build trust only with a steady membership. It's especially important to be sure everyone has absolutely *promised* to come to the first meeting.

Everyone who has tried to organize HSPs into groups has had the same experience—HSPs think they want to come, but as the actual meeting approaches, they get cold feet. There are good psychological reasons for this that you can imagine, so I will not go into them. It is normal, but annoying for the organizer. The only thing that works for certain is a deposit, but you aren't charging for this group. One solution is for the organizer to take a small deposit, to be refunded only if a member completes the group. Otherwise that money goes to the organizer who, after all, puts in a lot of volunteer time. You can explain to people why: "Experience shows that we HSPs really want to come, but get cold feet at the last minute, unless we have made a little financial commitment that we stand to lose."

Time and Place. Each session is planned to take two hours, with a fifteen-minute break. I envision your meeting once a week, although you could have an intensive version of two sessions a week, ending in three weeks. If you do these on a weekend, do not do more than two sessions in one weekend. HSPs will burn out. Evenings are logical times to meet, but HSPs working a regular week need lots of rest rather than excitement on weeknights, so a weekend morning might be better.

The meeting place can rotate among members' homes, or perhaps someone has a good location for all six sessions. The place should be private, without interruptions from family members, roommates, or even pets. In fact, there should be no one else at home (unless it is a very large house and the meeting room is well separated). There should be no concern about being overheard.

The setting should be comfortable. It also has to be easy for everyone to get to, with parking available if cars are driven. HSPs usually dislike fluorescent lights. You will want to inquire among the people coming whether they have allergies, for example to cats, or environmental sensitivities, for example to perfumes. The person having the group that week (not necessarily the facilitator or the organizer, by the way) can offer water and perhaps tea, but I think it is better not to offer food. "Having the group" should not become a burden.

Personal Preparation and Confidentiality

Assuming a group is organized and you will be going to a meeting soon, your main responsibility is to read the rest of these guidelines and the instructions for at least the first session, so that you are certain you want to commit yourself to the group.

Part of committing yourself is agreeing to keep private everything said in the group. When you think about it, you will realize it is important to you and will be to the others, too. If you want to talk about the group to people not in the group, you can make general comments or relate your own experience, but you should not share things said by others in the group, even with your partner. And since each member is agreeing to this, you can feel safer in knowing the others are reading this and making the same commitment.

Promptness and Calling In

It is very important that everyone comes on time and the meeting starts and ends on time. Five minutes of lateness by one person has to be multiplied by all members—if there are six members, and one is late for five minutes, that means twenty-five minutes of others' time is wasted by one person. So promptness is one more way to avoid conflicts or subtle resentments that have to be brought out eventually. The surest way to keep people prompt is to start on time, no matter who is there. That is one reason I begin sessions with discussing your journal entries, something you can begin more easily without everyone present. If some unforeseen event happens and you can't be on time or can't even come, call the location of the group and let the others know. It can be very disrupting and distressing to have members missing and not know why.

The Structure Is Your Friend—Be Loyal to It

The success of this group depends on your staying within the structure. It will protect you from all kinds of problems. But it will sometimes be annoying and will require everyone's resolve. Groups *always* go through a phase of attacking the leader, and a leaderless group attacks the structure. But the structure can't defend itself, so you each will have to do that.

The secret to keeping to the structure is the facilitator and the timekeeper working together so that it isn't one person always bringing the group back to the task. These two act as the group's conscience for that session. The jobs rotate, so that everyone or almost everyone will do it in a six-week group period, and no one person is always having to say, "time's up."

The Responsibilities of the Facilitator, the Timekeeper, the Host, and the Members

Once the group is organized, the organizer can be the facilitator for the first session, but beyond that the organizer should not have to have any continued responsibilities. The group will shoulder these, with the following distribution of tasks.

The *facilitator* should read the instructions for the session he or she will facilitate before the session and be prepared to clear up any questions members have. If anything seems unclear, he or she can resolve it before the session by phone with the timekeeper so the group does not have to. During the session, the facilitator leads the group in the tasks, reading the instructions if they are short, or explaining them, and guiding the group through. At the end of the session, the facilitator will help the group select the timekeeper and facilitator for the next session by drawing two names from a bag, drawing again if someone has already performed that role. (If toward the end someone has done both, don't even put that person's name in.)

The *timekeeper*, with the facilitator, gets the group started on time. The timekeeper keeps the time for entire tasks, each individual's speaking time during a task if it is divided among members, and announces the end of the break and the end of the session. Members often like receiving a warning (thirty seconds before the end of something less than five minutes long). When timing individuals, the timekeeper might ask each person if he or she would like that. It is best to use some kind of quiet timer or beeper to keep time for all six sessions.

When the group meets in a home, the *host* should see that there are no interruptions. That means turning the phone off and answering the door, turning away any nonmembers. Be sure everyone has access to water and knows where the bathroom is. Offering anything else is optional and best kept simple—maybe just tea or juice.

The *members* also have their responsibilities—to be on time, to help the facilitator and timekeeper keep to the structure (remember, debate over some little point may cost much in terms of group harmony), and to look after one another's emotional needs. Each member can watch for upset feelings in others and check in with anyone seeming distressed, during the group or even after the group. However, each member also must be responsible for his or her self. None of you are mind readers or professional therapists. And none of you want or should take on the responsibilities of another's entire emotional life. As your skill with group process grows, you as a member may also be able to make observations about what's going on in the group, saying what others were vaguely aware of but have not yet said. For example, "I wonder if we're not all feeling a little overwhelmed and need to just sit quietly for a minute." If the observation is not used by the group, don't feel too bad and don't push it. It does not mean you are wrong, but it does mean the group cannot at the moment act on your comment.

Permission Not to Speak

Each meeting is structured so that everyone has the chance to speak. But what if you don't want to say anything? Then *don't*. Just say, "I think I'll pass for now." What a good thing for an HSP to learn to feel free to do. In fact, the whole group should congratulate anyone who requests to pass. This group should be a safe, comfortable place for HSPs. Every member can sympathize when overarousal makes it hard to say anything.

On the other hand, do not join the group if you plan never to say anything. That will cause you and the group too much stress. Groups *always* worry about a silent member—is this person hurt, angry, standing back and judging us, planning to leave? The group will eventually have to focus on you, which is the last thing you wanted.

When someone passes, the group should come back to this person later and he or she should try to speak, or speak a little about why that's not so easy to do at that moment. The group should not dwell at length on this member—but the member should reassure them.

Time Spent with Each Member, or Again, the Structure Is Our Best Friend

The biggest trouble any group can get into is spending too much time with one member. At its worst, it becomes scapegoating. But even at its best, it is a tricky business. HSPs can become quickly overaroused by an entire group's attention and cease to be able to process what's being said. The other members, being less aroused, may not realize this. Later the person may remember the attention only as an unpleasantly overwhelming experience.

It's true that a group cannot help a member, and certainly cannot create deep change, without spending time focused on that member. *But deep change is not the goal of this group,* at least during these six sessions. You are not a therapy group and not even a support group. You are there to discuss, to learn from one another, to help one another some, but you cannot and must not set out to fix one another's deep psychological problems.

When the group focuses on one person, consciously setting out to be helpful, many other things can be happening *unconsciously.* For example, the person receiving the attention may be frustrating the group by giving it an impossible problem to solve, or may simply be starved for attention and needing to be the center of everyone's focus. Or those involved may be vying for that member's (or a third member's) attention, respect, or affection. It may become an unconscious competition over who is the better helper or wiser person. Finally, the group may be focusing on an individual in order to avoid other issues. A group with a skilled therapist or professional facilitator would recognize and work with these unconscious agendas so that the group could focus successfully on individual members, but your group does not have that kind of facilitator.

It is very human and compassionate to want to abandon the structure when someone is "into something big." It seems just too hard, too cold, to say "time to move on to the next person." But if the group is consistent about keeping to the time, everyone will understand, even the person feeling so much, who may really not want any more attention or benefit from it at this time. And if the group is not consistent, those not receiving extra time will feel hurt. See the problem? All the members need to be especially committed to the structure at these times, but in particular the session's facilitator and timekeeper need to help each other and say something like, "Wow, I know we are all really wanting to stay with you on this, and we are glad you could share this with us. But Elaine is watching, and you know what she says about sticking to the structure."

Honesty

The more honest you can be with your group, the more everyone will gain. This is especially true for being honest about your reactions to others and to the group. But honesty always has its shades. You want to speak the truth, but "speak the truth sweetly." Things can be said in a kind, thoughtful way or in an inconsiderate, ruthless way. But I don't have to say much about that to HSPs. I do need to remind HSPs, however, not to share personal matters before feeling safe to do so. Sometimes we try to please others by such revelations, or we are just hungry for intimacy. Take it slow.

Clearing the Air

Everyone joins a group with high hopes, and as with any relationship, the actuality is something a bit more down to earth. Things happen that you don't like and there are personalities you don't enjoy. When bad feelings about the group outweigh good ones, you will want to quit. The group can do two things to prevent its own demise: See that everyone is having as many good feelings as possible, and that they air and discuss the bad feelings so they can be resolved or minimized. Sometimes, through discussion, bad feelings can even turn into good feelings.

The problem with saying anything negative is that you may feel you will hurt someone's feelings, be criticized back (and who is above all criticism?), or everyone will disagree with you. So it takes courage. But the more you lead in this, the more others can do it too.

It helps a great deal if anyone airing a disappointment or resentment can be honored and appreciated for doing so, whatever the merits of the point. It also helps if the group can foster the attitude that conflicts in agendas and personalities are inevitable in any group, that such conflicts are always the best teachers, and it is how you work with them that matters. Above all it helps when you are the one with the grievance that you think about your own issues (complexes) and how your reaction here, today, may relate to your family life or other group experiences. They *almost always* relate rather tightly. The six-week group is not the place to go into this very much, but you can work on it privately. (The exception to this rule that it is good to be quick to "own the problem as your own" is when there's a problem member whom several others are struggling with too. Even then, in part you are reacting to that person in your typical way, but there is also an issue that goes beyond you and the other person, and the others with the same issue need your support.)

At the start of the fourth and sixth sessions there is a structured time to "Clear the Air."

Keeping a Log

One leaderless group I knew kept a log where members could write messages to the group—spontaneous feelings, news, complaints, whatever. Everyone read the log as they waited to begin or at the break. This is optional, but you might want to initiate this in your group. Every method of communicating seems to add to the group's well being.

Meeting Outside the Group

As you get to know each other, some of you may choose to meet outside the group—two people, three, four. Since you may have joined the group partly to meet people, this makes sense for you to do. But be thoughtful of others' feelings. Remember, HSPs notice such things even if you don't say anything. There's a new alliance, things shared that others did not hear, and then a certain sense of being left out. Keep this in mind.

Ritual

Watch for any spontaneous rituals that develop and enjoy them. Perhaps you all like to drink a certain tea, and each host begins having a pot of that waiting before the meeting. You can consciously develop rituals if you are good at this. For example, you might light sage or incense if this will not bother anyone, and purify the room before starting, or have some way of closing and opening the circle at the start and end of the meeting (see page 248 for more on rituals). But do none of this if it makes *anyone* even *slightly* uncomfortable. The group's harmony for these six sessions comes ahead of having ritual experiences.

Group Decision Making

There will be a few times when the group must make a decision, for example, on where to meet. When the group wants to make any democratic decision, it first has to decide if the issue requires everyone to agree or just the majority. It should require unanimous agreement if anyone has strong feelings on the issue, because forcing the no-voters to go along with the group would be upsetting to them. People are more important than any procedures, "frills," or good ideas.

For example, suppose someone wanted to photograph the group. Great idea! But I as a member would have strong feelings that anyone not wanting to be in a photo (perhaps for reasons of confidentiality) should be able to veto that idea, and not just by not being in the picture (making the person feel awkward). So with me in the group, a unanimous decision would be needed for a photo. But if the issue was whether to meet at John's house this week and Ann's house next week, or Ann's house this week and John's house next week, and no one can make up their mind and no one cares enormously, a simple majority vote could settle it quickly.

All voting should follow this procedure: Everyone takes an identical piece of paper from a little pad and uses the same kind of pencil, a No. 2. Make it clear what a yes or a no vote means. People write their vote and put the paper, folded once so they all look the same, into the paper bag always present. The facilitator counts them. When a vote needs to be unanimous, one no vote ends it, and the facilitator stops reading the votes after the first no. This way, no one knows if there was only one no (if there is, usually everyone knows whose it was).

The Stages of a Group

All groups work through certain issues, representing certain stages of group life, sometimes repeating them as needed. Most of this is unconscious, although once you know about these issues, you can make them conscious and point out when one might be influencing what's happening in the group. Although these stages will be *much* less apparent due to this group's tight structure, I am going to discuss them because they will appear to some degree, and may appear more if you continue your group beyond the six weeks or try something without so much structure.

The first stage is getting to know one another and setting the norms. Will it be okay to be late? (I hope not.) Will people be allowed to interrupt? Will an expression of annoyance be allowed or hushed up for the sake of harmony?

The next stage involves the subtle process of being sure everyone is on board. Quiet people's opinions are sought, to be sure they too are committed and happy. About this time there is also some competition among the competitive types, and those who don't like this kind of thing may let their own values be known. They want the group to be close and not fight. All of this is shaping the group's personality, and groups do develop their own personalities and resulting typical problems. For example, the competitive-style groups have trouble being close, while the ones liking closeness have trouble discussing their conflicts.

All of these stages are about finding out how safe the group is for *moi*, and soon in most groups (less in one as structured as yours), that brings up the issue of the leader, and each person's issues with authority. Typically, some will want to test the leader's strength, kindness, and role in the group. Some will need to express dissatisfaction with the leadership. Some will idealize the leader. In the case of this group, mostly you will see reactions to the structure as my leadership in absentia.

A later stage or phase is "pairing," when two people become close or intimate and the rest of the group is the witness to this sweet ideal. While some may feel left out, the group as a whole often enjoys vicariously these moments of inspiring, idealized intimacy. But be careful that these interludes do not become another way for the group to avoid its larger task of becoming a cohesive, helpful unit.

All of these stages and issues are just preparation for and sometimes distractions from the group's task, which in your case is learning all you can about yourselves by completing the session's tasks. Again, you will see less of these stages in your group, which is so structured and brief. But if your group continues, you'll notice these stages more.

One final point of interest, perhaps for you personally as you watch yourself in the group: Most people's hopes, fears, and disappointments regarding the group as a whole will reflect something of their relationship with their mothers; their issues regarding the leadership will often reflect something of their relationship with their fathers.

So here you go. I hope you are as excited about beginning as I am to type these words, imagining your beginning.

Bring to Every Session

Each member: This workbook, two sharpened No. 2 pencils.

Organizer (or see that someone brings):

1. A small chalkboard, large tablet, or "white board" (something about 18 × 24 will do) and appropriate writing implement for it. This is needed in the second, third, and fourth sessions, but *not*

for the first session, so you can ask if anyone has one or collect money to buy one.

2. Small (about 2 × 4 or 3 × 5) pads of identical paper, one for each member.
3. Some extra sharpened No. 2 pencils.
4. A paper bag.
5. For the first meeting only—transparent tape and marking pen to make name tags using paper from the small tablets. Or bring name tags.
6. Something for the first timekeeper to use in keeping time—a timer with a soft tone is best.

The First Session—Getting to Know One Another

The purpose of this session is to help you get to know one another and then to learn how others are experiencing you, a rare opportunity. And in the process of giving feedback, you will get to know one another even better.

First Half (55 minutes)
Getting started (10 minutes)
1. Start on time.
2. Make name tags with paper from the tablet and tape them on yourselves. Use the marking pen and make letters *large,* first names only.
3. If everyone is present, take care of "housekeeping"—where the bathroom is, where the glasses are for water. If not, delay this until everyone is present and go ahead to 4.
4. Draw names to decide who will be the timekeeper (the organizer can be the first facilitator, or a name can be chosen for that, too).

Introductions (15 minutes)
If there are six members, 2 minutes each equals 12 minutes, plus time to get started. Give more or less time to each person according to the number in your group, so that this task still takes about 15 minutes.

Purpose: To get to know one another.

Method: Each person should say his or her name and whatever he or she wants others to know first about himself or herself. (The next session will involve talking at length about each person's work, so talking about one's career can be kept short.) Good topics might be how you feel about being an HSP and coming to the group. Be sure to mention if you already know anyone in the group and the nature of your relationship.

Reading guidelines (25 minutes)
Purpose: To refresh your memory of the guidelines, to experience them *in* the group, and to be sure everyone has read them.

Method: The facilitator should have the group read the guidelines out loud, by going around in a circle and each person reading a paragraph, beginning with "Personal Preparation and Confidentiality" on page 274 and stopping before "The Stages of a Group" on page 281. It's best not to discuss or make comments on the instructions as you go along—it'll take too long. Just read them aloud clearly at a reasonable pace so all can absorb the meaning. This reading out loud may seem a little sophomoric, but think of it as a ritual of commitment to the group, and an easy way to pass the time while you get used to one another. And you will be surprised at how many new things you will notice, hearing them out loud.

More housekeeping (5 minutes)

Discuss where you will meet next time and any other practical issues. Those who wish to can exchange phone numbers.

Break (15 minutes)

Some will want to chat, some will want to go off alone. Either is fine. But don't leave and fail to come back without telling someone you are doing that. Imagine how that would distress the others.

Second Half (50 minutes)

First impressions (About 42 minutes)

For six people, this means 12 minutes total writing about the other five people; then each member receives feedback from the other five for 1 minute each, making 30 minutes, so this will take 42 minutes in all. With a smaller group, allot only 10 minutes for writing and more time to each person for feedback. A larger group will need to spend more than 42 minutes—take time from the "Introduction" task by shortening the time alloted for each person.

Purpose: To receive feedback about how others experience you. Feedback from those you have never met can be especially surprising. But even if you do know some of the others, you may never have received feedback from them about how they perceive you. This can be a powerful experience. But if you think this activity is not for you, "pass" on *receiving* the feedback.

Steps:

1. In about 12 minutes, write your three "first impressions" of each person, *using a separate piece of paper for each person.* (Since you'll probably each write about one another in different order, this way when it comes time for a particular person to receive feedback you can pull out your slip on this person.) If you notice something about how the person is with his or her sensitivity, be sure to say that.

   Do not worry about my asking you to prejudge people—everyone does it to some degree, and everyone can benefit from knowing how others first perceive them. And not all of your feedback has to be "nice," if you are experiencing something about a person that makes you uncomfortable. Just be sure to state it diplomatically, gently, and as your personal reaction, *not* as how this person really is. You have no idea. Write, "I find myself worrying that you may not like me," *not* "You seem to be the sort of person who judges people."

2. The facilitator has each person (including him- or herself) take turns receiving all the feedback from each other person. The person receiving all this feedback listens silently, and just says "thank you" at the end. The feedback is something to think about later.

Remember, what you will hear is not "true" of you, but only true of the impression you made on these people who do not know you. You will be hearing others' projections—what characteristics they watch for, what in others matters to them. (Technically, we project something we deny in ourselves. I might say "You're angry" when I'm the one who is angry, but I deny it or don't know it yet. Or I might say, "You seem to have taken a lot of care in how you dressed tonight" when how I dress is an issue for me that I tend to deny. Maybe I don't like people who attend to appearances. I make a point of not being that way. It's one of my complexes, as discussed on pages 125, 185, and 206). All projections, however, require some "hook" or outer appearance that makes the projection seem valid, even if it isn't. So a first impression from someone is at least feedback about the kinds of projections you invoke.

There's also a chance to learn from the feedback you give to others— what characteristics do you attend to that others don't, and perhaps look for so much that they aren't even there? In other words, what do you project?

For those of you who do know each other, the feedback you give should still be about how the person is in this session, almost as if you were seeing him or her for the first time. And be careful not to say anything that would reveal something about the person to those he or she does not know as well as you—nothing like, "I can see you are sad tonight, but I know that is because of your divorce."

Journal writing (5 minutes)

This should be a silent time. Use the space below to write about your reaction to giving and receiving this feedback or about your hopes and fears regarding the group and how it feels so far. At the start of the next session you will have the chance to share whatever you would like of this with the group.

_____

_____

Ending (3 minutes)

Draw names for the next session's facilitator and timekeeper; thank this session's timekeeper, facilitator, and host; say good-bye; and end on time (even if it means less time for journal writing).

The Second Session—The Difficult Problem of Vocation

This session has the purpose of exploring the issues of vocation (what you feel you were born to do) and work (how you support yourself, how you manage in your workplace). Vocation and work are very difficult problems for HSPs, given our culture. Indeed, one purpose of this session is to help you see that many of the problems you have in this area are common to most of you and are partly a social problem, not just your personal problem or personal fault.

First Half (50 minutes)

Begin on time. "Housekeeping decisions," like where to meet next, are always delayed until later, when everyone has arrived.

Journal sharing (10 minutes)

Purpose: To allow members to share what's going on with them (and leave a little time for late people to arrive).

Method: Every session will start this way. As time permits, members can talk about or read from their journal entries written at the end of the last session. Excerpts read should probably be less than a page. Or members can simply bring up any general thoughts or feelings about the group so far.

Sharing your stories

(30 minutes—divided among you equally—5 minutes each if six people.)

Purpose: To let members hear how other HSPs are managing to find and follow their vocation and support themselves.

Method: To focus their stories, members should try to answer these questions:

1. What they feel is their vocation or calling—what they feel they were born to do.
2. How they follow their vocation (or why they don't).
3. How they support themselves—does their vocation support them, or does something else?
4. How they get along in the workplace.
5. How being an HSP has affected all of the above.
6. In general, the problems and successes they have had in the vocational area.

If one of these points is really the whole story for you and takes up all of your allotted time, that's fine.

Housekeeping (10 minutes)

Use this time to deal with any practical issues, such as where the next meeting will be held.

Break (15 minutes)

Second Half (55 minutes)

A chance to discuss vocation with other HSPs

(30 minutes—6 minutes to decide on topics, although it may take less; then discuss each for about 8 minutes.)

Purpose: To share experiences regarding what is for many of you the most difficult aspect of being an HSP.

Steps:

1. To focus the group, the facilitator asks the group to name three issues that they heard come up in the first half that seemed important to several people and worth discussing. If more than three seemed important, the group can vote.

2. To vote, members have two votes and vote for the two topics that are most important to them. Alternately, they can vote for one topic, by giving both of two votes to that topic. This gives the topics a weight, and the three receiving the most votes, indicating the most need or interest, are discussed. (Spend no more than 6 minutes on the deciding and voting process.)

3. Discuss. The timekeeper divides the remaining time, about 24 minutes, into three equal parts for the three topics, or gives slightly more time to those topics receiving the most votes, indicating the most interest.

Explaining your sensitivity in the workplace

(15 minutes—5 minutes each, helping three members.)

Purpose: To help one another find positive ways to describe and defend your sensitivity.

Steps:

1. Facilitator, and members too if possible, should read ahead of time the tasks on pages 17 and 143 to help guide the discussion.
2. Facilitator asks for a member to describe a situation in which he or she would like to explain or defend better the trait of sensitivity to an interviewer, supervisor, colleague, employee, or whatever. This could also be a past situation the member wishes had been handled better.
3. Other members suggest ways this might be done.
4. After about 5 minutes, move on to another person—you'll do three situations in all.
5. If no one volunteers, discuss the topic in general, or why it is not a problem for anyone, or why no one wishes to talk about it!

Journal writing (7 minutes)

In silence. Write about whatever feelings or thoughts you have as a result of this session.

_____

_____

_____

_____

_____

_____

_____

_____

_____

_____

_____

_____

___

___

___

Ending (3 minutes)

Draw names for the next session's facilitator and timekeeper; thank this session's timekeeper, facilitator, and host; say good-bye; and end on time (even if it means less time for journal writing).

The Third Session—Health, Body, Balanced Living, Coping

This is another critical topic for HSPs. Everything depends on the state of your health, your body. The body supports the clarity of your thinking, the wholeness of your mood, and thus the happiness of those around you too. HSPs cannot use their bodies the way the other 80 percent of the world does, or thinks it can. But the pressure to behave like a non-HSP is enormous. In this session your goal is to create support for a different, gentler approach to your wonderful, sensitive body.

First Half (55 minutes)

Begin on time. Delay "housekeeping decisions" until later.

Journal sharing (**10 minutes**) See page 288.

Sharing ways to cope with overarousal (**30 minutes**)

Purpose: To learn from one another new ways of taking care of yourselves—sharing your problem areas first, then your best solutions for each.

Steps:

1. The facilitator spends 10 minutes asking the members *only* about the specific kinds of difficulties they have avoiding, controlling, or recovering from overarousal. As members state these difficulties, the facilitator lists these on the board or large tablet, with space under each. Perhaps one member is a young mother wondering how to manage her sensitivity. The facilitator writes, "managing with children." Another is a businessman having trouble sleeping when he travels. The facilitator writes, "sleeping when traveling." A third is a professional woman who can't get herself to take time off. The facilitator writes, "making ourselves take time off." (10 minutes, or until there are about eight issues listed.)

2. Going back over the list, other members offer how they have dealt with each difficulty. Facilitator writes the solutions in the space left under each. (20 minutes)

Deciding to change (**5 minutes**)

Purpose: To take the time to decide how you want to change your life or grow as a person.

Method: Individually, in silence, thoughtfully contemplate and then write down how you would like to change—for example, what new coping methods you would like to introduce into your life, such as saying "no" to requests, finding time to meditate or exercise, scheduling downtime, exploring job options, or setting better boundaries with a difficult person.

Housekeeping (10 minutes)

Break (15 minutes)

Second Half (50 minutes)

Helping one another take better care of yourselves (37 minutes)

Purpose: To give one another support while you try to live a life more in harmony with your sensitivity; also, to meet in pairs for a change.

Steps:

1. Break into pairs. Facilitator puts all the names into a bag and draws out two at a time, creating pairs. (If there's an odd number, one set can be triad.) Each pair finds a spot to sit that's a little separated from the others. (5 minutes.)

2. Once in pairs, spend 10 minutes with one of the pair as supporter and the other person supported. The person to be supported states how he or she wants to take better care of his or her body, or other ways he or she wants to grow in this area of self-care, and why it has been difficult so far, and what might help. The supporter mostly listens, but may suggest further ideas, shape the goal into something reasonable, or help formulate a supportive plan with small steps of change (but *don't* impose your own health ideas). (10 minutes for one person.)

3. Switch roles. (10 minutes for other person—triads divide time into 7 minutes each.)

4. Return to the group, where each member reports in 1 minute or less on what happened for him or her while being supported on the topic. The rest of the time can be spent discussing anything else on this topic, or anything else that has come up in the group. (12 minutes.)

Journal writing (10 minutes) See page 286.

———————————————————————————————

———————————————————————————————

———————————————————————————————

Ending (3 minutes)

Draw names for the next session's facilitator and timekeeper; thank this session's timekeeper, facilitator, and host; say good-bye; and end on time (even if it means less time for journal writing).

The Fourth Session—Close Relationships

The purpose of this session is to explore together your trait's impact on your close relationships. Close relationships are a major contributor to even the most introverted HSP's health and happiness, but they are also a contributor to great distress and low self-esteem. At least some of these hurtful relationship experiences go back to childhood, which we will discuss in the next session. In this session you will focus on adult relationships, having a chance to ask one another questions and share what you have learned with others.

A large part of this session is also devoted to clearing the air in the group, discussing any joys or discomforts. You might call this practice in actually getting closer to others rather than talking about how you do it elsewhere!

First Half (55 minutes)

Begin on time. Delay "housekeeping decisions" until later.

Journal sharing (**10 minutes**) See page 288.

Clearing the air (**35 minutes**)

Purpose: To discuss any issues arising in the group that might be in the way of your enjoying one another. This activity is one of the most important for learning something about group process and how you personally react to others and to groups.

Steps:

1. Spend 5 minutes writing down anything that has happened in the group that has been especially good for you and anything that has not been helpful or comfortable for you. Keep in mind that you will put your name on this and it will be read out loud.

   Wondering why this method and not an open discussion? I have learned that people find it a little easier to be honest in writing, even when they know it will be read out loud. Also, it keeps the comments focused.

   You might write a comment to the whole group—for example, you enjoyed their support about your work issues in the second session, or you felt ignored by the group at the end of the last session. Or you might write to an individual about something this person said or did, to you or someone else. Typical comments would be "Lynn, I loved how you kept us from digressing in that session when we were discussing ways to cope," or "It made me uneasy, Peter, when you criticized Jackie in the last session."

2. Put your name on what you have written and put it into the paper bag.

3. The facilitator reads out loud all the messages (his or her own included) on the slips of paper in the bag. (5 minutes.)

4. The rest of the time (25 minutes) is spent letting the group or individuals involved discuss each message. Enjoy the praise and the group's successes; try to resolve any grievances or hurt feelings. With the latter, remember an apology works wonders and defensiveness does not. But no one need apologize for what they feel. We can be mistaken, however, about what we thought someone else would feel, and we are all often wrong about *why* someone felt or did something.

Housekeeping (10 minutes)

Break (15 minutes)

Second Half (50 minutes)

A chance to discuss your close relationship issues with other HSPs

(37 minutes—10 minutes to decide on topics, although it may take less; then about 9 minutes to discuss each.)

Purpose: To share experiences about the impact of being highly sensitive on your close relationships.

Steps:

1. For 5 minutes the facilitator asks the group members to pose any kind of questions to the group about being highly sensitive in close relationships— anything they would like to hear other HSPs talk about. As the members call out their questions or topics, the facilitator writes these down so the group can see them. Some questions I've heard brought up:
   - "Do the rest of you have trouble getting enough time alone in a close relationship?"
   - "How do you meet other HSPs?"
   - "How do you make peace with the idea that you may never remarry?"
   - "Are we better off with another HSP or with a non-HSP?"

2. Having heard all these good questions, the facilitator has the group vote on the three questions they would most like to spend time discussing. Members have two votes, and vote for two or one question (by giving both votes to one). The three questions receiving the most votes are discussed. (Voting should take about 5 minutes.)

3. The timekeeper divides the time left (about 27 minutes) into three equal

amounts, or gives slightly more time to those questions receiving more votes, indicating more group interest. The group discusses these.

Journal writing **(10 minutes)** See page 286.

_____

_____

_____

_____

_____

_____

_____

_____

_____

_____

_____

_____

_____

_____

_____

_____

_____

_____

_____

_____

_____

Ending (3 minutes)

Draw names for the next session's facilitator and timekeeper; thank this session's timekeeper, facilitator, and host; say good-bye; and end on time (even if it means less time for journal writing).

The Fifth Session—Reframing Your Childhood, Reparenting the Sensitive Child

The purpose of this session is for you to share with one another some stories of your sensitive childhood. Not much can be changed or even told in one two-hour session, and yet I always find it surprising how much people do recieve from discussing this topic even a little. It is a deeply personal, vulnerable area for most of us, however, so I waited until late in your group to have you broach it. Come to this session with an attitude of reverence and unconditional love for the sensitive child each of you was.

First Half (55 minutes)

Begin on time. Delay "housekeeping decisions" until later.

Journal sharing **(10 minutes)** See page 288.

Reframing a childhood experience **(35 minutes)**

Purpose: To take one experience and understand it freshly, in the light of your sensitivity, and share it with others so that they can be a witness to what truly happened.

Steps:

1. On a piece of paper from the pad, put a "1" for Side One and then spend 5 minutes writing down an experience you had as a child that you know hurt your self-confidence, made you feel flawed, defective, or guilty, and that you now know was really all about your sensitivity. *Be brief and write clearly*—someone else will read out loud what you wrote. Do not put your name on what you write; do not write anything you do not want read out loud.

2. On the other side of the paper put a "2" and spend 5 minutes writing about how you now understand this event, in light of your sensitivity. (This is all a shortened version of "Reframing Your Past," page 24.)

    An example:

    1. On my sixth birthday my parents gave me a surprise party, complete with a clown. He had a spring for an arm with a punching bag at the end. Hitting me in the stomach, he yelled, "Here's the birthday boy." Twenty kids followed, heading straight for my favorite toys. I ran to my room and locked the door. My parents begged me to come out. Then my father told me I was being selfish, ungrateful, and cowardly, and couldn't understand how I could be his son.

2. I realize now I was overwhelmed by all the stimulation. I couldn't possibly help what I did. I was not being selfish, ungrateful, or a coward. I was just behaving normally for a sensitive child. I wish my parents had known about this trait in me and had planned a quieter celebration.

It is common for people to have trouble doing this task. Just trying to think of an event, you may become emotionally flat, unable to concentrate, or agitated. Take note of your response, but do not force yourself to do this activity. Just sit back and try to breathe easy. You can still be part of the second half.

3. Again, do *not* put your name on what you wrote. Put your piece of paper into the bag. (Total to here, 10 minutes.)

   Why this roundabout method of putting these responses in a bag and drawing them out to read them as if they were anonymous (when probably most of you will guess who wrote what)? First, it is a bit like giving it into another's keeping by letting another read it. Second, the whole group would probably want to shower each member with sympathetic responses, but there simply is not time to do that for each of you. And third, even if there were time, you would soon be drawn into very deep issues for which your group is not ready.

4. When everyone who wants to has put in a slip of paper, the facilitator passes the bag and everyone draws out one. If you draw your own, put it back, unless you are the last person—then keep it but act like it isn't yours.

5. Read over to yourself what is written and decipher the words so that you can read them out loud fluently. (People's wise defenses often show up here too, in illegible handwriting.)

6. Each person reads aloud the slip they drew. The group soaks in what they have heard, holds it quietly, then may want to comment on whether they can add to the reframing.

   In the example given above, suppose that instead of what I wrote for Side Two, a group member wrote only, "I realize my parents were doing the best they could" (a common response), or "I wish I had come out of my room the way they wanted me to." This member needs the group's help to reframe this experience more in the way that I did.

(Steps 4 to 6 should take about 25 minutes.)

Housekeeping (10 minutes)

Break (15 minutes)

Second Half (50 minutes)
Free discussion time (36 minutes)

Use this time to talk about your childhoods or the feelings the task in the first half brought up, plus any other childhood stories you want to share. But everyone should be careful not to focus too long on any one member—I am counting on all of you to manage this well. This should remain a group-focused experience.

Read aloud instructions for next session (3 minutes)

Bring *one* of these two:

1. Something creative you have done, or that you appreciate that someone else has done. This might be a tape of music (but be sure the host has a tape player—or bring one), a photograph, a work of art, a poem. Or you can play an instrument, sing, or dance. You can bring photos of the children you care for or of a vacation you have taken. You can bring a vase of flowers from your garden or a printout of a Web site you have created. But again, the item you deeply appreciate can be something done by someone else, too. The point is to celebrate our sensitive, subtle perception of the world. This is not any kind of competition.

2. Plan to share one of your spiritual experiences or your philosophy of life or how you handled a loss or death—either you can talk about it, or share some object or creative expression which represents it for you.

    Whatever you plan to share, be certain it can be shown and talked about in about 3 minutes. So, for example, there will not be time to read a short story. It is very awkward to cut someone off in the midst of sharing something important. Make it easy on your timekeeper by keeping the time limit in mind.

Journal writing (8 minutes) See page 286.

Ending (3 minutes)

Draw names for the next session's facilitator and timekeeper; thank this session's timekeeper, facilitator, and host; say good-bye; and end on time (even if it means less time for journal writing).

The Sixth Session—Celebrating Our Sensitivity and Ending This Group Experience

The purpose of this session is twofold—to celebrate the side of ourselves that is creative, sensitive to subtleties, and in touch with spiritual sources, and to end these six weeks in a conscious way (even if the group is going to continue). The topics are actually very related, as HSPs feel endings keenly and generally have a well-developed sense of loss and death compared to others in the population, who tend to deny these issues. The way we need to deal with this greater awareness is to express our feelings, including our joy in the moment, through creative outlets and through developing our natural spiritual talents.

First Half (45 minutes)

Begin on time.

Journal sharing (10 minutes) See page 288.

Clearing the air (35 minutes)

Purpose: To express what you wish to express to one another before this six-session group ends.

This is a very difficult point for the group. It is over, as what it was. Most of you have had fantasies of continuing the group, and it may work out in some form. But it will never be the same as it has been. Believe me, if you meet for a potluck a month from now, *it will not feel the same.* So let's get to work on an ending.

Steps:

1. Spend 5 minutes writing down anything that has happened in the group that has been especially good for you and/or anything that has not been helpful or comfortable for you. This can be anything that happened during the entire time the group has met or since the fourth session, the last "Clearing the Air." You can address the whole group or a particular member. Keep in mind that you will put your name on this and it will be read out loud.
2. Put your name on what you have written and put it into the paper bag.
3. The facilitator reads out loud all the messages (including his or her own) on the slips of paper in the bag. (5 minutes)
4. The rest of the time (25 minutes) is spent letting the group or individuals involved discuss each message. Enjoy the praise and the group's successes; try to resolve any grievances or hurt feelings.

Break (15 minutes)

Second Half (60 minutes)

Voting whether to continue the group (20 minutes)

Purpose: To decide whether to continue the group, and to do so in a way that is anonymous and protective of one another's feelings.

Steps:

1. Discuss for 15 minutes *how* you might continue the group—weekly, every two weeks, meeting times and places, whether it would be structured using tasks from this workbook or structured around other topics members bring in; whether it would be free form about anything bothering people or process-oriented with a hired facilitator. Obviously if you know you would not want to continue no matter what the group's structure, do not push for a particular outcome of this discussion.

2. Vote on whether you want to be in the group if it is continued. This vote must be unanimous for the group to continue. (Otherwise, if only one or two voted yes, they would feel very rejected.) Vote in a completely anonymous way, putting identical slips of paper into the bag. You are voting on whether to continue the group in the way you decided in the discussion, but exactly *as constituted*—that is, with the members of this group. (So if this group of people or someone in this group is not right for you, you will vote no about continuing the group. You might vote no for other reasons too, of course.)

3. If there is disagreement about the type of group, meeting time or place, and so forth, conduct more than one vote for continuing the group under the various conditions you can't decide among—for example, once a week, free discussion versus once a month doing tasks from the workbook—but these conditions are always for the group as constituted. If one of these votes is unanimously for continuing, then the group continues in that form.

4. The facilitator reads out the slips. If he or she encounters a no, he or she stops reading the votes and destroys the contents of the bag. The group as it is now composed will end with this session. Members can call one another, or call some but not all, and continue to meet in any way they wish. But this group is over today.

   If there is a no, please put the safety of everyone's feelings above honesty, and *do not* discuss why you or anyone else may have voted no. Remember that a no could mean that a person is just too busy to give up two hours a week any longer, or that the person has received what they wanted and desires to do something different with his or her time. The group could have been wonderful for all of you, but there can still be good reasons to end.

Celebrating our sensitive perception (30 minutes)

Purpose: To experience one another's wonderful trait, firsthand. To know one another in yet another way.

Steps:

1. Each person shares what he or she brought (see instructions at end of guidelines for the fifth session). The timekeeper divides the time evenly among those not passing on this activity—and do gently encourage everyone, even those who brought nothing.

2. About half of each segment of time should be used for the person to talk about what he or she brought or wished to share, and half is used by the group to give what was brought an honest, warm reception (here's the time to speak the truth that is the very sweetest). So both parts of each person's segment must be very brief.

3. When I do this with a group, I let people decide on their own if they want to go first and when to go next. This in itself allows our intuition to come into play to create the experience as a whole.

4. Put anything anyone brought into the center of your circle.

Ending (10 minutes)

Purpose: To end consciously, rather than drift away and avoid the feelings, as HSPs can do.

Steps:

1. Stand up in a circle around the things that have been set there. Do not hold hands—some may not want to, and it would be difficult to refuse if some of you begin it. But look into one another's eyes if you want to.

2. The facilitator asks members to say whatever they wish—anything that, if not said, would leave them feeling incomplete. Everyone should be very aware that this is the end of the group, at least as it has been. This is your last chance to speak to the group as it is now.

3. Everyone does not have to speak, however. Anyone can speak more than once if something more comes to mind.

4. *Everyone* should be aware of the time—don't leave it all to the timekeeper—so that you *end on time*, or nearly so. This is important.

Journal writing Do this on your own time, but as soon after the session as possible.

_____

_____

_____

_____

_____

_____

_____

_____

_____

_____

_____

_____

_____

_____

_____

_____

_____

_____

_____

_____

_____

_____

_____

_____

A final note from your invisible facilitator: The group was not quite what you expected, was it? It was better in some ways, disappointing in others. You probably feel anything but "complete." Your feelings are racing around. I hope with time you come to remember these sessions as especially useful to your life. I wish you well.

Resources

Introduction

References to research relevant to this trait can be found in the notes at the end of *The Highly Sensitive Person* and in the reference section in the following article, available at all university libraries:

"Sensory-Processing Sensitivity and Its Relation to Introversion and Emotionality," by Elaine N. Aron and Arthur Aron, *Journal of Personality and Social Psychology,* 1997, Vol. 73, No. 2, 345–368.

Chapter 1

Two sources for further work with sensing the body:

Eugene Gendlin, *Focusing* (Bantam Books, 1981).

Betty Winkler Keane's *Sensing* (published by Harper and Row in 1979; available from the author at 30 Lincoln Plaza, New York, NY 10023).

Chapter 2

About aggressive cultures:

Riane Eisler, *The Chalice and the Blade* (Harper San Francisco, 1995).

A classic on the research on "inhibited" children:

Jerome Kagan et al., *Galen's Prophecy* (Basic Books, 1994).

A book teaching active imagination:

Robert Johnson, *Inner Work* (Harper San Francisco, 1989).

A book teaching voice dialogue, to be used by pairs:

Hal Stone and Sidra Winkelman, *Embracing Ourselves* (Nataraj, 1993).

Chapter 3

A source for "sound conditioners":

Marpac, 2907 Blue Clay Road, P.O. Box 3098, Wilmington, NC 28406, 910–763–7861

To find out about Transcendental Meditation in your area: 1–888–LEARN TM.

For help with anxiety, phobias, or posttraumatic stress:

Anxiety Disorders Association of America, a nonprofit organization created by leaders in the field: 301–231–9350.

For help with dealing with difficult people:

Robert Bramson, *Coping with Difficult People* (Dell, 1981).

Charles Keating, *Dealing with Difficult People* (Paulist Press, 1984).

For information on noise-canceling technologies (the "noise buster"):

Noise-Cancellation Technologies, One Dock Street, Stamford, CT 06902; 800–869–6647

Chapter 4

A book on how you should have been raised, good for reframing and reparenting yourself: Janet Poland, *The Sensitive Child* (St. Martin's Paperbacks, 1995).

Chapter 5

Books and resources on social skills and shyness:

Pamela Butler, *Self-Assertion for Women* (Harper San Francisco, 1992).

Sharon Bower and Gordon Bower, *Asserting Yourself* (Perseus Press, 1991).

Jonathan Cheek et al., *Conquering Shyness* (Dell, 1990) (out of print but in many libraries)

Phil Zimbardo, *Shyness: What It Is, What to Do About It* (Perseus Press, 1990).

Palo Alto Shyness Clinic: Director, Lynne Henderson, Ph.D. 4370 Alpine Rd., Suite 204, Portola Valley, CA 94028, 650–851–2994. www.shyness.com

Chapter 6

Some books on finding your true vocation:

Marsha Sinetar, *Do What You Love, the Money Will Follow* (Dell, 1987).

Barbara Sher, *I Could Do Anything If I Only Knew What It Was* (Delacorte, 1994).

Chapter 7

Some resources for couples:

John Gottman, *Why Marriages Succeed or Fail . . . And How You Can Make Yours Last* (Simon and Schuster, 1995).

Harville Hendrix, *Getting the Love You Want: A Guide for Couples* (HarperCollins, 1988).

Claude Steiner, *Achieving Emotional Literacy* (Avon, 1997).

Excellent weekend workshops for couples and a source for other materials: The Seattle Marital and Family Institute, P. O. Box 15644, Seattle, WA, 98115–0644, or call 888–523–9042. The institute is run by John Gottman, Ph.D.

Chapter 8

Jung Institutes are in New York, Philadelphia, Toronto, Boston, Chicago, Dallas, Santa Fe, Seattle, Los Angeles, San Francisco, and Washington, D.C.. There is also an interregional organization for other cities that can be reached by calling one of the institutes in these cities.

A book to take to your therapist if you are working on the effects of any kind of single trauma:

Edna Foa, *Treating the Trauma of Rape* (Guilford, 1998).

Chapter 9

Some books combining alternative and regular medicine, by M.D.s:

Ronald Hoffman, *Intelligent Medicine* (Simon and Schuster, 1997).

Michael Norden, *Beyond Prozac* (HarperCollins, 1995).

A book combining every kind of treatment for anxiety and phobia:

Edmund Bourne, *The Anxiety and Phobia Workbook* (Five Communication, 1997).

The classics on SSRIs. More or less "pro":

Peter Kramer, *Listening to Prozac* (Penguin, 1993).

Very "con":

Peter Breggin and Ginger Ross, *Talking Back to Prozac* (St. Martin's Press, 1994).

Chapter 10

Some books on dream work:

Gayle Delaney, *Breakthrough Dreaming* (Bantam, 1991).

Robert Johnson, *Inner Work* (Harper San Francisco, 1989).

Carl G. Jung, *Dreams* (Princeton University Press, 1974).

Kathleen Sullivan, *Recurring Dreams* (The Crossing Press, 1998).

Edward Whitmont and Sylvia Perera, *Dreams: Portal to the Source* (Routledge, 1989).

Some books on creating rituals:

Jeanne Achterberg, Barbara Dossey, and Leslie Kolmeier, *Rituals of Healing* (Bantam, 1994).

Sam Keen and Anne Valley-Fox, *Your Mythic Journey* (Tarcher, 1989).

Malidoma Patrice Some, *Ritual: Power, Healing, and Community* (Swan/Raven, 1993).

About living a life that is true to your inner voice:

⟶Marsha Sinetar, *Ordinary People as Monks and Mystics* (Paulist Press, 1986).

Chapter 11

The classic text on group psychotherapy also discusses group process:

Irving Yalom, *The Theory and Practice of Group Psychotherapy,* 4th edition (Basic Books, 1995).

For information about *Comfort Zone*, the HSP newsletter, write P.O. Box 460564, San Francisco, CA 94146–0564.

Appendix: Symptoms of Posttraumatic Stress, Depression, and Dysthymia

(Adapted from DSM-IV)

What follows is not meant to substitute for a professional assessment of your situation, but to help you recognize if you may need that. These lists have been adapted from the *Diagnostic and Statistical Manual of Mental Disorders,* 4th edition, or *DSM-IV*, published by the American Psychiatric Association and used to determine diagnoses for treatment purposes.

I. Assessing for Posttraumatic Stress

Use this list to help you decide whether you might be experiencing "clinically significant" (time-to-get-help type of) suffering from a trauma.

1. An event has given you an experience of a strong sense of threat and of intense fear or horror. And since the event, you are not doing well—at work, in relationships, or both. The event could be recent, or it could have taken place a while ago and this is a delayed reaction. But you know this sense of not doing well has to do with the event. Given that, go on with this self-assessment.

2. The trauma is persistently reexperienced. Check any items below that apply to you:

   ☐ You have recurrent and intrusive distressing recollections of the event—images, thoughts, or perceptions.
   ☐ You have recurrent distressing dreams of the event.
   ☐ You sometimes act and feel as if the traumatic event were recurring, as if you are reliving the experience. This might be during illusions, hallucinations, or flashback episodes, perhaps when waking up or when intoxicated.
   ☐ You experience intense psychological distress when exposed to cues, inner or outer, that symbolize or resemble an aspect of the traumatic event.
   ☐ You have physical stress reactions when exposed to those cues.

3. The next questions are about whether you avoid things associated with the trauma, or feel a numbing to life in general that was not typical of you before the trauma. Check the items below that apply to you.

   ☐ You try to avoid thoughts, feelings, or conversations associated with the trauma.
   ☐ You try to avoid activities, places, or people that cause you to recall the trauma.
   ☐ You can't recall important aspects of it.

- [ ] You have markedly less interest in activities that were significant to you before the trauma.
- [ ] You feel detached or estranged from others since the trauma.
- [ ] You generally seem to have fewer feelings—of love, joy, anger, fear, etc.
- [ ] You have a bad feeling about your future, or you do not expect to have a normal life span.

4. The next questions are about symptoms of increased arousal that were not present before the trauma (you can see why HSPs would have more of these, being more easily overaroused). Check any of these that apply to you:

- [ ] Difficulty falling or staying asleep.
- [ ] Irritability or outbursts of anger.
- [ ] Difficulty concentrating.
- [ ] Hypervigilance—that is, being unusually nervous, expecting trouble.
- [ ] An exaggerated startle response.

You would be said to have PTSD if you answered yes to 1, and checked just *one* item under 2, *and* checked at least three under 3, *and* at least two under 4, *and* these symptoms have been present for more than a month (if it has been less than a month you would probably be diagnosed as having an "acute stress reaction").

This is a justifiably conservative diagnostic process. Fewer items checked does not mean you are not being affected by a trauma. If in doubt, please get a professional opinion.

II. Assessing for the Presence of Depression
Check those which apply to you.

- [ ] Most of every day you feel depressed—sad, empty, hopeless—or you cry easily or seem sad to others.
- [ ] Most of every day you have lost most of your interest or pleasure in all or almost all of the things you do.
- [ ] You have lost or gained weight without meaning to (a change of more than 5 percent of your weight in a month), or your appetite has gone away or increased suddenly.
- [ ] You can't sleep (especially waking in the middle of the night or too early in the morning) or sleep too much.
- [ ] You are slowed down or nervously speeded up to a degree that others would notice or have noticed.
- [ ] You feel fatigued or lack energy.
- [ ] You feel worthless or more guilty than would make sense to anyone else hearing your thoughts.
- [ ] You can't think, concentrate, or make decisions.
- [ ] You think about wanting to die (this does not have to be nearly every day).

If you checked five items or more, *and* if one of them was among the first two items on the list, *and* if the five have been present *nearly every day for the same two-week period, and* represent a change in you from before, *and* that change is causing you distress or interfering with your life, then you would be diagnosed as being in the midst of a major depressive episode. That means you owe it to yourself and others to get help.

If you don't meet all of these criteria, but do meet many of them, then you still need help finding out what's going on and working on it, especially if you checked the last item or any of the items are strongly true.

III. Assessing for Dysthymia

There is also something called "dysthymic disorder," which acknowledges that a little depression for a long time can be as bad for you, your brain, and those around you as a severe depression for a shorter time. Check if this applies to you:

☐ A depressed mood for most of the day, for more days than not, for at least two years. This mood and the following symptoms have not been absent for more than two months during those two years.

If the above is true, check any of these which apply to you when in this mood:

☐ Poor appetite or overeating.
☐ Insomnia or sleeping more than you need.
☐ Low energy or fatigue.
☐ Low self-esteem.
☐ Poor concentration or difficulty making decisions.
☐ Feelings of hopelessness.

If you said yes to the first item *and* checked two or more of the remaining ones *and* all of this makes you feel distressed or impairs how well you function in life, then you would be diagnosed as having dysthymia. As with depression or PTSD, you should be getting help from a professional.

NATIONAL BESTSELLER

The groundbreaking bestseller from the popular HSP specialist—now reissued with a new preface addressing the tremendous response from readers nationwide.

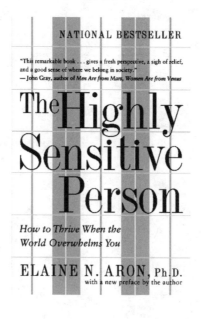

NATIONAL BESTSELLER

"This remarkable book . . . gives a fresh perspective, a sigh of relief, and a good sense of where we belong in society."
— John Gray, author of *Men Are from Mars, Women Are from Venus*

The **Highly Sensitive Person**

How to Thrive When the World Overwhelms You

ELAINE N. ARON, Ph.D.
with a new preface by the author

The Highly Sensitive Person provides relief and insight for thousands who have struggled with a lifetime of inaccurate labels such as "overly shy," or "too emotional." At last identifying the traits that comprise a highly sensitive person, clinical psychologist and researcher Elaine Aron's book is the first written specifically for the 50 million Americans who are considered to be HSPs, proving to them that they are not alone and helping them lead richer, fuller lives.

 IN TRADE PAPERBACK FROM BROADWAY BOOKS